MOROCCO
Jews and Art in a Muslim Land

MOROCCO
Jews and Art in a Muslim Land

DANIEL J. SCHROETER, AMI BOUGANIM, OUMAMA AOUAD
LAHRECH, HARVEY E. GOLDBERG, AND MOSHE IDEL

EDITED BY VIVIAN B. MANN

MERRELL

IN ASSOCIATION WITH

The Jewish Museum

NEW YORK

THE JEWISH MUSEUM IS UNDER THE AUSPICES OF

THE JEWISH THEOLOGICAL SEMINARY

Published on the occasion of the exhibition *Morocco: Jews and Art in a Muslim Land* at The Jewish Museum, New York, September 24, 2000 – February 11, 2001

First published 2000 by
Merrell Publishers Limited
42 Southwark Street
London SE1 1UN
www.merrellpublishers.com

Text © 2000
The Jewish Museum
1109 Fifth Avenue
New York
New York 10128
www.thejewishmuseum.org

Images © copyright holders; for details see right

Library of Congress Control Number: 00 133476

British Library Cataloguing-in-Publication Data
Morocco : Jews and art in a Muslim land
1.Art, Jewish – Morocco – Exhibitions 2.Jews –
Morocco 3.Judaism in art – Morocco 4.Morocco –
Civilization
I.Mann, Vivian B.
704′.03924′064
ISBN 1 85894 110 5 (hardback)
ISBN 1 85894 111 3 (paperback)

Produced by Merrell Publishers Limited
Edited by Iain Ross
Designed by Roger Davies
Printed and bound in Italy

FRONT COVER Interior of the Dahan Synagogue, Fez

BACK COVER Charles-Émile Vernet-Lecomte, *Femme Juive de Tanger*, Paris, 1886; see cat. no. 96

FRONTISPIECE Bracelet of Simḥah Pinto and Sun and Moon Bracelet, Tangier, early 20th century; see cat. nos. 65, 67

OPPOSITE Amulet, Morocco, 1861–62; see cat. no. 34

PAGES 6–7 Francisco Lameyer y Berenguer, *La Mariage Juif à Tangier*, Madrid, 1875 (detail); see cat. no. 95

PAGE 8 Interior of the Nahon Synagogue, Tangier

PAGES 10–11 Eugène Delacroix, *Fanatics of Tangier*, Paris, 1837–38 (detail); see cat. no. 91

PAGES 14–15 Menorah papercut, Morocco, c. 1900; see cat. no. 100

PAGES 18–19 *Hzams* (belts), Fez, 19th – early 20th century; see cat. nos. 151, 153, 156

PAGE 20 Detail of a Torah Mantle, "dedicated by Meir the son of Abraham Hakohen for the elevation of the soul of Rabbi Reuben, the son of Joseph Hakohen, 5646 [1885/86]," Morocco; see cat. no. 2

PAGE 22 Raymond Crétot-Duval, *Entrance to the Mellah of Salé*, Morocco, 1925 (detail); see cat. no. 98

CONTENTS

STATEMENT BY SA MAJESTÉ
LE ROI DU MAROC

The Jewish Museum's exhibition pays tribute to one of the most remarkable experiences of tolerance of our time, and also to one of the most encouraging lessons of modernity, through the long-standing history and memory shared by Muslims and Jews in Morocco.

The blending of cultures resulted in a sympathetic understanding that unified the people of Morocco, to the extent that My Honorable Grandfather, His Majesty Mohammed V, answered the Nazi commander who demanded a list of Jews: "We have no Jews in Morocco, only Moroccan citizens."

These close intergroup relations are reflected in the art of the Kingdom. The architecture of mosques and synagogues, the music of Muslims and Jews, the patterns and designs of textiles, stucco, and tiles all reflect this commonly held artistic tradition. In the south, two millennia of Berber–Jewish coexistence resulted in a fusion of cultural expressions. Jews and Berbers wore the same clothes and jewelry and prayed in similar buildings.

Today, a new relationship has evolved between Morocco's Muslims and Jews, and the Jewish-Moroccan culture that began in Fez, Rabat, Essaouira, and Marrakesh has become an international culture, sustained by a permanent relationship with the people and the land of Morocco.

The reverence felt by Moroccan Jews all over the world for their homeland was expressed in their fervent loyalty to My August Father, His Majesty King Hassan II, and continues to be apparent in frequent visits to the Kingdom and in the continuation of Moroccan tradition. In Paris, Caracas, Montréal, and in Israeli cities, Jewish brides wear elaborate wedding costumes made in Tangier, Rabat, and Tetuan as they enact specifically Moroccan wedding rituals. The veneration of righteous individuals, an important element of Muslim and Jewish culture, has been transferred abroad, but is also the major factor drawing Jewish Moroccans to their homeland.

While The Jewish Museum's exhibition celebrates a rich past, it also points to a creative present in which new relationships between Muslims and Jews are being created.

Mohammed VI

KING OF MOROCCO

COMMITTEE OF HONOR

André Azoulay
Conseiller de Sa Majesté le Roi du Maroc,
Sponsor of the Exhibition

M. Mohamed Achaari
Ministre des Affaires Culturelles du
Royaume du Maroc

M. Maurice Arama
Art historian

Mme. Sonia Azagury
Collector

M. Mohamed Benaïssa
Ministre des Affaires Étrangères du
Royaume du Maroc

Mohamed Othman Benjelloun
Chef du Cabinet, Ministère des Affaires
Culturelles du Royaume du Maroc

M. Serge Berdugo
Secrétaire Générale du Conseil des
Communautés Israélites du Maroc

Ms. Patti Cadby Birch
Art historian

Dr. Paul Dahan
Art historian

M. Hamid Fardjad
Filmmaker

Dr. Ivo Grammet
Art historian

Mr. Warren Green
Director, American Friends of the
Alliance Israélite Universelle, New York

Mr. Robert J. Hurst
Chairman of the Board of Trustees, The
Jewish Museum, New York

His Excellency Abdeslam Jaïda
Ambassadeur, Consul-Général du
Royaume du Maroc à New York

Professor Simon Levy
Directeur du Musée du Judaïsme
Marocaine de Casablanca

His Excellency Abdallah Maâroufi
Ambassadeur du Royaume du Maroc à
Washington, DC

M. Edmond Rahman El Maleh
Writer

M. Larbi Messari
Ministre de la Communication du
Royaume du Maroc

M. Hassan Sebbar
Ministre de Tourisme du Royaume du
Maroc

Mr. Ami Sibony
President, American Friends of the
Alliance Israélite Universelle, New York

His Excellency Ahmed Snoussi
L'Ambassadeur du Royaume du Maroc
auprès de l'Organisation des Nations
Unies à New York

Professor Ady Steg
Président de l'Alliance Israélite
Universelle, Paris

M. Jean-Jacques Wahl
Directeur Général de l'Alliance Israélite
Universelle, Paris

LIST OF LENDERS

Anonymous

Albright-Knox Art Gallery, Buffalo

Maurice Arama

Sonia Azagury

Serge Berdugo

Dr. Michael M. Cernea

Dr. Paul Dahan

Isabelle C. Denamur

Dr. Ivo Grammet and Guido Bellinkx

Linda Gross

William Gross

Juliette Halioua

Mr. and Mrs. Abraham Halpern

Israel Museum, Jerusalem

Samuel J. LeFrak

The Library of The Jewish Theological Seminary of America, New York

The Metropolitan Museum of Art, New York

The Minneapolis Institute of Arts, Minneapolis

Dr. Alfred Moldovan

Musée Archéologique, Rabat

Musée d'Art et d'Histoire du Judaïsme, Paris

Musée Batha de Fès, Fez

Musée Israélite de Fez, courtesy of Edmond Gabay, Fez

Musée du Judaïsme Marocain de Casablanca

Musée Sidi Mohamed Ben Abdellah, Essaouira

Museum of International Folk Art, Santa Fe

Rabbi and Mrs. M. Mitchell Serels

Hechal Shlomo
The Sir Isaac and Edith Wolfson Museum of Jewish Art, Jerusalem

Ami Sibony

Anna Stern

14

FOREWORD

The Jewish Museum's exhibition program has often examined a particular aspect of the Jewish Diaspora, bringing into sharp focus through art and artifacts the distinct Jewish cultures that have emerged over centuries. In various exhibitions over the past decade, we have explored the experience of Jews in Italy, on the Iberian peninsula, in the Ottoman Empire, and in Germany – all part of an ongoing investigation of all sectors of Jewish culture in the world.

Morocco: Jews and Art in a Muslim Land continues this important tradition. The story of Jewish Morocco will surprise many with its longevity, the intricate intermingling of Muslim and Jewish culture and rituals, and the exquisite beauty of its artistic creations. Our pride in presenting this exhibition and the accompanying publication has been further enhanced by the honor that comes to us with the patronage of King Mohammed VI, who has enthusiastically endorsed our efforts.

The publication of *Morocco: Jews and Art in a Muslim Land*, to accompany the first American comprehensive exhibition on Jewish Morocco, offers a valuable opportunity to explore and elaborate on this history through both scholarly analysis and personal reminiscences. The historical context of Jews in Morocco is discussed in 'Jewish Communities of Morocco: History and Identity' by Daniel Schroeter. In his reminiscence 'Cradle of the Wind,' Ami Bouganim, a Moroccan-born French writer and educator, recalls his childhood in Essaouira, the hopes of its Jewish community, and the impact of the Alliance Israélite schools on Moroccan Jewry. In 'Esther and I: From Shore to Shore,' Oumama Aouad Lahrech, a writer from a distinguished Muslim family, tells of growing up in the cities of Rabat and Salé that are linked by the Bu-Regreg River. The essay intertwines her own history with that of her best friend, Esther Bitton, and with that of Esther's family. 'Customs of the Jews of Morocco' by Harvey Goldberg analyzes the receptivity to other cultures that accompanied Moroccan Jewry's basic loyalty to the tenets of Judaism and those customs unique to Moroccan Jewry. 'The Kabbalah in Morocco: A Survey' by Moshe Idel traces the arrival of Spanish kabbalistic teachings in Morocco during the mid-thirteenth century and their subsequent diffusion, as well as the roles of astrology, magic, and alchemy in pre-modern Morocco. Finally, in 'Memory, Mimesis, Realia,' Vivian B. Mann, together with Maurice Arama (on paintings) examines the role of Moroccan Jews as both the subjects and makers of art, and the impact of other cultures on the arts of Morocco.

No exhibition of this breadth and scale could be created without the contributions and exceptional work of remarkable people. Dr. Vivian B. Mann, Morris and Eva Feld Curator in Judaica at The Jewish Museum, curator of the exhibition and catalog editor, has brought not only her incredible enthusiasm and extraordinary breadth of knowledge, but also the benefit of years of dialogue with colleagues, collectors, and friends in Morocco, Israel, Europe, and the United States. She is to be congratulated for her impressive achievement. The exhibition's beautiful design was created by Stuart Silver, Honorary Trustee of The Jewish Museum and noted exhibition designer, whose enthusiasm for Morocco's architecture and the country's blend of cultures yielded an exquisite setting for the exhibition. Integral to the realization of the design was the wonderful work of Dan Kershaw, Consulting Exhibition Designer. Because the architecture as well as the landscape of the cities and countryside of Morocco are so much a part of our story, a film was commissioned for use in the exhibition.

Filmmaker Hamid Fardjad has brought visitors closer to Morocco with his exceptional work.

The Jewish Museum is very thankful to the many private and public lenders to this exhibition (listed on page 13). In addition, we are deeply indebted to many Ministries within the Moroccan government for their invaluable assistance in facilitating research, loans, and logistical support, and to Royal Air Maroc for transportation assistance to and from Morocco.

We are also tremendously grateful for the support of the exhibition and catalog given by a number of generous funders. I extend initial thanks to the Museum's Board of Trustees, whose support of and enthusiasm for the institution's mission has encouraged ambitious scholarly endeavors such as *Morocco*. Vital assistance for the accompanying film project has been given by Mrs. Patti Cadby Birch, a testament to her deep love for Morocco and its culture, and by the Centre Cinématèque, Rabat. The American Friends of the Alliance Israélite Universelle, whose story is so integral to the exhibition, has been wonderfully generous. Deep gratitude is extended to long-standing and generous supporters: The Louis and Harold Price Foundation, The Lucius N. Littauer Foundation, the Wolfensohn Family Foundation, Natalie and Charles de Gunzburg in memory of David Amar, the Honorable Ronald S. Lauder, The Morris S. and Florence H. Bender Foundation, The Joe and Emily Lowe Foundation, the Milton and Miram Handler Foundation, Josabeth and Paul Fribourg, and The Norman and Rosita Winston Foundation, as well as the Maurice Amado Foundation for their support of the accompanying catalog. I thank all these donors for their belief in this project and their confidence in the Museum's mission. Further special assistance came from Ruth Blumberg, long-time supporter of The Jewish Museum, Arthur Sibony, President of the American Friends of the Alliance Israélite Universelle, and Juliette Halouia, collector, all of whom have been especially supportive of the inclusion of Sephardic culture in the programming of The Jewish Museum. I would also like to thank Jessica Hirshbein, whose enthusiasm for the museum and the project was most important throughout.

Finally I wish to thank Ruth Beesch, Deputy Director of Program, and all of the staff who were involved in this project: Operations, Development, Curatorial, Registrar and Collections Management, and Media and Public Relations Departments for their extraordinary work in bringing this project to life. It is my sincere hope that this exhibition will bring much deserved and continued attention to the magnificent culture and legacy of Morocco.

JOAN ROSENBAUM
Helen Goldsmith Menschel Director
The Jewish Museum, New York

LIST OF DONORS

Morocco: Jews and Art in a Muslim Land was made possible through the generous support of:

Mrs. Patti Cadby Birch

The American Friends of the Alliance Israélite Universelle

The Louis and Harold Price Foundation

The Lucius N. Littauer Foundation

Wolfensohn Family Foundation

Nathalie and Charles de Gunzburg in memory of David Amar

The Honorable Ronald S. Lauder

The Morris S. and Florence H. Bender Foundation

The Joe and Emily Lowe Foundation

Milton and Miriam Handler Foundation

Josabeth and Paul Fribourg

The Norman and Rosita Winston Foundation

Royal Air Maroc

and other generous donors

The catalog was published with the aid of a grant from the Maurice Amado Foundation.

INTRODUCTION

The artistic and spiritual cultures of Morocco are a blend of many: the cultures developed by those native to the land, the Berbers, and the arts and modes of spirituality brought by successive waves of settlers – the Phoenicians, the Romans, the Jews, and the Arabs. By the seventeenth and eighteenth centuries, a rich and blended culture had developed in which Muslims and Jews participated as both artisans and patrons of each other's art, and in which Jews and Muslims shared paths to spirituality. *Morocco: Jews and Art in a Muslim Land* is an exhibition that examines the ways in which Jews participated in the creation of the dominant Islamic artistic culture of Morocco, as well as in common modes of spirituality with their Muslim neighbors. It concludes with a presentation of the changes in Moroccan Jewish life attendant on the establishment of French schools by the Alliance Israélite Universelle, beginning in 1862, a development that contributed to the formation of a Moroccan diaspora in the twentieth century. Today, the Jewish-Moroccan culture that began in one country has become an international culture, nurtured by deep roots and a continuing relationship with the land of Morocco.

FIG. 1 Bracelet with high bosses, Ida ou Semlal, Anti-Atlas, late 19th – early 20th century; see cat. no. 88

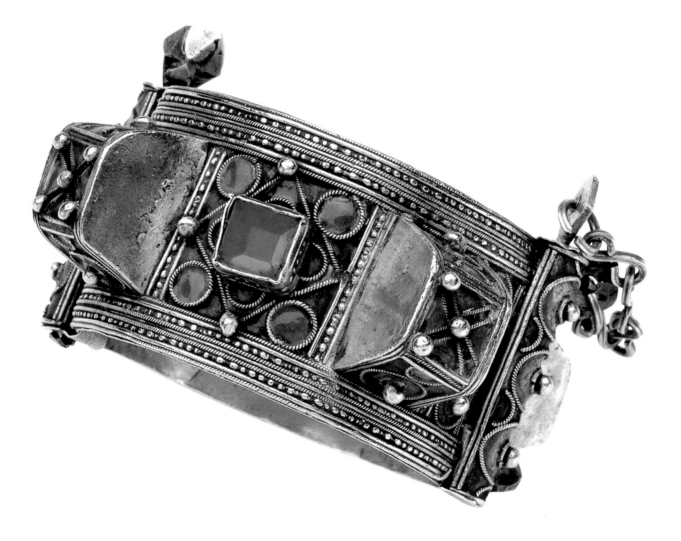

The conceptualization of *Morocco: Jews and Art in a Muslim Land* owes, first, to the many consultants and curators who gave of their knowledge: Alia Ben Ami, Israel Museum; Issachar Ben Ami, Hebrew University, Jerusalem; Nitza Behrouzi, Eretz Israel Museum, Ramat Aviv; Harvey Goldberg and Moshe Idel, Hebrew University; Simon Levy, Musée du Judaïsme Marocain de Casablanca; Daniel Schroeter, University of California, Irvine; and Yaron Tzur of Tel Aviv University.

There were many who helped by introducing me to collectors and those knowledgable about Jewish Morocco. I thank William Gross of Ramat Aviv for introducing me to Dr. Paul Dahan of Brussels and to Dr. Ivo Grammet of Essaouira, both of whom participated in shaping the exhibition and who gave freely of their expertise. Through Dr. Dahan, I met Maurice Arama, who contributed to the catalog, and Guy Joubert, who was exceedingly generous with contacts and resources. Yvette Raby smoothed the way during my first research trip to Morocco and introduced me to Hamid Fardjad of Casablanca, who became an invaluable member of the curatorial team. It was he who conceived the role that audio-visual components could play in the exhibition and who fought for their realization, out of a deep love for his adopted country. Stuart Silver, exhibition designer, came to Morocco and was inspired, creating an outstanding design, which was beautifully realized by Daniel Kenshaw. The organization of preparations for the exhibition was in the capable and very efficient hands of Laura Mass, Project Assistant, whose continual good humor made working with her a pleasure. Laura was ably assisted by Sage Litsky, Exhibition Assistant in the Judaica Department.

Aḥaron aḥaron ḥaviv. There is a Hebrew saying that, translated literally, means "the last is the most dear." We are very grateful to André Azoulay, Conseiller auprès de Sa Majesté Le Roi du Maroc, for his encouragment, support, and for his vision of what this exhibition and catalog might express about the contribution Jews can make in a hospitable and tolerant Arab land.

VIVIAN B. MANN
The Jewish Museum, New York

JEWISH
COMMUNITIES
OF MOROCCO

History and Identity

DANIEL J. SCHROETER

N

SPAIN

ATLANTIC
OCEAN

MEDITERRANEAN SEA

Tangier

Tetuan

Larache
Chefchaouen
Mellila
Ouezzane
RIF
Tlemcen
Ouergha
Oujda
Taza
Sebou
Rabat   Salé
Volubilis
Tahala
Ouad Moulouya
Casablanca
Meknes   Fez
Azemmour
SAIS
Sefrou
Mazagan   *CHAOUIA*
(El Jadida)
Ifrane
Bu-Regreg
MIDDLE ATLAS
Safi
Oum er Rbia
Demnat
Errachidiya
*TAFILALET
REGION*
Essaouira
(Mogador)
Marrakesh
HIGH ATLAS
SIROUA MOUNTAINS
Goulmim
Ksar es-Souq
Ouarzazate
Erfoud
Agadir   Talouine
Sous
*OUAOUZGUITE
REGION*
Dra' valley
Sijilmassa
Aït Baha   Taroudant
Ida ou Semlal
ANTI-ATLAS   Akka
Tiznit
SOUS
Tamgrout
Iligh
M'Hamid
IFNI
PRE-SAHARA
Dra' valley
Ziz River Valley

Goulmim

0   100   200 km
0   50   100 miles

Ancient Origins

The Jewish communities of Morocco have ancient roots. It is unknown when the first Jewish communities were established in the northwestern corner of Africa, but like many communities formed by the far-flung Jewish Diaspora, Moroccan Jews locate their origins in the ancient kingdom of Israel. Legends recount that during the reigns of David and Solomon, 'Jewish' merchants reached the southern parts of Morocco: the Anti-Atlas and the Dra' valley. Traditions on the arrival of Jewish settlers range in time from the deportation of the ten tribes of Israel by the Assyrians in the eighth century BCE to the conquest of Jerusalem and the destruction of the First Temple in 587 BCE. The first Jewish settlers of Ifrane in the Anti-Atlas – reputedly the oldest continuously existing Jewish community in Morocco, where Jews lived until the 1960s – are traditionally thought to descend from refugees fleeing Palestine at the time of the destruction of the Temple (587 BCE). Crossing Egypt, they eventually reached the Anti-Atlas region in 361 BCE.[1] By attributing their origins to the symbolic and formative 'First Diaspora,' Moroccan Jews not only establish their links to the Jewish world and the ancient Land of Israel, but also legitimize their very deep roots in Moroccan soil.

The Maghreb, the northern part of Africa stretching from the western half of Libya to the Atlantic Ocean, is native to the Berbers (*Amazigh*; plural, *Imazighen*).[2] The term 'Berber' (*Barbaroi*) was originally used by the Greeks to refer to the native inhabitants of Africa, as well as of other non-Greek lands. Little is known of the origins of the Berber language, with its many dialects, nor of where the Berbers themselves originated. Some scholars have argued that they migrated from the western Mediterranean during the Bronze Age, but evidence for this theory is inconclusive.[3] The religious beliefs and practices of the Berbers before the Muslim conquests of the seventh century are little-known, except in so far as certain customs, integrated into Islamic practice, can be attributed to pre-Islamic origins. The customs of Jews living among Berbers likewise show their connections to this indigenous culture.

Were there also Jews who were Berbers? Moroccan Jews maintain traditions about Jewish kingdoms and free Jewish tribes before Islam became the dominant religion in the region. But these stories do not refer to Jews as Berbers. Traditions about Berber Jewish tribes are first found in the writings of Arab historians in the twelfth century. A few centuries later, Ibn Khaldun wrote about Berber tribes following Judaism, recounting the story of the Jewish 'priestess' Kahina, who led the resistance to the Arab conquests of the seventh century. The legends of Jewish Berber tribes resisting the expansion of Islam, together with the customs of contemporary Jews living among the Berbers, have convinced some modern scholars that a significant number of North African Jews descend from Berber tribes who converted to Judaism in late antiquity. This theory, however, is based entirely on anachronistic evidence, leaving the question of the possible Berber origins of North African Jews unanswered.[4]

North Africa also witnessed a series of foreign invaders from at least as far back as the ninth century BCE, when the Phoenicians established colonies along the coast, the most famous of which was Carthage in present-day Tunisia. It is plausible that some Jews found their way to the North African Punic colonies and then moved to the southern confines of Morocco. There is no doubt, however, that Jewish communities

FIG. 3 Map of Morocco

Page 25

FIG. 2 Rabbi riding with his grandchild to his fields, Oulad Mansour, High Atlas, March 1950. Photograph by Elias Harrus. The Jews of Oulad Mansour, unlike those of other communities in the High Atlas, were mainly farmers.

FIG. 4 Man in *akhnif* (man's cape), Ouaouzguite, 1935–36. Photograph by Jean Besancenot.

were established in Morocco during the Roman period. The Romans destroyed Carthage in 146 BCE and became the dominant power along the North African coast, contesting with Berber tribes for control of the interior. The Jewish Diaspora spread throughout the Hellenistic Mediterranean world of the Roman Empire, its growth increased by the destruction of the Second Temple in 70 CE and the subsequent expulsion of the Jews from Palestine. North Africa became an arena for intensive missionary activities: an emerging Christianity and a developing rabbinical Judaism contested for converts.[5] It is plausible that among the Jewish settlers arriving in Morocco during the Roman period there were missionaries who successfully converted some of the Berber inhabitants to Judaism. The oldest archeological evidence of Jews living in Morocco, inscribed stones, date from the third century CE, from the Roman site of Volubilis, near Meknes.[6]

Jewish communities, whether descended from the inhabitants of ancient Palestine or from Berber tribes converted to Judaism, were probably scattered throughout Morocco by the time of the Arab conquests of the seventh century. Legends about 'Jewish kingdoms' abound in Ifrane and the southern Dra' valley. We are told that the original settlers were merchants of King Solomon's time, and that their descendants greatly multiplied, eventually taking control of the region around the fifth century

FIGS. 5, 6 *Akhnif*, Siroua, c. 1930; see cat. no. 141

BCE. The Jewish community preserved traditions, possibly dating from the twelfth century CE, of great battles fought between Christians and Jews in the Dra' valley.[7] Jewish hegemony in the Dra' valley was supposed to have lasted until the eleventh century CE, when the region was taken over by Sanhaja Berbers under the Almoravid dynasty. While there is little evidence to support these traditions, they do reflect the ancient roots of Jewish communities in the Dra' valley and Anti-Atlas.

Morocco and the Islamic World

The number of Jewish residents in Morocco increased greatly when the region was brought into the Islamic world. Jews moved to Morocco from other parts of the Middle East and Mediterranean basin as Arab rule extended from Iraq to Spain in the seventh and eighth centuries. They settled largely in the Berber districts of southern Morocco. These regions, the Berber inhabitants of which had converted to Islam, were fertile grounds for Kharijites, as sectarian movements that emerged in various parts of the Middle East and North Africa in the early centuries of Islam were often called. The Kharijites rejected the hereditary right of Arabs to lead the Muslim community and opened the door to converts of all races and groups. Berber Kharijite states emerged in southern Morocco, building their bases of power in part by monopolizing the trans-Saharan trade. The city of Sijilmasa, a southern oasis in the Ziz valley, was founded in 757 CE by a Kharijite movement called the Sufrites, which extended its hegemony westward over the Dra' valley. Jews living in the region came under the protection of the Kharijite state. Sijilmasa developed into a thriving city and major center for international trade, linking traders from Moroccan communities in the Dra' valley, Sous, Atlas, and Fez not only with the trans-Saharan trade, but also with traders from far beyond the Maghreb.

Evidence for the existence of a Jewish community at Sijilmasa dates from the tenth century. Not only merchants lived there, but also rabbinical scholars of some stature. Sijilmasa's community formed part of a broad network of Jewish merchants and scholars linking various parts of the wider Mediterranean world, Iraq, and the Indian Ocean.[8]

Jews settled in the city of Fez shortly after its foundation in the early ninth century. The city became the capital of the Idrisids, the first Moroccan-based Sunnite Islamic dynasty. Fez's Jewish population increased rapidly, reaching, according to one estimate, 90,000.[9] The eleventh-century Arab traveler and geographer, al-Bakri, wrote that Fez "has more Jews than any other town of the Maghreb; from there they go to all the faraway countries. The people of the Maghreb have a proverb: '*Fas bled bla nas*' [Fez is a town without people]."[10] So numerous were the Jews that it was as if the city had no Muslim inhabitants.

Marrakesh was the second major Muslim city to develop in Morocco. It was founded in 1062 as the capital of the Almoravids (*al-Murabitun*), a Berber dynasty that built an extensive empire, including the Maghreb and Spain. During the Almoravid period Jews lived at Aghmat, on the northern flank of the High Atlas, about forty-five miles southeast of Marrakesh; they were forbidden to reside in the new capital, although they would come there to trade. It is unclear whether Jews lived in Marrakesh in 1147, when it was conquered by the Almohads, another Moroccan Berber dynasty that succeeded the Almoravids and extended its hegemony over much of the Maghreb

FIG. 7 Jewish woman's headdress,
Dra' valley, late 19th century; see cat. no. 77

31

FIG. 8 *Sefer Abudarham*, Fez, 1521;
see cat. no. 5

and Spain.[11] The founders of the Almohad dynasty were intolerant of non-Muslims, and Jews were subjected to forced conversion. This was the only period in Moroccan history when Jews were not allowed to practice their religion. Maimonides of Cordova was living in Fez at the time of the Almohad persecution. He left for Egypt, urging other Jews to quit areas where forced conversions were taking place. Many Jews continued to practice Judaism secretly, and it is also likely that Jews found refuge in the isolated villages of the mountains to the south of Marrakesh, where they remained until the second half of the twentieth century. The Almohad persecutions, however, did not last, and by the 1220s Jews were living in Marrakesh and openly practicing Judaism. The Marinid dynasty, which took over in the mid-thirteenth century, made Fez its principal capital, but a sizeable Jewish community also developed in Marrakesh, Morocco's southern royal capital.[12]

Morocco was an integral part of a wide network of highly mobile Jewish communities in the Mediterranean world during the Middle Ages, and major intellectual and religious currents affecting other parts of the Jewish world profoundly affected Moroccan Jewry. In the ninth century, the Karaites, a group that rejected the hegemony of the rabbinical leadership and its reliance on the Talmud as a source of authority, spread throughout the Mediterranean basin, including Morocco. North Africa was particularly receptive to sectarian movements, as is evident not only in the period before the rise of Christianity, but also in the emergence of the Kharijite states after the spread of Islam. It is likely that Karaite and Rabbanite controversies erupted in Morocco's major communities. And while Rabbanites prevailed in the cities, especially in Fez, which was already a major center of rabbinical scholarship in its early period of Jewish settlement, Karaite practices survived for centuries.[13] In the sixteenth century, Leo Africanus observed of the Atlas that 'Great numbers of Jewes remaine in this region, which live as stipendarie soldiers under divers princes, & are

FIG. 9 *Mellah* (Jewish quarter) of Tissent, Aït-Bouli, High Atlas, 1952. Photograph by Alfred Goldenberg.

continually in armes; and they are reputed and called by other Jewes in Africa Carraum [Karaites], that is to say, heretiques.'[14] It is not certain that the Jews of the Atlas actually affiliated themselves to the Karaite branch of Judaism, but in some of the more remote communities in Morocco, heterodox practices were able to thrive outside the reach of the rabbinical leaders of Morocco's major communities.

At the same time, Jewish communities in the far south were connected not only to the major urban communities of Morocco, but also had a profound influence on religious developments throughout the Maghreb. With the development and expansion of the Kabbalah, Jewish mystics in the Sous, Tafilalelt, and especially the Dra' valley became well-known throughout Morocco for their kabbalistic works.[15]

The Sephardic Diaspora

Morocco was closely linked to developments in Spain, where the largest and most prosperous Jewish population in the world lived during the Middle Ages. But, as the *Reconquista* by the Catholic monarchs progressed in Spain, Jews were increasingly persecuted. After a wave of anti-Jewish violence in 1391, many Jews sought refuge in Morocco, where the ruling dynasty, the Marinids, was more hospitable to them. Spanish or 'Sephardic' Jews settled throughout the country, particularly in the northern cities (such as Tetuan), which became major destinations for Iberian refugees. Fez received a large number of Jewish immigrants, and as the city's Jewish population grew, the Marinid Sultan 'Abd al-Haq b. Abu Sa'id decided to confine the

FIG. 10 *Mellah*, Fez, fall 1998. Photograph by Anna Stern.

Jews to a special quarter near the palace in 1438. The immediate cause of the sultan's decision was a Muslim massacre of the Jewish community, following allegations that Jews had placed wine in the mosques of Fez. The sultan intervened by relocating the Jews to a quarter next to the imperial city in 'New Fez.'[16] But the broader context of the inter-religious tension may well have been competition between Jews and Muslims over urban space, especially in light of the growing immigration of Spanish Jews. The spot chosen by the sultan was called the *mellah* (see fig. 10), and soon the new Jewish quarter swarmed with thousands of arrivals from Spain, following the expulsion of Spanish Jewry in 1492. The term *mellah* came to be used for other quarters in Morocco where Jews resided in a designated, enclosed district of the city. In the sixteenth century, the Jews of Marrakesh were obliged to live in a *mellah* built by the Sa'dians, a dynasty that took control of Morocco in that century and centered its power in the southern capital. In the nineteenth and twentieth centuries, the term *mellah* came to mean any Moroccan Jewish quarter, or by extension, any individual Jewish community in Morocco.[17]

In many of the places they settled in Morocco, the new arrivals from Spain were collectively know in Hebrew as the *megorashim* (or 'those expelled'), to distinguish them from the native Jews, the *toshavim* (or 'residents'). In northern Morocco, the refugees usually formed the majority of the community. In Fez, which contained Morocco's largest Jewish community during this period, Spanish refugees exercised enormous influence on the religious and cultural life of the community. Their influence was also significant in southern and eastern communities. In Debdu, a community in eastern Morocco where the majority of the town's inhabitants were Jewish, Jews of Spanish origin appear to have formed the dominant family groups.[18] In Marrakesh, the Spanish refugees were concentrated in one area and maintained separate synagogues. A French observer noted in 1903: "In Marrakesh there are both native and Spanish Jews. Each sect possesses synagogues and a *Talmud-thora* of its own …"[19] Over the centuries, however, the descendants of Spanish Jewry in many Moroccan communities assimilated aspects of the indigenous Jewish culture, and this gave birth to a new, uniquely Moroccan cultural synthesis.[20]

Jewish Society under the 'Alawids

In the seventeenth century, the 'Alawid dynasty emerged from the *shurafa* (sing. *Sharif*; a descendant of the Prophet Muhammad) of the Tafilalet region of southeastern Morocco and succeeded in gaining control of the country. This dynasty still reigns. The center of power moved back and forth between Marrakesh and Fez, except during the reign of the powerful Sultan Mawlay Isma'il (1672–1727), who made the city of Meknes his capital. In 1679, he ordered a *mellah* to be built, and the Jewish community of Meknes developed into one of the most important in Morocco. In 1807, Sultan Sulayman decreed that Jews who had until then lived side-by-side with Muslims in Tetuan, Salé, Rabat, and Essaouira should move into *mellah*s. Other cities may have been affected as well.[21] Since it was incumbent upon Muslim rulers to protect *dhimmi*s (literally, 'protected persons') in times of disorder or inter-religious tensions, the sultan acted to protect Jewish communities by establishing *mellah*s, and perhaps also to placate popular hostility towards the Jewish population.

FIG. 11 A Jew from the village of Oulad Mansour negotiating the purchase of a cow from a Muslim seller at the market, Demnat, High Atlas, May 1950. Photograph by Elias Harrus.

Jews in the major cities under the control of the sultan were therefore reliant on royal authority to assure the safety of the community. But the sovereign also relied on Jews to perform important and necessary services, such as the collection of customs duties, minting coins, and diplomacy. Jews also served as royal merchants, receiving monopolies to trade in certain goods with European countries. Following the Almohad period, there were no longer indigenous Christians in Morocco, and the interdependency between the sultans and the Jews, the only *dhimmi*s, was therefore particularly strong.

Jews were an integral part of the social landscape of Morocco, serving as intermediaries between rural and urban societies. In several locales Jews farmed as late as the twentieth century, for example, in the community of Oulad Mansour on the northern flanks of the central High Atlas (see fig. 11).[22] Nahum Slouschz, the first scholar to write extensively about the history of North African Jews, observed Oulad Mansour in 1913: "Of its twenty-five families, fifteen or sixteen live by cultivating the soil … they raise wheat, barley and fruit, above all figs and dates." In many regions, Jews owned land and cattle, employing Muslim sharecroppers and shepherds. Almost everywhere, whether in the larger cities or rural villages, Jews were engaged in commerce or crafts. In small communities throughout rural Morocco, Jews were frequently the only craftsmen, "employed in the trifling mechanical occupations which the Brebes [Berbers] require," according to an English physician who visited Morocco in 1789.[23] As elsewhere in the Muslim world, jewelry was predominantly a Jewish profession. In the Anti-Atlas community of Tahala in the region of Tafraout, approximately half the Jewish population were jewelers, according to mid-twentieth-century observers.[24] Throughout Morocco, Jews were merchants and peddlers, forming a vast trading network.

One can often trace the emergence of new Jewish communities to changed trade routes, which, in turn, reflected shifts in political power. Morocco was linked to a wide network of international trade. Prior to the twentieth century, the largest commercial cities of Morocco were not along the seacoast, but in the interior of the

FIG. 12 Jewish jeweler, Tahala, Anti-Atlas, May 1958. Photograph by Elias Harrus.

country, where its most important industries were located. Jews were involved in linking these cities with the rural hinterland, often as traders traveling from one weekly market to the next. Since Jews were not part of the tribal system, with its many political rivalries, they possessed a neutrality that meant they could serve as vital intermediaries.

Jews were also involved in long-distance trade. Morocco was one of the major northern termini for the trans-Saharan trade, and Jewish merchants served as suppliers and financiers of the major caravans leaving from Marrakesh, Fez, and other towns at different stages of the caravan routes. Jewish communities were scattered along the trade routes to the very northern edge of the Sahara, where the large annual caravans made their desert crossings. From the southern capital of Marrakesh, the Jewish community was tied to various smaller Jewish communities south of the Atlas and along the southwestern trade routes in the Sous, such as Iligh, Akka, or Goulimime. In the Dra' valley, a region famous for its dates, Jewish communities acted as links in the trans-Saharan trade route. They were found in numerous locations: for

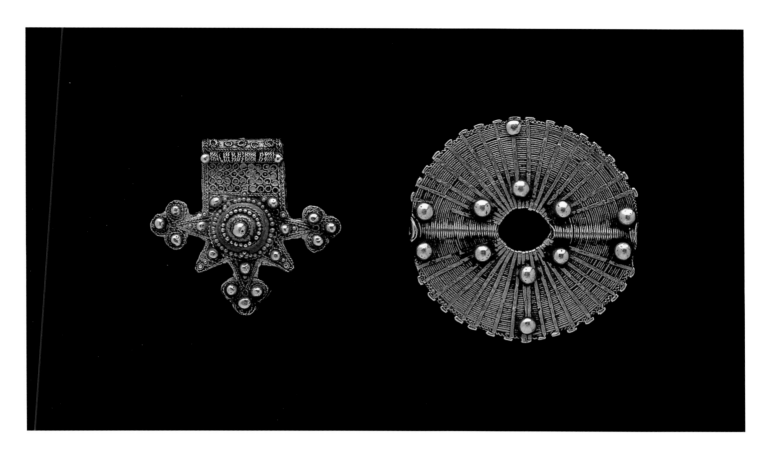

example, the two communities of the Ktawa region, Beni Sbih and Bni Hyun, and the most southerly Saharan community of M'hamid Ghozlan. Fez was linked by southeastern trade routes to the Tafilalet, where Jewish communities were found in Qsar Suq, Errachidiya, and other towns in the southeastern Ziz valley.

Some of the commerce with sub-Saharan Africa was for local consumption, such as the trade in slaves and gold, or served the Saharan people, such as the trade in salt. But the trans-Saharan and domestic trade routes were also linked to trade with Europe. In exchange for gums, almonds, olive oil, and ostrich feathers, Moroccans imported European manufactured goods (especially textiles) at the time of the industrial revolution. From the southeastern routes, goods were transported first to Fez and then to the northern Mediterranean towns of Tetuan and Tangier, where they were exchanged for European goods. The central authorities often had a difficult time controlling the flow of goods exchanged in the southwestern Atlantic seaports. European powers frequently sought to strike commercial deals with regional powers, which disconcerted the central government (the *Makhzan*), who forsaw the loss of both political control and potential revenues.

In 1764, Sultan Sidi Muhammad b. 'Abdallah founded the port of Essaouira (known as Mogador in Europe) with the aim of channeling the European trade through a closely controlled royal port and deriving customs revenue through the expansion of foreign trade. Jews were instrumental to his plan, and members of major Jewish mercantile firms from all over Morocco settled at the new port to conduct trade.

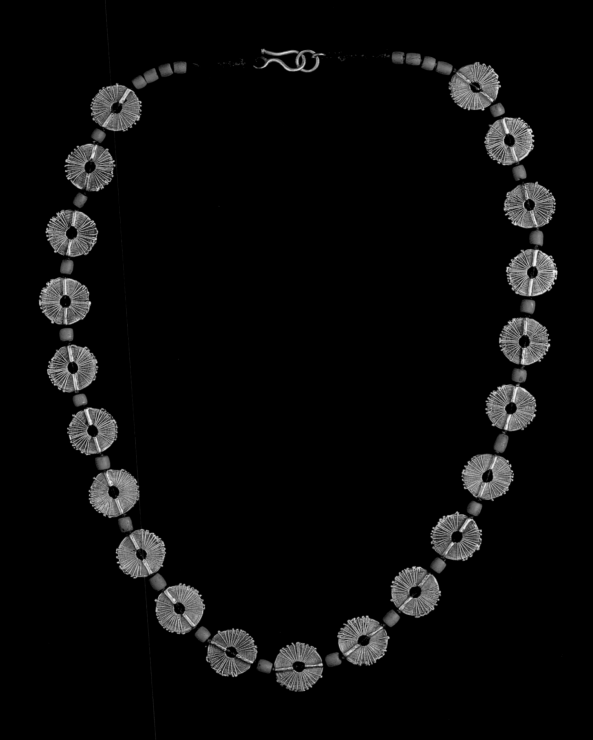

Essaouira grew to become Morocco's principal seaport, a position it maintained until the late nineteenth century. Its Jewish community became one of Morocco's largest and constituted between 30% and 40% of the town's general population. The city became a magnet for Jews living in southwestern Morocco, and the merchants of Essaouira were also connected to the communities of Marrakesh, to other seaports, and to the trade routes in southern Morocco.[25]

Moroccan Jews in the Wider World

Moroccan Jews were also part of the wider Jewish world. Although acculturated to their local rural environment, the Jews of even the most remote regions in the Atlas maintained connections with larger communities in the cities, and through them with the Jewish world beyond Morocco. From the sixteenth century on, the élite merchant families traveled frequently between Morocco and Europe, readily moving between the major Sephardic communities in Europe, such as those in London, Amsterdam, or Livorno, and Moroccan trade centers. Commerce and scholarship often went together, and rabbis and merchants were linked to the Sephardic world as a whole. Moroccan Jews were also among the principal settlers in Ottoman Palestine, forming communities of 'Westerners' (*ma'aravim*) in Jerusalem, Safed, Hebron, and Tiberias.[26] A time-honored tradition among fund-raisers for *yeshivot* (rabbinical academies) of the Holy Land was to send out emissaries (*shliḥim*) to the far-flung Diaspora communities. Morocco was a major destination for many emissaries, some of whom had been born there. The emissaries not only collected funds in the major cities of Morocco, but also circulated in the small towns and villages of the countryside.[27] As a result, the Moroccan countryside is scattered with the venerated tombs of rabbi-emissaries who died on the road, graves that have been converted into pilgrimage shrines by local Jewish inhabitants.[28]

On the eve of modern times, Moroccan Jewry was a diverse population, consisting of more than two hundred communities, large and small. The majority of Jews spoke the Moroccan Arabic dialect, but with added linguistic features that differentiated Jews from Muslims. In Morocco, as elsewhere in the Arab world, this language was called Judeo-Arabic, and when written, it used Hebrew characters. Some communities with heavy settlements from Spain, such as Tangier, Larache, and Tetuan, maintained a Judeo-Spanish dialect known as Haquitía, while others adopted the language and customs of the indigenous, Arabic-speaking Jewish inhabitants. In Berber-speaking regions, Jews were usually bilingual, speaking Berber with their Muslim neighbors, and Judeo-Arabic at home. In a few of the most isolated communities of the High Atlas, some Jewish communities spoke Berber only.

These variations point to the differing origins of Moroccan Jews, as well as to their long history of migration. Jewish names in Morocco also reflect the diversity of their origins, with names derived from Arabic, Berber, Spanish, places of origin in Spain or the Middle East, or the professions in which Jews specialized.[29]

The role of Moroccan Jews as merchants made them the primary intermediaries between Morocco and Europe. From the Sa'adian period of the sixteenth century, and continuing in the 'Alawid period (beginning in the seventeenth century), the majority of Moroccans conducting trade with Europe were Jews. European traders relied on a string of Jewish merchants in Moroccan coastal towns – Rabat, Safi, Essaouira,

FIG. 14 Necklace, Tafilalet, early 20th century; see cat. no. 83

39

FIG. 15 Eugène Delacroix, *A Jewish Woman of Tangier in Festive Costume*, 1832; see cat. no. 93

Opposite

FIG. 16 Anonymous, *Moroccan Peddler in London*, mezzotint: colored, c. 1800; The Jewish Museum, New York, gift of Dr. Harry G. Friedman (F5895)

Tetuan, or Agadir (depending on the period) – who maintained multiple ties with other Jews in the interior of the country. Some of the élite families in Morocco were part of a wider, transnational network of Sephardic merchants. Moroccan Jewish merchants resident in European ports formed an extensive trading network and a web of associations and familial ties that dominated North African trade in the eighteenth century. There was a constant flow of merchants back and forth from Tunis, Algiers, Tripoli, Tetuan, Essaouira, and Gibraltar. Since there were no permanent embassies or consulates representing Morocco in European countries, Jews often represented Moroccan sultans on diplomatic and commercial missions. Jews from Morocco and elsewhere in North Africa, who joined the Sephardic community in London, for example, were called 'Berberiscos' (i.e. from the Barbary) by the 'native' Sephardim. Gentiles called them 'Barbary Jews.' It was not only diplomats and merchants who were known in Europe; in London, for example, Moroccan peddlers were a familiar part of the Anglo-Jewish landscape, noted for their 'Turkish'-style dress and for their sale of spices, rhubarb, and Moroccan slippers.[30]

While Moroccan and European Jews were part of the same transnational Jewish world, by the eighteenth century European Jews began to distinguish themselves sharply from their coreligionists in the Maghreb. Samuel Romanelli, a learned Italian Jew from Mantua, was able to spend several years in Morocco by using his considerable linguistic and intellectual skills, preaching in synagogues and working for Moroccan merchant firms. He lived among the Jews of Tetuan, Marrakesh, and Essaouira, and visited many other communities. His popular account in Hebrew, which was published in several editions in Europe, is among the most detailed portraits of Moroccan Jews of the eighteenth century.[31] While nominally subordinate to his Moroccan patrons, he revealed in his book his sense of superiority to his coreligionists, whom he regarded as relatively primitive and superstitious. Romanelli's account offers more of an insider's view of Moroccan Jewry than non-Jewish European accounts of this time, but at the same time, his picture of native Jews mirrors the orientalist images of Barbary (as the Maghreb was called in Europe) current at the time, wherein the European civilization of the Enlightenment is contrasted sharply with the irrational and tyrannical East. Regarding Moroccan Jews, he wrote: "a veil of obscurantist faith corrupts their hearts and blinds their eyes."[32]

Europeans who traveled or lived in Morocco usually had closer contact with Jews than with Muslims. Because of their intermediary role between Europe and Morocco, and their minority status, Jews were more receptive to Christian visitors than Muslims, who were apprehensive of contact with foreigners. Almost all the published accounts of Morocco in the eighteenth and nineteenth centuries contain some descriptions of Jews and Jewish customs, especially those of Tangier and Tetuan, which were the cities most visited by Europeans. Some offer detailed descriptions of Jewish weddings, and many describe the beauty of Jewish women. "In no part of the world, perhaps, are more beautiful women to be seen than among the Jewesses at Tangier," wrote an English observer, echoing the remarks of many travelers.[33]

Muslim authorities frequently required Jews to accommodate Christians who were in Morocco on diplomatic business. During their diplomatic missions to the sultans in Fez and Marrakesh, Europeans were often housed in the Jewish quarter. For example,

41

the painter Eugène Delacroix, who was attached to a diplomatic mission, was fascinated by the Jews he met in Tangier during a visit in 1832. He stayed at the family house of the dragoman of the French Consulate, Abraham Benchimol, who was his interpreter and guide and one of a number of Jewish subjects that the artist painted from life in Morocco.[34] Christians relied on Jews not only as interpreters and commercial agents, but also for contacts in the interior of the country, because the lucrative markets and centers of royal power were inaccessible to them. Europeans in Essaouira relied on Jewish middlemen to ransom European captives whose ships had run aground on the treacherous southwestern coast. Sometimes Jews were given control of collecting customs duties or tolls. In 1823, Meir Macnin, a Jew from Marrakesh who had spent many years as a merchant and diplomatic agent for Morocco in London, was given complete control over the export of goods from Larache, El Jadida, Casablanca, and Safi, as well as the exclusive right to export oxen from the ports of Tangier and Tetuan.[35] He also became the chief conduit in Tangier through which all communications to the sultan were made by foreign embassies. Europeans sometimes complained that practically no diplomatic or commercial business could be accomplished in Morocco without the assistance of Jews. Despite the ambivalence of Europeans toward Moroccan Jews, Jewish merchants continued to be employed as consular representatives in Moroccan ports, or dragomen in European embassies. Even Spain, which still banned Jews from Iberia, did not hesitate to employ them as consular representatives.

European Intervention and Influence

The growing influence of Europe in Moroccan affairs during the nineteenth century deeply affected Moroccan Jewry, whose élite already had close ties to European countries.[36] The opening of Morocco to foreign trade, and the arrival of a greater number of foreign traders (especially after the Anglo-Moroccan treaty of 1856, which stipulated the protection of both British subjects and their agents in Morocco), resulted in Moroccan Jews coming in greater numbers under the auspices of foreign powers and consulates.[37] They were considered by European powers and merchants as vital intermediaries in the conduct of commerce in the country, especially since foreign merchants were largely restricted to coastal cities far from the towns and markets for which most of their goods were destined. Thus, Jewish middlemen with connections to the string of Jewish communities in the interior of the country were instrumental in opening up lucrative domestic markets to foreign trade. Merchants in the ports employed middlemen not only in the major cities of Fez and Marrakesh, and in other coastal towns, but also scattered throughout the countryside, in the Tafilalet, Dra' valley, and Sous.

Foreign embassies in Tangier often found it useful either to employ leading Jewish merchants as their consular representatives in port cities, or to extend patents of protection to Moroccan Jews that granted their protégés extraterritorial rights, guaranteed by commercial treaties with the European powers.[38] Jewish communities, both in the coastal towns and in the interior, looked increasingly toward the European powers for their well-being and protection, in addition to relying on the traditional protection of the sultan. In the 1880s, the Jews of the town of Demnat in the Atlas

Opposite

FIG. 17 Théo van Rysselberghe, *Portrait of Abraham Sicsu*, c. 1880; see cat. no. 99

43

FIG. 18 Medal commemorating journey of Sir Moses Montefiore and Isaac Adolphe Crémieux to campaign against anti-Jewish measures in Damascus. Artist: GNR, Berlin, 1840; The Jewish Museum, New York, gift of Samuel and Daniel M. Friedenberg (FB802)

appealed to the European consulates against the arbitrary actions of the town's governor. The case of the Demnat Jews became a cause célèbre among foreign diplomatic missions in Morocco.[39]

European Jewry also began to intervene in Moroccan affairs. Prior to the nineteenth century Moroccan Jews had seen themselves as part of a wider Sephardic Jewish world, encompassing Europe and the Middle East, but post-Enlightenment European Jewry increasingly saw Moroccan Jews as 'Eastern' or 'Oriental' Jews, who were less developed and in need of philanthropic support to achieve emancipation and to modernize their community through superior schooling. If the Damascus Affair in 1840 – a notorious Syrian blood libel case – was an important turning point in mobilizing European Jewry for an international lobbying campaign to defend Jews in distress,[40] it was Spain's attack against Morocco in 1859–60 and its occupation of Tetuan and the surrounding region that inspired the first major philanthropic campaign on behalf of Moroccan Jewry. Nearly three thousand Jewish refugees fled Morocco for Gibraltar as the result of the Spanish attack, including a fifth of Tangier's Jewish community; the Jews of Essaouira also fled to sea or into the countryside. (It was not, however, the first time that the plight of Morocco's Jews had caught the attention of Europe's emancipated Jewish citizenry. In 1844, following a French bombardment of the ports of Tangier and Essaouira, the *mellah* of the latter port was pillaged, and as a result a charitable fund was established that was presided over by Sir Moses Montefiore, the leader of London's Jewish community; figs. 18, 19.) A fund-raising campaign in 1859–60 to support the refugees of Tangier and Essaouira was so successful that a surplus remained that was used for further charitable works in Morocco.[41]

A few years later, when a Jewish boy was executed in Safi, and other Jews were imprisoned for allegedly poisoning a Spaniard, the now venerable and elderly Sir Moses Montefiore embarked on one of his last international missions. He met with the sultan, Sidi Muhammad b. 'Abd al-Rahman, who issued a royal decree (*dahir*) proclaiming that Jews in Morocco were protected by justice under Moroccan law.[42] Montefiore and European Jewry may well have had in mind the Ottoman decrees that effectively eliminated *dhimmi* status and gave Jews and Christians, at least in theory, equal rights. In Morocco, however, even the theoretical concept of modern citizenship did not exist, and Sultan Muhammad IV merely reformulated the traditional role of the Islamic state as protector of *dhimmi*s. But for Moroccan Jewry, the Montefiore visit was of the utmost importance. They witnessed a powerful foreign Jew, backed by the European powers, gaining an audience with the sultan and speaking on their behalf. The sultan's decree, clearly intended to placate the foreign powers, also made the Moroccan sovereign a grudging partner with European Jews in guaranteeing the protection of the Moroccan Jewish communities.

The single most important influence in the transformation of the Moroccan Jewish community was the Alliance Israélite Universelle (AIU), founded in Paris in 1860. The declared purpose of this French Jewish philanthropic organization was to work towards the "emancipation and moral progress" of Jews around the world. The Alliance became one of the most active lobbying groups in the Jewish world, attempting to improve the status of Jewish communities. But its most important

influence lay in the establishment of a network of Jewish schools, primarily in the Mediterranean basin. These Jewish schools, with their mainly secular curriculum, provided a modern education, to 'regenerate' the 'backward' Jewish communities.[43]

Morocco was the largest field of operation for the Alliance.[44] Its first school opened in the northern Moroccan town of Tetuan in 1862 (fig. 20, p. 46), and schools in other Moroccan cities were soon established. Although Alliance pedagogy met with some resistance from traditional rabbinic leaders, who saw these modern educators – often backed by the power of the French Consulate – as a challenge to their leadership, the Jews of Morocco came to accept the schools as a permanent feature of their communities. By the time the French and the much smaller northern Spanish protectorates were established in 1912, the AIU had schools in many of the coastal towns, including Tetuan, Tangier, Larache, Rabat, Casablanca, Safi, El Jadida, and Essaouira, and in major cities of the interior: Marrakesh, Fez, and Meknes.

Growing foreign influence in Morocco, and the particular role that Jews played as intermediaries in developing international trade, led some Moroccan Jews to emigrate to European countries, the Americas, or other parts of the Middle East and North Africa. This stream of emigration began to accelerate in the late eighteenth century. In the mid-nineteenth century, regular steamship lines included Moroccan ports in their networks, and transportation to Europe and even to the New World became much easier. The travel of many Moroccan merchants to Europe for trade (for example, to London, Manchester, Livorno, and, later, Marseilles) gradually led to emigration as well. Moroccan Jews would settle in the British enclave of Gibraltar, on the southern Iberian Peninsula, in London, or in Manchester, and become naturalized British subjects. Others were able to obtain French passports in Algeria with growing frequency and ease once France occupied that country in 1830. Some Moroccan Jews remained abroad as part of a permanent diaspora community, while others would return, their new status as foreign nationals a cause of considerable tension and conflict with the *Makhzan*.[45]

In the nineteenth century, small numbers of Moroccan Jews began to settle in Portugal, from which Jews had been banned since the time of the Inquisition.[46] Even more significantly, the Spanish invasion of northern Morocco in 1859–60 and the

FIG. 20 School of the Alliance Israélite
Universelle, Tetuan, 1862. Photograph by
N. Boumendil.

occupation of Tetuan may have set in motion a process of emigration to South
America, especially to Argentina and Brazil, that continued throughout the second
half of the nineteenth century. The Spanish occupation, though it lasted only a few
years, and the increased number of Spanish emigrants in Northern Morocco, revived
to some extent the waning Spanish cultural identity and the Judeo-Spanish dialect,
known as Haquitía, spoken by the Jews of Tetuan, Tangier, and elsewhere in the north.
These communities took pride in what they believed to be their purer Spanish origins,
referring to the Jews of Fez and Marrakesh as *forasteros* ('outsiders'). Emigrants from
northern Morocco brought their dialect to the New World, as Jews from Tangier,
Tetuan, and other Moroccan towns settled in the cities of Argentina, Venezuela, and
Brazil, and in smaller numbers in other Latin American countries. Moroccan Jewish
immigrants made their livelihoods in commerce and peddling, and also sought to
take advantage of new opportunities in the Amazon Basin, with the growing demand
for Brazilian rubber after 1880.[47]

Conditions also appeared more favorable in Palestine because of Ottoman reforms
and the growing influence of foreign consulates in Jerusalem, some of whom offered
protection to Jews.[48] A growing number of Moroccan Jews, from the cities as well as
the mountains, joined the already existing North African communities in the Holy
Land. While the largest number settled in Jerusalem, Jews of North African origin
formed the majority of Sephardim in Safed, Tiberias, Jaffa, and Haifa. Moroccan Jews
often combined religious motivation with commerce. Not only merchants moved to
Palestine, but also peddlers, artisans, and even the indigent.[49] Emigration was often
impermanent. The frequent return of emigrants to Morocco, together with new
departures, created a sense of a transnational Moroccan Jewish community by the
nineteenth century.

Under Colonial Rule

Colonial rule began formally in 1912. Morocco was divided between the French, who
came to rule most of the country, and the Spanish, who ruled the northwestern tip
(Tangier was later made into an international zone). While the treaty establishing the
Protectorate proclaimed the sovereignty of the sultan over all the Sharifian territories
and maintained the principle of indigenous government, real authority was vested in
the colonial powers. Under the guise of maintaining sovereignty, the French
authorities would issue royal decrees (*dahirs*) that the sultan was obliged to sign. The
first Résident Général of the French Zone, Maréchal Lyautey, who represented France
from 1912 to 1925, was particularly influential in establishing the Protectorate system
under which Morocco was to be governed for nearly forty-five years.

Some Moroccan Jews, especially the younger generation that had been educated in
the schools of the AIU, or those who enjoyed the status of protégés of foreign powers,
sought advantages under French auspices. But their hopes of attaining full rights and
even French citizenship were not realized. Unlike the the French citizenship awarded
Algerian Jews en masse by the Crémieux Decree of 1870, the status of Moroccan Jews
remained poorly defined. Westernized Jews, especially those with foreign protection,
had hoped to be subject to adjudication in the European courts that were established
by the French and the Spanish, independent of the indigenous courts, to judge cases

FIG. 21 Moses Ganbash, *Shiviti* with Topographic Map of the Land of Israel, Istanbul, 1838–39; The Jewish Museum, New York, F5855

involving Europeans. But in both the French and the Spanish Zones, the Jews were still considered to be subjects of the sultan and under Sharifian jurisdiction, even if, in reality, the French administration came to dominate in inter-religious affairs, taking over the control and supervision of the *Makhzan* authorities. The French authorities distinguished between the juridical authority of the state and the religious courts. Cases between Moroccans, regardless of their religion, were to come under the jurisdiction of the *Makhzan*. This implicitly did away with the concept of the Islamic state. Jews were no longer subject to the stipulations governing *dhimmi*, nor to the inequities of the *shari'a* courts, which were based on Islamic law. Nevertheless, they were formally recognized as 'indigenous,' a status resented by Westernized Jews. The position of the Jewish population as a whole remained ambiguous, since there was as yet no clearly formulated notion of nationality. In other words, the Protectorate authorities effectively did away with *dhimmi* status, but failed to provide a coherent legal framework for Jews.[50]

At the beginning of the Protectorate, Jewish communities maintained considerable internal autonomy. In principle, the Protectorate granted the rabbinical courts (*beit din*) jurisdiction over disputes involving civil, personal, and commercial matters. Gradually, however, their competence was reduced to matters concerning personal litigation, marriage, divorce, and inheritance. Furthermore, in 1918 the administration issued a *dahir* that reorganized Jewish communal structure. The domain of responsibility of the community 'committee' was specified: administration of religious affairs, charitable organizations, and management of pious foundations (*heqdesh*). The committee was made up of a president of the local rabbinical court or a rabbi, and a number of notables, appointed by the Grand Vizier from lists compiled by the community. The committee was appointed for two years and could be renewed. In effect, the *dahir* gave the administration direct control of the running of the community, through the Inspecteur des Institutions Israélites, an official of the Direction des Affaires Chérifiennes. While the ostensible reason for the reorganization was to modernize the administration of native institutions, the effect was simply to render the community subservient to colonial rule without providing it with the means to adapt to change.[51]

Although under colonialism Jews did obtain certain rights not previously held, the self-governing status that Jewish communities, as *dhimmis,* had enjoyed under Islamic law was undermined. The formal roles of the official representatives of the Jewish community and of the rabbinical courts were restricted. Informally, rabbinical leaders continued to exercise considerable moral authority over Jewish communities, and their intervention was often sought in disputes outside their official responsibilities.

In 1915, the French authorities established a system of public schools for Jews, with the intention of eventually replacing the AIU network. A number of Alliance schools were taken over, but the AIU increased its efforts to recruit students for its schools, unwilling to relinquish the influence that it had gained in the pre-Protectorate period. In 1924, the French authorities decided to give the Alliance control of most of the Franco-Jewish schools. With the help of annual subsidies from the French, the Alliance was able to maintain its preponderant role in secular education for Jews in Morocco.[52] The AIU continued to expand its network into the small towns of the countryside, which the organization referred to as the *bled* (in Moroccan Arabic, one's native region or locality). In the wake of the French conquest of additional areas, new schools were opened. It was not before the 1930s, however, that the southern parts of Morocco were firmly under French control. In 1932, the Alliance opened a school in Demnat; after World War II, when the French authorities extended their control over the southern flanks of the Atlas and the Saharan oases, the Alliance began opening schools in these areas too. Through financial assistance from the American Joint Distribution Committee, a new network of schools was established in predominately rural areas of Morocco.[53] The AIU was still launching new schools until the 1950s, in communities such as Akka, Iligh, and Goulimime, only a few years before the mass migration from these regions began. When these schools were opened, the AIU realized that it was likely that these communities would emigrate, and so they regarded the education of the children for life in the modern world as their primary task.

The Alliance, more than any other institution, was responsible for creating the modern Jewish élite in Morocco. But there were other schools that joined with the Alliance in the education of Jewish youth. Technical education was provided by the Organization for Rehabilitation through Training (ORT), and the American-based Sephardic religious institution, Otsar Hatorah, together with the Lubavitch movement, founded a network of religious schools.[54] Locally based *yeshivot* also developed to educate a new generation of rabbis, *dayanim,* and other religious functionaries of the Jewish communities.

Colonial rule also set in motion a process of urbanization and natural population growth that greatly affected Jewish communities. The Moroccan economy's new ties

to Europe meant that the coastal cities drew more and more population from the interior of the country. Of particular importance was the development of Casablanca, which in the nineteenth century had been a small town. The French decided to develop Casablanca as their main seaport and commercial center, and it rapidly grew to become Morocco's largest city. Casablanca drew Jews from all over Morocco, especially from the south, and became home to the largest Jewish community in the country. By 1952, the Jewish population of the city numbered almost 75,000, about 10% of the total.[55]

Other cities also grew rapidly during the colonial period. The city of Rabat, together with Salé on the opposite bank of the Bu-Regreg river, was home to older Jewish communities, and contained *mellah*s that were created in 1807. When the

French chose Rabat as their administrative and political capital, a large settlement grew outside the old city ramparts. Its Jewish population grew from about 2400 in 1913 to about 12,000 in 1947.[56] The Jewish population in the town of Oujda, a medium-sized city near the Algerian frontier, likewise increased during the Protectorate, from about 1190 in 1910 to about 3175 in 1952.[57]

The Jewish population of the cities of the interior also changed during colonial rule. Marrakesh, the historical capital of southern Morocco, became a magnet for surrounding rural communities and the far-flung Jewish communities of the south.[58] During the years after World War II, however, the Jewish population of Marrakesh dropped dramatically, from about 25,000 in 1936 to about 16,000 in 1952.[59] Fez's Jewish population remained fairly steady, while Meknes witnessed some growth. In Marrakesh, Fez, and Meknes, and in other cities of the interior, some Jews left the *mellahs* for the new neighborhoods built in the colonial French style outside the ramparts of the *medina*, the historical core of the city. A gap grew between this new, increasingly frenchified bourgeoisie and the Jewish residents of the *mellah*, where Jewish migrants from rural Morocco usually settled.

Scattered throughout the interior were new towns, often built next to smaller, older settlements, that served as commercial or administrative centers for the French. In these towns, such as Beni Mellal or Midelt, in the midst of important agricultural regions, or Errachidiya (an important military base en route to the Tafilalet) in the southeast, major Jewish communities developed. Jews in these new colonial towns, which were built next to new roads and new trade routes, continued in their middlemen roles as merchants, shopkeepers, and sometimes transporters.

FIG. 24 Interior of Synagogue, Amzrou, c. 1950. Photograph by Z. Schulmann.

While some of the bigger cities witnessed large increases in their Jewish populations as a result of internal migration, the Jewish communities of the rural hinterlands usually continued to exist, and sometimes expanded, as new modes of transportation and networks of trade developed. Smaller rural communities averaged between twenty to thirty families (or between one hundred and one hundred and fifty people), while small towns in the interior typically had Jewish populations of between five hundred and three thousand. And while a number of small rural communities disappeared in the 1930s and 1940s, the result of emigration to the cities, most of the rural town *mellahs* continued to exist until the 1950s. By the time the mass migration of Moroccan Jewry began in the 1950s, there were probably between 230 and 250 Jewish communities, large and small, in almost every region of Morocco, with a total Jewish population of close to 280,000.[60]

Independence and Emigration

Moroccan Jews had always maintained close attachments to the Holy Land. Most of the European founders of the modern Zionist movement were, however, ignorant of or disinterested in the Jews of North Africa as potential partners in settling Palestine. A scattering of Moroccan Jews formed Zionist organizations at the end of the nineteenth century that affiliated with the World Zionist Organization, despite the low priority given to the Moroccan groups.[61] However, Zionism never developed into a mass political movement in Morocco as it did in Eastern Europe. To a certain extent, those Jews who were part of the more modern political culture that Zionism entailed were drawn to France and French culture, as espoused by the teachers of the Alliance schools. But the Jewish masses in Morocco were also aware of developments in Palestine, and the efforts to create a Jewish nation struck deep religious chords.[62] Thus, active participation in political Zionism was not a precondition of immigration to Palestine: other factors led to the mass immigration to Israel in the 1950s and 1960s.

The foundation of the State of Israel in 1948 marked the first major wave of immigration to Palestine. The French administration placed obstacles in the way of Jewish emigration, but by 1949 it realized that the stream of departures could not be stopped, and it therefore allowed the Jewish Agency to create an organization, Cadima, to conduct emigration to Israel.[63] Zionists were now able to operate openly and prepare the population for departure. As the struggle for Moroccan independence grew in the 1950s, anxiety over the future mounted among Jews. In 1955, a year before Moroccan (and Tunisian) independence, North African Jews represented 87% of the new immigrants in Israel.[64]

As Morocco approached independence, a few Moroccan Jews joined the nationalist movement, but most stayed on the sidelines without actively participating in politics.[65] Others prepared to leave the country, and a more massive emigration began. After independence, the Zionist movement could no longer operate legally, and emigration was organized clandestinely, sometimes resulting in tragedy. The most notorious event took place in January 1961 when a ship smuggling forty-three Jews out of Morocco sank: all the Jewish passengers drowned.[66] The restrictions on emigration were relaxed following the unexpected death of Mohammed V in 1961. His son, King Hassan II, quietly allowed Jews to emigrate, while later, in the last decades of the twentieth century, he encouraged Moroccan Jews who had settled in Israel to return to Morocco. King Hassan II died in the summer of 1999, and his son and successor, King Mohammed VI, has continued this open-door policy.

Moroccan Jews have lived in several worlds in the twentieth century. On the one hand, most remained loyal to Mohammed V, despite the obstacles he placed in the way of emigration. The king was much venerated by the Jewish population, who considered him to be fulfilling the traditional role of protector. During World War II, when the Vichy regime established in Morocco attempted rigorously to apply the racist Statutes des Juifs, Mohammed V was believed to have refused to cooperate with the French Protectorate authorities. While his role as protector of the Jews in the war may not have been as proactive as many Moroccan Jews believed, his sympathetic attitude towards his Jewish subjects left his image untarnished.[67] Upon his death in 1961, the Jewish masses poured out into the streets in a great display of public mourning, a scene remembered by Muslim Moroccans today.

After independence, some Jews continued to see their future in Morocco, and a number of prominent leaders have held government positions. The future of the Alliance Israélite Universelle and other international Jewish organizations operating in Morocco was not clear. Threatened by government takeover, the Alliance was able to negotiate its continuing presence in independent Morocco by integrating its course of study into the national curriculum, subsidized by the Moroccan government.[68] Renamed 'Ittihad-Maroc' (Alliance-Morocco), a network of schools continued to function and to educate a new generation of Jewish youth. But emigration forced the

FIG. 25 'Black Panther' demonstration at the Western Wall, Jerusalem, 1971

closure of the rural schools, and the number of pupils in the Alliance's schools in the cities also diminished as mass emigration continued into the 1960s.

Moroccan Diasporas

The majority of the 280,000 Jews in Morocco emigrated to Israel, where they settled mostly in 'development towns' along Israel's borders, or in the poorer, working-class districts of Israel's main cities. In Israel today, Jews of Moroccan origin, including those born of Moroccan parents, number nearly 500,000. In the 1950s, a decade of heavy immigration from the 'Eastern communities' of Asia and Africa (*edot ha-Mizrah*), Moroccan Jews were pressured to assimilate, their North African culture not valued by the dominant Ashkenazi element of the Israeli occupation. But in recent years, Moroccan Jews have sought to revive their ethnic heritage, taking greater pride in their history. This heritage includes the veneration of saints, and pilgrimages (*hillulahs*) to the graves of holy men on the anniversaries of their deaths. During these celebrations, pilgrims light candles, chant liturgical poetry, dance, and drink a Jewish-Moroccan eau-de-vie (*mahia*). It is believed that the saints perform miracles, such as the healing of the sick or the curing of infertility. The greatest pilgrimage that developed in Israel is to the grave of Simeon bar Yohai, who is the second-century CE rabbi popularly assumed to have written the book of Zohar. On the annual festival of Lag B'Omer, over 100,000 people flock to Meron in Galilee, where the grave of the ancient rabbi is located. Another greatly venerated rabbi is the Moroccan-born Israel Abu Hatzera, known as Baba Sali, who died in the Negev town of Netivot in 1984. His picture is found in homes, shops, and restaurants throughout the country, as well as in prayer books, calendars, and even on mundane items such as key-holders. Since his death, the *hillulah* to his grave has become the second largest such gathering in Israel, again with over 100,000 participants.[69] The shrine of Rabbi David u-Moshe in the High Atlas of Morocco was traditionally the goal of thousands of pilgrims every year, and, at the end of the twentieth century, many Moroccan Jews living in Israel still return to visit his grave. In 1973, a man in Israel had a dream that Rabbi David u-Moshe appeared and asked to live with him in a tiny room in his apartment in Safed. This room became the site of a *hillulah* drawing some 20,000 pilgrims per year.[70] This transfer of Rabbi David u-Moshe to Israel is one example of how Moroccan culture has taken root in Israeli soil.

Yet Moroccan Jews are part of a wider, transnational community that stretches across continents. While the destination of the largest number of emigrants was Israel, the hardship of life there and the promise of greater prosperity in Europe or North America influenced a number of Moroccan Jews, some of whom were already middle-class, to emigrate to France, Canada, and, in smaller numbers, to the United States, Belgium, Switzerland, Spain, and other countries. For those Moroccans who were more influenced by and attached to French culture, France or Montréal appeared more attractive than Israel. In France, Moroccan Jews and their offspring probably number over 100,000. Heavily concentrated in Paris, Moroccan Jews have moved into traditional Ashkenazi districts, or settled in new suburbs north of the city. In Montréal, Jews of Moroccan origin number about 20,000 and have developed a range

FIG. 26 *Hillulah* compound of Rabbi David u-Moshe, Timzrit, near Agouim, High Atlas, 1998. Photograph by Rose-Lynn Fisher.

of community institutions independent of the already existing Anglophone community. Moroccan Jews have not restricted their settlement to French-speaking Québec, but have also settled by the thousands in Toronto and other Canadian communities. Several thousand Moroccan Jews have also settled in New York, Washington, DC, Los Angeles, and other cities in the United States.[71]

In the last two decades, Jews from this far-flung Moroccan diaspora have returned to visit Morocco in growing numbers. Often through organized tours, Moroccan-born Israeli, French, and Canadian Jews combine tourism with pilgrimage, visiting their birthplaces and the countryside shrines of Jewish saints.[72] These shrines, some of which had fallen into disrepair, have in recent years been refurbished; new hostels have been set up to accommodate the pilgrims and existing accommodations improved. Jews from other countries of the Moroccan diaspora have joined their Israeli counterparts in forging a new sense of a wider Moroccan Jewish identity.

Moroccan Jewry, like so many other communities of the Diaspora, is exceptionally cosmopolitan. At the crossroads of the Mediterranean and the Atlantic, Morocco has, since antiquity, experienced a constant ebb and flow of peoples, resulting in a rich and unique cultural synthesis. Polyglot Jewish merchants, scholars, and travelers have served as links to the wider world since the early Middle Ages: they connected sub-Saharan Africa, the Middle East, India, Europe, and, in more recent times, North America. Sharing the universal beliefs and practices of their coreligionists in other countries, their Judaism has never been doubted. Even in the seventeenth century, an English Christian observer of the religious practices and beliefs of Moroccan Jews remarked: "There are not to be found among them [any] who publickly own the Samaritan Schism, in rejecting all books of Scripture, but the pentateuch of Moses …

FIG. 27 Repairing household wares, Oulad Mansour, High Atlas, March 1950. Photograph by Elias Harrus.

nor are there any to be met with who adhere to the *Old Bible,* without *Talmud-Traditions.*"[73] Yet, Judaic and cosmopolitan as they are, Moroccan Jews have, paradoxically, also been very parochial, rooted in indigenous culture and sharing with their Muslim compatriots characteristics that would immediately identify them as Moroccan. The veneration of saints, a practice that existed in all the Moroccan communities, is perhaps the most striking example of the particularity of Moroccan Jewish culture; yet this seemingly heterodox practice has not prevented Moroccan Jews from adhering to religious practices found everywhere in the Jewish world. Nowhere has this paradox been so apparent as with the thousands of Jews who lived in the Atlas and valleys until the early 1960s. Here, the Jews were an integral part of the social fabric, sharing a range of customs and beliefs with the Berber inhabitants, but always maintaining their distinctive Jewish identity. Despite the rugged terrain and inaccessibility of many of the areas where Jews lived, these communities were never totally isolated but were part of the wider currents of Jewish history.

According to Moroccan law, natives who leave Morocco cannot lose their nationality. With only about 4000 to 5000 Jews remaining in Morocco at the beginning of the twenty-first century, there is a particular poignancy to this principle. The vast majority of Moroccan Jews are scattered throughout the world. A new generation is being born outside Morocco, with the largest community living in Israel, but with substantial numbers in France and North America. These Moroccan Jews and their children are forging new identities in the countries where they live. Few consider the possibility of building a future in Morocco. But whether Israeli, French, or Canadian citizens, many still regard themselves as part of a wider Moroccan Jewish culture, linked by their continued or rediscovered attachments to their places of origin.

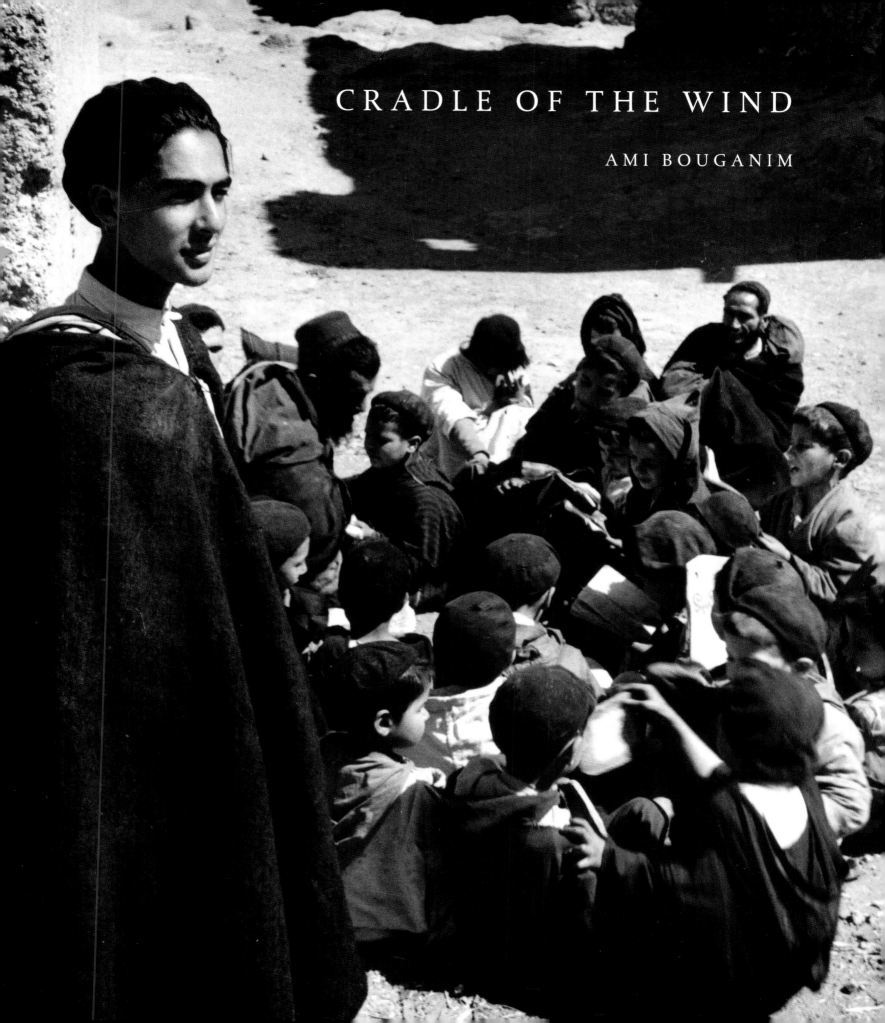

CRADLE OF THE WIND

AMI BOUGANIM

FIG. 28 Portuguese Ramparts, Essaouira, March 1999. Photograph by Yvette Raby.

I was born in Essaouira-Mogador, the fifth in a large family, three girls and four boys, rocked by the same winds that had visited and turned the heads of my forefathers and their forefathers before them. Indeed, I feel I have been entrusted – without really knowing by whom or by what – with the tricky mission of putting these winds, their pranks, and their boisterousness into words. Maybe because I was born on a particularly stormy night when three or four palm trees had their leaves stripped off, and a trawler vanished without a trace of memory in the unfathomable baggage hold of the ocean. Maybe because Elijah the Prophet – who heralds the coming Messiah – was there that night in the city and only came to see me in my swaddling clothes to observe my consternation, transform my tears into laughter, and burden me with the illusion that literature is the source of salvation. More likely because the famous demons of Mogador held a synod over my cradle and decided that I was sufficiently like them – exhibiting almost all of their moral qualities and dispositions – to try to get them out of this overly prudish (for their tastes) city and represent them the world over. But that day, those rascals were so bad-tempered and evil-minded that they failed to provide me with the gift and talent I needed to accomplish my secret mission.

Three or four days later, my father, delighted to have enriched his lineage with a second male heir after three vain attempts that had produced only girls, invited his prayer companions to come and exorcise the demons who lie in wait for newborn infants, especially when they are born to the most vulnerable community in the world, the community of God's chosen few, in particular in Mogador, the peninsula of the Diaspora, exposed to all the dark eclipses of the heavens and all the malevolent winds of the earth. They must not have prayed with sufficient fervor or deference as regards my father (who behaved as though he were the virtual prophet of Mogador) since for the last fifty years I have been playing with words and produce only bad ones, nasty and somber comments on the literary deficiencies of humanity as a whole

FIG. 29 Amulet for a newborn son, Morocco,
20th century; see cat. no. 113

and my own inhibitions in particular. Mogador, of course, is rightfully proud of
having more than one minor scribbler who doubtless dedicated who knows what
poem or narrative to it, but I alone identify with its winds and demons with such
frivolity and derision.

So do not attribute the perversity of this narrative to the synagogue criers who
never stopped trying to drag me to their kabbalistic séances and submit me to their
exorcisms, the rabbis I never stopped heckling so they would put a little humility into
their ragged beards, my poor teachers whom I hounded with insidious questions and
disarmed with my criticisms, my unfortunate mistresses whom I besieged with my
desires, or even less, my poor father, who died like everybody else, waiting for the
Messiah although I was right there beside him. The only ones who deserve the blame
are the demons of Mogador, who slip so craftily into the most solemn and ponderous
of my writings, making a laughing stock of my most serious poems, philosophical
stances, and stirring orations.

In that terrible and glorious year, Mogador had fully come to terms with its elderly
and senile. The unfortunate city survived on its memories, ruminating on its past
glory, consular titles, and grandiose colonial illusions. Forty years after the founding of
the Protectorate, it was still waiting for the event that would lift it out of its degrading
retirement and assign it a new historical mission. Maybe the landing of the Chinese or

FIG. 30 Rooftops, *medina*, Essaouira,
March 1999. Photograph by Yvette Raby.

the Martians, maybe the discovery of an oil field or a diamond mine. Maybe the conquest of Mogador by the Canadians or its incorporation into the Principality of Monaco. Ships no longer entered the harbor; they anchored in the open sea where the tugboats and barges unloaded their cargos of China tea and loaded them with Sous almonds. Mogador no longer knew the terrors of bombardment or the thrills of boats docking. She was on the fringes of history, banished from the heavens, at the windswept crossroads, and she vegetated like old maids who wait behind the closed shutters of their houses for a princely suitor's proposal made under their balconies and carried by the matchmaking winds. The more she declined, the more she dreamt; the more she dreamt, the more she waned away.

The people of the Kasbah, descendants for the most part of the king's courtiers and their rabbis, refused to resign themselves to decadence. Even though they had ceased to speak much English, they continued to live at the pace and in the manner of the English. Their houses looked like museums, filled with antiques and knicknacks encrusted with memories, and their features were like coats-of-arms, pretty and ugly at the same time. The French now lived in villas they had built for themselves on the coast. Naturally, like all colonists the world over, they gave the impression of being there without being there, but they had their Mogador too: a typically French way of worming their way through the ramparts, meeting its people, braving its authorities. They were as caught up with the place as the Jews or the Muslims, they were infected with the prudish insinuations of the wind, the dark ocean spray, the whispering of the monkey trees. They were in Paradise and relieved their boredom by Muslim-bullying, Jewish vexations, fancy balls, and reading newspapers and magazines that described – weeks and months later – the fads and crises that had shaken the wide world from which they had retreated in order better to observe its infatuations and antics. They did not work; they oversaw their properties or their canneries. They were the new masters of the city without being its heirs – intruders perhaps, who had nevertheless changed their ways. The winds now had French names, the sea carried echoes of the Marseillaise, my father wore a black beret, and my mother sang me lullabies from Lorraine.

I have resigned myself to entertaining my readers with a confession as to the circumstances of my birth. For some time, even the idea of revealing more than three or four obligatory lines in small type would have seemed pretentious and devoid of any interest. Until a few months ago, I never assumed there was any importance to my brief passage in this world, any genius in my intuitions, or even talent in my literary sales pitch that could make me believe for an instant that my life could be of interest to strangers. Naturally, I have revealed intimate details here and there, cleverly blending the true and the false the better to breach the trust of my readers; emphasizing certain features, playing down others, practicing my literary skills with the complete impunity a bad writer can produce by mixing genres and covering up his tracks. However, I never committed the sin of believing that my works would share the same destiny as the sacred texts. First of all, my life is as bleak as a monk's, fuller than the life of a scientist, and as pedantic as that of a pedagogue. Second, over the last few years I have had to earn my pittance by compiling bad biographies and saying good things about everyone, to the extent that this type of book and character nauseates me. So if I finally decide to reveal my life to you, it's because I've recently had a revelation that authorizes me to stake my claim as the Messiah, without having to worry about reprisals from heaven. I have no doubt that this first avowal, the greatest of all avowals, which conditions the value of all the rest, will elicit mockery, invective and even maybe – hopefully – anathema, and I am nonetheless intimately, resolutely, and irremediably convinced that I am the best candidate of my generation to profess to this caustic title. I am not joking, I speak with full knowledge of the facts. I spent decades looking for my Messiah, in books of course, in temples and academies, in newspaper columns and on television screens, in the markets and the streets, and even in monasteries, in libraries, research institutions, and cancer wards, vagrants' benches and city sidewalks, and every time I discovered a likely candidate and examined him for signs of messianity, I saw that I had more convincing ones. Exhibiting symptoms of divine dementia, I found my own attitudes and ecstasy more promising than theirs. Exhibiting signs of miraculous powers, saving the incurables, curing neurasthenics, and opening sterile entrails, I found my prowess in the domain even more remarkable. I found my gifts even more amazing and perspicacious. Time and time again, I was convinced of being able to do better than the most impressive statesmen, the cagiest schemers, the most prolific writers, the most remarkable scientists, the sharpest salesmen, the most talented actors.

Finally, one day I decided to drop my Mogadorian reserve to amass the most glorious laurels in all the physical and intellectual fields. From disaster to disaster, from torment to torment, from bitterness to bitterness, I finally realized that I was no worse than any of the others and that I could cite my messianic childhood without blushing. In any case my whole life would have unfolded with the intimate belief that to have been born in a murky city, dangerously exposed to the waves of the dark ocean which threaten at any time to bury it in a shroud of ooze and mud, the arena of

FIG. 31 Synagogue of Rabbi Ḥayyim Pinto, Essaouira, 20th century

the contradictory winds that whirl around whoever ventures out into the street, the hideout of all the demons who have chipped away at men's minds since the beginning of creation, the theatre of miracles where only calamities take place, the den of all sources of visions hatched out of boredom and megalomania. I could claim these haunting memories, these illusions, these mirages, and these perversions as mine and present myself, in all legitimacy, as the Messiah of Mogador with no fear of being refuted by history – from which this city would be permanently and irremediably freed – by its people who would have lost their memory, or even less so by its winds, which despair today more than ever that someone will extract more meaningful confessions from them than all the insanities and stupidities that have been attributed to them up to now.

I can't tell you exactly who my mother and father were, for the simple reason that they themselves did not really know who they were or what kind of beast they had produced. Both had grown up in the *mellah* at the turn of the century in one of the alleyways that crawled under the buildings and sprawled underground in search of safety and perhaps light, in one of those rickety houses where the staircases threatened to collapse at any time in one of the inner courtyards where silence was a virtual miracle. The visitor who dared set foot in this labyrinth of misery and pity had no idea that it was one of the most privileged retreats of the divinity, who indulged every day in a discordant concert of litanies and incantations. The authorities had opened the portals of the *mellah*, but its people, locked for centuries in their dreams and nightmares, could not bring themselves to cross the threshold for fear of losing themselves in the wide world. They were waiting for a guide who would lead them to the Promised Land; they never despaired of His delay, and called for His coming in all their prayers. A long wait, which perhaps turned into stagnation, and surely into sweet senility. Their beards had grayed, their voices had become hoarse, and their gazes narrowed. Nonetheless, they were still the incarnation of God, a fallen divinity, broken and groping in the dark muddy streets. I don't know why they had reached such an extreme. Perhaps because their divinity, intractable and finicky, did not accept half-measures and carried out His intentions fully, propelling the decline of His earthly representatives into uselessness and debility, as it would propel their massacre into genocide and their restoration into military triumph. But the people of the *mellah* were just as unable to exonerate their divinity as they were to agree on His motivations and intentions. They were set in their bleak boredom, ruminating over promises with silver linings, fretting over terrible prophecies, enthusiastic when reading the sweet Psalms, mumbling interminable incantations in Aramaic, and only abandoning the mundane to declaim, excited and impatient, their Song of Songs and rekindle their desire for divinity. They prayed and multiplied, from Sabbath to Sabbath, since the beginning of time and to the end of time.

On the other side of the city, the Kasbah seemed to glitter. It was the link to the outside world, it received its furniture from Manchester and its dresses from Paris, bought everything and sold everything. It was as religious as the *mellah* and no less versed in the sacred texts, and it felt no less obligated to give charity to the poor and

FIG. 32 Jew of Mogador, 1935. Photograph by Jean Besancenot.

the stranger, the widow and the orphan. However, it remained shockingly unmoved by the misery of the *mellah* and its people, whom it clearly considered to be primitives, only relinquishing alms to protect its reputation in the eyes of visitors. It was perhaps a mortuary of the rich, from which emanated a distrust for these Judaized Berbers that was shared by almost all of the exiles from the Spanish expulsion, most of whom were descendents of the high aristocracy. In any case, it was a terrible powerlessness of the sacred texts, which failed to penetrate the moral or social awareness of these courtiers and descendents of courtiers, who needed to journey to London and Paris to be moved by the fate of their coreligionists. In the Kasbah, the divinity made Himself at home at the turn of the century and had let Himself become very Britishly stilted in manners, politesse, and starch. The same divinity? Another divinity? The messiahs, as my flesh and blood testify, only emerge in the name of new divinities to protest the human perversion of the previous ones …

Both of my parents had passed through the gates of the *mellah* to sit on the school benches of the Alliance Israélite. My father, perhaps a descendant of the Oufrane Berbers who had settled in Mogador in the middle of the eighteenth century, was a strange man. The only thing I knew about him was that he was God-fearing, had his primary school diploma, a hardware store, and chattered in the Berber dialect. (Naturally this very mundaneness detracts from my claims to messianity, since the man was clearly not descended from King David, but some unknown lines are more unpredictable and more illustrious than pathetic royal lineages.) From God, my father received a holy fear of failing to observe one of the religious commandments, closely supervising his offspring so as to prevent any deviation, correcting their behavior and continually restoring them to the paths of the straight and narrow.

From the Alliance, he received a curious Basque beret that supposedly covered his real or imaginary ringworm and that he never removed – neither for the Casablanca city dweller's hat nor the worker's cap of Netanyah. From his hardware store, he had only nails, which he was later to bequeath, plus interest, to a morose local rabbi in return for a promise to build a synagogue in his memory. He received the dubious merit of willing me the Berber dialect, to which I gladly attribute to my human condition when I am disconsolate about my Jewish fate, rebel at my Arab nature, and am distressed by my disordered French. I also inherited from him a scabrous sense of humor that instinctively puts into my mouth all sorts of questions, each one more preposterous and futile than the last, which have the merit of disorienting my audience and giving them doubts as to my sanity: for example, whether they believe in God; whether they will write a will one day; whether they prefer grilled or fried grasshoppers; or whether they know that they are condemned to die. Above all, I inherited some of his psychopathic excuses, which I will say nothing about so as not to profane his memory. I will only say that the older I get the more I seem to know him; since I reached the age of resembling him, I discover more and more often his features in my mirror, surprise myself more and more in finding his gestures and mannerisms in my movements, perceive more and more often his laugh in my laughter, and these reunions give me both remorse and satisfaction, remorse because I did not thank him for giving me life, and satisfaction for not having perpetuated his lineage. My father was just an ordinary shopkeeper who borrowed from courtiers

FIG. 33 Teacher of religious studies with pupils, Tazenakht, northern Anti-Atlas, March 1954. Photograph by Elias Harrus.

converted into small private bankers. He vanished regularly to collect merchandise from Casablanca, and, after his return, the store would fill up with pots and pans, bolts and locks, screws and nails, hammers, saws and pliers, axes, shovels and pickaxes, hand-turned grinders, mousetraps, and oil heaters. New bags of chickpeas, peanuts, chunks of washing soda, sticks of cumin, cinnamon, sesame seeds, and ground pepper were stacked up. Merchants came to hear the latest news from the big city, and after them came a parade of mountain folk who bought more from enjoyment than from need.

He stood behind the counter from dawn to dusk, with a break between one o'clock and two o'clock for the midday prayer, a meal generally composed of our leftovers, and his daily half-cigarette, which he smoked with the great delight of partaking of a semi-sin and a semi-pleasure. This stalwart father of mine never ceased telling us how hard he worked to feed us, clothe us, send us to school, believing his pedagogical duty was to make us feel how much of a burden we were. I suspect he never really knew what work was, at least until he left for Israel; not even one day of tedious tasks or brimstone from a boss. Clients, naturally, he had from the city and elsewhere, but also all the idle of Mogador. First, the courtiers, who had not worked for generations, living off who knows what, the most penniless finally resigning themselves with more or less good grace to trade with the people of the *mellah*, without, however, pushing their renunciation so far as to venture into its reeking alleyways. They put on their suits and ties, wore white moccasins, and held a rolled-up newspaper in their hands. Every day like clockwork they made their tour of inspection of the Kasbah to catch up on the news with the shopkeepers and check on their holdings at the same time; without fail they ended up at the English Speakers' Club or the Circle Français. They did not even pretend anymore to be waiting to embark or give the impression of having just disembarked, and were so bored that they leaped at the opportunity of the first domestic incident to give it the scope of a cosmic scandal. An unexpected decease plunged them into moroseness that resuscitated their imaginarily ailments, and they busied themselves intently rewriting their last will and testament from the perspective of imminent death. A locust invasion, enormous waves, an eclipse of the sun, prompted them to perform their penitential exercises to ward off catastrophes even more terrible than the annunciatory signs had heralded. They kept their warehouses, now empty, only because they were a company name, a mark of grandeur and nobility, an excuse to hope – and because they found no buyers. The doors, closed with chains and heavy padlocks, were pierced with small circular apertures that allowed cats, the great mouse-hunters of Mogador, to chase the rats that attacked the foundations. From time to time, one of them purchased a shipment of almonds, mobilized a cohort of sorters, and began searching the world over for a buyer; once in a while, one would even go to Casablanca to take the boat to Manchester or Marseilles, but most of the time he prepared for his own departure, his share of some obscure inheritance, or attempted to prevent one of his sons or grandsons from marrying a foreigner.

My father received them in his shop with all the due respect the people of the *mellah* could muster, despite their resentment of these ex-courtiers of the king. He offered them stools, took an interest in their health, which he knew was delicate (it

FIG. 34 Jew of Mogador (David ben Barukh), 1936. Photograph by Jean Besancenot.

was the custom to complain about bad health to protect oneself from the evil eye), and asked them about world news. When they were particularly generous they left him their newspapers, which he plunged into immediately, leaving aside his weekly Torah portion, his Psalms, and his Book of Splendors. After the courtiers, he received the college of rabbis, on their collection rounds. To one he paid the price of a sermon, to another the price of his blessing or the religious instruction he gave to his offspring. Then came the procession of beggars who scrutinized you from head to foot even when they were blind, with one eye beseeching, the other eye threatening, claiming their alms with the assurance of those who know that their riches are guaranteed in the world to come, and, united with the heavens through their poverty, feel authorized to administer curses or blessings. In this realm of consuls, vice-consuls and consular agents, they were the most illustrious and miserable of God's ambassador-consuls. They were cantankerous, vehement, servile, with all the attributes of godliness. They were, behind their rumpled beards, their grating voices, and their rags, still divine. They did not beg for themselves or their families, but for the salvation of the giver and the perpetuation of the divine presence among men.

The child, perched on a stool, a fistful of peanuts in one hand and sesame pods in the other, couldn't always tell the difference between the rabbis and the beggars. Both were the true masters of the city now, more so than the Arabs and even more than the French. Maybe with the lunatics, the countless lunatics of Mogador, who ran after the wind with more daring than the most visionary of rabbis and the bravest of beggars, beyond the bounds of time and reason, routing the gods from their hideouts in the sanctuaries, proclaiming their treason on the streets and in the marketplaces, attempting to extract them from their prostration in a city deserted by history and occupied by demons. At last came the rabbi, a bag in one hand and a cane in the other, reciting endless blessings under his breath; the child got off his stool, emptying his hands into the bags of peanuts and sesame seeds. He grabbed a fold of the man's heavy black robe and was trundled through the gates, past walls, streets, squares and markets, shops and more shops, horses and camels, dogs and cats, to Prison Street where he lived. And in the shadows of a room that gave out on to blackness, around a simple oil lamp, he told the long story of an old man's wait, one that had already lasted more than two thousand years …

ESTHER AND I

From Shore to Shore

OUMAMA AOUAD LAHRECH

TRANSLATED FROM THE
FRENCH BY YAEL AZAGURY

In my father's memory

My heart is now open
to welcome all forms.
The gazelles' grazing grounds
And the monks' monastery!
A shrine for its idols
The Ka'aba for he who circles it
The Torah Tables
And also the Koran's leaflets!

Ibn Arabi,
What the Seeker Needs: Essays on Spiritual Practice, Oneness, Majesty and Beauty, 1992

Our memory is our future's promise: 'Tell me
what you remember and I will tell you who you
will become.'

Edmond Jabes,
The Book of Resemblances, 1990–92

When I started piecing together my scattered memories of Morocco's common Judeo-Muslim heritage, of our shared destinies that keep meeting and then branching off again, I had not yet made a commitment to conjuring up the dead. And yet it was images of cemeteries that first came to mind, helping me to unravel the thread of my own recollections as a Muslim, often deeply buried in the labyrinth of my memory. The recollections of my friends, who have made invaluable contributions to this testimony, have enabled me to follow the trail before it goes cold and to revive the fabric of our past. Going back to the sources and engaging with inspiring books, men, and women also gave substance to a past shared by two communities, and shed light on forgotten events.

On a cold and gray November morning, the image of the Jewish cemetery in Rabat reminds me of the death, about ten years ago, of someone I loved. The man buried on that day was Ḥayyim Bitton, father of my inseparable childhood friend Esther, and the symbol of a vanished era. With his death, an important page had been definitively turned; with him, a large piece of the Judeo-Muslim share of common experiences may well have passed away forever. Of course, remembering him also brings nostalgia for those moments shared with Esther, whom I met at the French school. And yet, when Esther and I separated after graduation in the late 1960s, I never felt the same emptiness that had been left by the death of her father, Monsieur Bitton. Not only was his death a personal tragedy for me, for his family, his children, and his wife, but it was also a turning point in terms of Jewish presence in Morocco.

There was a great softness in this man whose personality was at once simple and profound; he was rather secretive and not easily approached, melancholic, and nostalgic for something undefinable: maybe lost places, or past times. I thought he came from some other world, like a refugee from time and space. And yet, in my mind, he embodies an ill-known and sometimes deliberately hidden dimension of

Moroccan identity and history: a deeply Jewish Moroccan identity. It was only through him that I became aware of the ancestral Jewish presence in our country. Ironically, this deep-rootedness made him seem unique in my eyes when I was a child and later an adolescent; he did not seem like anyone else I used to meet in Rabat or Salé, be it in Muslim, Jewish, or Christian circles. He was different, like a small island in the middle of a cosmopolitan urban society. His native languages were Berber and Arabic, and he rarely used French: when he did, it was always with some difficulty. He had never been to school: he learned French on his own and rather late, and also improved his Hebrew. His personal Judeo-Arabic library was a source of constant amazement to me, with French classics like *The Count of Monte Cristo* in Arabic written in Hebrew characters. He managed to transmit to his children his thirst for knowledge and culture, only without this profoundly Arab dimension. This was a generational change that I experienced myself, as a result of French acculturation due to the Protectorate.

Monsieur Bitton was also fond of music, particularly Judeo-Arab music. Thanks to him, I learned to appreciate singers like Sami Al-Maghribi, Sapho, and especially the fabulous Reinette l'Oranaise, whose songs he used to play when I visited the apartment his widow still occupies in 'the new *mellah*.' When the French departed in 1956, the Jews left the *mellah* for neighboring areas, as Muslims abandoned the *medina* to settle in formerly exclusively French zones.

The story of Ḥayyim Bitton's life, though it came to me only piecemeal, made him seem even more endearing. A Berber, born in 1915 in the Ourika valley south of Marrakesh, he was named in honor of Rabbi Ḥayyim ben Diwan, who was worshipped because of the many miracles he performed in the region. Rabbi Ḥayyim ben Diwan is one of many Moroccan saints revered both by Jews and Muslims, and embodies the perfect symbiosis between the two religions. Muslims call him Moul

FIG. 36 Jewish woman nursing, Iligh, Anti-Atlas, March 1953. Photograph by Elias Harrus.

Anrhaz. According to legend, the earth opened to receive the mortal remains of the saint, and he was transformed into a green bird upon the visit of someone who was paying homage at his tomb. This brought good luck to the pilgrim, who became rich, and as a sign of gratitude he built small bungalows for the visitors to the tomb. I wonder whether Monsieur Bitton's saintly namesake could have influenced his fate, which was marked by extreme solitude and a great deal of suffering until his late marriage.

Motherless since his birth, he had only vague memories of his father from his early childhood in the High Atlas. Raised partly by his grandmother, partly by his stepmother, he ran away from home when he was very young to escape the latter's harshness when the former passed away. With most of his relatives dead, and no ties left in his native village except a distant half-brother, he initiated a precarious itinerant life that led him to Marrakesh and, eventually, to Casablanca, where he wound up completely alone at the age of seven. Not knowing where to go, he was sitting on the sidewalk in the big city when a Jew whose wife worked with a furniture dealer miraculously saved him. The man's name was Shulman, an Ashkenazi Jew who had come to Morocco in the early years of the century, working first as a porter. The Shulman family generously adopted Ḥayyim and gave him shelter, in exchange for which he would perform household chores: running errands, for instance. At the same time, young Ḥayyim became a carpenter. After he had honed his skills as a cabinet-maker, he acquired a paid job in a furniture business, which eventually allowed him to lead an independent life in Casablanca. Later on, he settled in Rabat, between the *mellah*, where he lived, and the *medina*, where he bought a small furniture shop. His late marriage with the very young Annette Ohana was the greatest achievement of his life. Marrying his beloved probably involved endless negotiations and the overcoming of strong resistance, since she was a descendent of the prestigious Meknassi family, who agreed only reluctantly to this union with a 'stranger.'

And indeed, the word 'stranger' is probably the most appropriate for this man out of time and space, a character straight from an Albert Camus novel, haunted by a tragic existential feeling. A whiff of despair, the result of a lifetime of hardship and misfortune, would always cling to him, even after he had married, and established a family of his own. To his daughter Esther, whom he loved above all, he gave his mother's name, in memory of the mother he had never known and whose absent image undoubtedly haunted him his entire life. He also gave off an air of dignity and stoic wisdom, masked by a certain coldness – or perhaps indifference – that gave this humble Berber Jew the air of an aristocrat.

It is not unusual to be a Berber Jew – or an Arab Jew, as many claim to be today – in Morocco's ethnic landscape. Berber Jews are known as *toshavim* or indigenous Jews, who can be counted as Morocco's first inhabitants, while the *megorashim* are the Spanish Jews expelled from Spain after 1492.

The dates of the settlement of the first Jewish communities, as well as of the conversion of Berbers to Judaism, still remain unknown; early Moroccan history is blurred by myth and legend. According to one of these legends, some of Israel's 'lost tribes,' who had been exiled after Nebuchadnezzar's destruction of the First Temple of

FIG. 37 Three merchants: two Jews and a Muslim, near Ighil N'Ogho, Anti-Atlas, February 1958. Photograph by Elias Harrus.

Jerusalem, settled in Morocco as early as the sixth century BCE. Our ignorance of the chronology or the logistics of this settlement doesn't change the fact that Jews have been rooted in Morocco since time immemorial.

Monsieur Bitton was a descendant of the *toshavim*, as was his wife. The Ohana family, whose origins can be traced back to the remote history of the inhabitants of the Anti-Atlas, was allegedly one of the first tribes of Moroccan Jews, originally hailing from the region of Ifrane, in the Dra' valley. One side of the family settled in Meknes. Esther was brought up within view of her maternal grandfather's immense house in Meknes's *mellah*. It was that house her mother had to leave in order to marry a 'stranger.' The Arab–Israeli war in June 1967 gave it the final blow. I still remember the tragic days when the Ohana mansion was deserted, and then occupied and devastated by a mob gone wild, while its owner was in Casablanca with his family. Later on, when things had calmed down, and the authorities – that is, the Qaid – had expelled the invaders, Shalom Ohana refused to go back to his home and sold it for nothing. Like most lavish residences in the *medina*, the Ohana mansion, having been divided up and ruined, is now occupied by several impoverished families: a sad end for such a magnificent and much-loved building.

Thanks to Esther's parents, I saw Moroccan Jews as simultaneously powerful and humble, thriving and modest, or, to use the terms of the Moroccan social hierarchy, both as *rûmiyyîn* – Westernized and modern – and as *baldiyyîn* – natives, or, to put it derogatively, provincial and backward.

The financial and political power of the Ohana family – a few years ago Joseph Ohana was an elected representative of the city of Essaouira – is common knowledge. It has marked the history of Judaism in Morocco in a profound way: on September 7, 1999, another Jo Ohana inaugurated a restored synagogue in the heart of Casablanca, in the presence of numerous representatives of Jewish and Muslim communities, such as the mayor of the city, and Morocco's Chief Rabbi, Rabbi Monsonego.

Above left

FIG. 38 Jewish marriage in Rabat, c. 1910–20. Photograph by J.-B. Morana.

Above right

FIG. 39 House of the Ohana family, Meknes, c. 1920. Photograph by Rafaël Ohana.

What most impressed me in Monsieur Bitton was his impassive endurance, the sense that he was almost detached from the world and from life – something that reminded me of my father's attitude. It might have been his strong sense of his Berber origins that lent him this detachment; his wife, and the majority of other Jews, were more Westernized and, especially, more French. I can remember another example from the Ohana family of someone like him: one of Esther's old aunts, Hassibah, who is over ninety years old and still sings the Song of Songs in Arabic. In fact, Ḥayyim Bitton was not simply a Moroccan with Berber roots, as many Muslims and Jews are. He was profoundly Berber and somehow uprooted in an urban environment: almost as if he had never really left his native village in the Atlas.

I cannot separate the image of Esther's father's tomb in the Jewish cemetery in Rabat from those of two other cemeteries in Salé: the Jewish cemetery, which I visited a few months ago, that contains the tomb of the saint Rabbi Raphael Ancaoua; and the Muslim one, where my father, who had a great love for Rabbi Ancaoua, was recently laid to rest. In family conversations, and especially in the presence of Esther's father, we talked endlessly about the saint, who was Chief Rabbi of Salé until his death in 1935. The figure of Rabbi Raphael, as we then used to call him, was inseparable, in my father's memory, from that of his grandfather Hadj Ali Aouad, a prominent Slawi (inhabitant of Salé) figure. The friendship between Hadj Ali Aouad and Chief Rabbi Raphael Ancaoua was unfailing.

To bring back memories of a time I knew only through my father's eyes, I turned to the – sadly rare – surviving acquaintances of Rabbi Raphael. Then, I used a valuable bibliography to help me reshape the scattered fragments remembered by each one.

But before I begin to recount the legendary story of these two venerable Slawis, it might be helpful to remember some historical and geographical facts about Salé,

FIG. 40 Jean Besancenot, *Juive de Salé, Costumes du Maroc,* Paris: Horizons de France, 1942

whose fate has always been tied to Rabat's fate, for better or for worse. Thus, we shall follow the course of the Bu-Regreg river, which connects the two rival cities that were built downstream on the river's mouth. According to a famous saying, the 'cities with two shores' will merge only when the Bu-Regreg flows with milk, and the sand of its shores turns into raisins.

My life between the Bu-Regreg's two shores has proceeded as peacefully as the course of the river, or so it has seemed. Nevertheless, I can't forget that Rabat, my adoptive town, with all the arrogance of a capital city, has relegated Salé, my hometown, to the role of a dormitory-suburb, or even a kind of dump. Institutions such as the jail and the psychiatric hospital are in Salé, and not in Rabat. And yet, ironically, Rabat was for centuries considered 'Salé's suburb.'

With a vibrant Judeo-Muslim community within its walls by the late nineteenth and early twentieth centuries, Salé had nothing in common with the city we now know, a place marginalized by the central power because of the strong pride and attempts at independence of its inhabitants. One of the most glorious episodes of its history was the unexpected declaration of the Republic of Salé in the seventeenth century: the flag, under the corsair banner, can be admired at the Musée de la Marine in Paris. Disgraced, Salé is now going through a painful pauperization process. Still, this has not been enough to undermine Slawi pride, even though the city's decay created feelings of sadness, disappointment, fierce reserve, and even arrogance among those who stayed there. My father, for example, was one of them. It is perhaps this deep nostalgia for something lost that made him seem, in my eyes, like Monsieur Bitton, although their destinies were so diametrically opposed as far as family and finances were concerned. My father was heir to a family of rich and fine intellectuals and was thus able to acquire – first in Morocco and later on in France – a completely bilingual culture. He was a great admirer of Leon Blum. He started working only at a late age, when he was past forty and already had a large family of his own. It was then that he took the important decision to move from his home, the great family house in Salé, to Rabat.

Although crossing the Bu-Regreg is, today, hardly an extraordinary commute for thousands of modern nomads who live on the right bank and work on the left, it used to have a certain significance in the history of the two rival cities, which occasionally united in a naval race against their common Christian enemy. Holding out for Rabat and its surroundings, Salé was the leader of a maritime *djihad* – holy war – conducted by famous corsairs who, from the sixteenth to the nineteenth century, used to hunt and terrify the Christians from the shores of the Atlantic Ocean to the edges of Iceland. It was a way of taking their revenge on the Christians who, in 1492, had expelled the Moors from their earthly heaven: al-Andalus. Even though they did not participate in the Andalusian saga, my ancestors, out of Muslim solidarity, helped the Spanish exiles in their *djihad* against the Christians. Two of my foremost corsair ancestors were *Raïss* – great commanders – who scoured the shores of the Atlantic. Through its control of naval affairs, the Aouad family, descended from the Beni Hilal – an Arab tribe that invaded the Maghreb in the tenth century – acquired a prominent position and is now justly proud of its glorious past, like most other great Slawi families.

This digression helps underline the importance of and the prestige enjoyed, even outside the city, by the two main figures in Salé's recent history: Rabbi Raphael Ancaoua and my great-grandfather Hadj Ali Aouad. What a beautiful friendship there was between these two men! One was a great rabbi who continues to be respected by both communities – his *hillulah* attracts hundreds of pilgrims, and his shrine is kept by Muslims – and by Jewish Moroccans the world over: David Levy, head of Israeli diplomacy, allegedly paid his respects at his tomb, three or four years ago, on a rainy January morning. The other was a *cadi* – a legal advisor, as important in Islam as a rabbi is in Judaism, and with an impressive religious knowledge. My father used to tell me that his grandfather knew all of Iman Boukhari's *hadiths*, in other words that he could give a reading – with commentaries – of one of the greatest religious sources after the Revealed Book, almost without pausing, in a record time of six days. The *hadith*, a broad tradition incorporating the Koran and the deeds and sayings of the Prophet, is the equivalent of the Talmud.

It is said that passers-by would prostrate themselves before one of the few Jewish saints who was beatified while he was still alive, and whose name, Ancaoua, means 'purity' in Arabic. My father would greet him only by kissing his hand. Jews and Muslims both venerated him for his premonitions – knowing when he would die, he had apparently gone to the cemetery to be buried – for the miracles he had performed, and, lastly, for his terrifying curses. Even Muslims came to him for advice, or to have him intercede in a delicate matter. The following anecdote is a good example of his radiant sense of justice: when a Muslim was fooled by a Jew to whom he had loaned money and who refused to pay him back, pretending he had never been given it, Rabbi Raphael was the only one able to give him justice. After summoning the two plaintiffs, he handed down his verdict with the sharpness of a guillotine: "If you are innocent, you will be blessed; if you lie, you will lose your sight," he said to the Jew, who became blind on the spot, to the great relief of the Muslim plaintiff.

My father would constantly tell us about Rabbi Raphael's frequent calls, on all occasions, to Hadj Ali's home. The rabbi was not very tall and rather skinny, dressed in a black (the distinctive color for Jews) *djellaba* – a wide traditional dress with long sleeves and a hood that went down beyond his knees. He wore a black skullcap on the back of his head, and a sort of shawl around his head and neck. He had a long white beard, unlike my great-grandfather, who would have his trimmed every Friday at the *hajjam,* or barber. (He must have looked astonishingly similar to the photograph of a rabbi I acquired on a recent visit to the saint's tomb). When the great man arrived, he was announced to Hadj Ali: "*Hada lhazzane* [It's the rabbi]," to which my ancestor would reply: "*Qolo yadkhoul* [Show him in]." Before entering the room where the *cadi* was, the great rabbi would, like everyone else, take off his *babouches* (slippers). The host would then welcome his guest with: "*Marhaba blhazzane* [Welcome to the rabbi]."

"Yak kolchi bikhir [How are you]?"
"Iyyah a sid el fquih, Allah y toualina omrak [Fine, dear master, may God grant you a long life]."

As a sign of friendship, the rabbi would bring delicacies and sweets, which were much appreciated by everyone, especially by the youngest members of the family. When the two men were sitting down, an old man who had come with the rabbi would put on the table a large platter covered with a sheet. He would then proceed to unveil the sweets and delicacies: there was, for instance, the famous Kippur bread, stuffed with almonds, the *rkaka,* or unleavened bread with neither salt nor yeast, that Mme Bitton still sends me. There was also *maâkouda,* pastry made with eggs and potatoes and shaped in little cubes with almond paste. Sipping mint tea, the two patriarchs would then discuss city affairs, especially the legal and religious matters with which they were charged. Meanwhile, the children would stuff themselves with the Jewish pastries they were so fond of and so eagerly expected every time Rabbi Raphael visited.

Perhaps the symbolic value of these offerings should be emphasized. For Moroccans, whether Jewish or Muslim, 'sharing bread' – any kind of food, really – is a sacred gesture that creates enduring ties. It is like an oath of fidelity that can only be broken by an act of betrayal. Holiday celebrations therefore provide Jews and Muslims with an opportunity to express mutual respect and appreciation while exchanging gifts of sweets and delicacies. The *mimouna,* a celebration marking the end of Passover, is a good example of this spirit of sharing. For this very happy holiday – *mimouna* means 'luck' or 'good fortune' in Arabic – people from the *medina* bring bread to their neighbors in the *mellah,* as well as numerous pastries and delicacies such as the traditional fish dish, *bed* or *shad* depending on the region. This feast goes on until late at night, while Jews and Muslims sing and dance under the auspices of Lalla Mimouna, a saint who is believed to bring good luck.

History will remember Rabbi Raphael as one of the most prominent Moroccan rabbis of this past century, in the same way that Hadj Ali Aouad is one of the most memorable and respected figures in Salé's recent history. They were two high dignitaries, feared and respected not only for their social and religious authority, but also for their strong personalities and their prestige in both the Jewish and the Muslim communities. When Rabbi Raphael died at the age of eighty-seven, representatives from the royal palace, French and Moroccan authorities, and thousands of Jews from all over Morocco attended his funeral. Madame Bitton remembers her father's hasty trip from Meknes to be there. Jews, Muslims, and Christians gathered for a last farewell to this saint. Some say that rabbis even came from France. Was my great-grandfather present for this last ceremony? I am not really sure. But given the deep friendship between the two men, only his extreme old age – he was nearly one hundred years old when he died, just a year after his loyal companion – could have prevented him from being there.

The story of this exemplary friendship between two patriarchs of different religions has undoubtedly imbued the relationship between the two faiths with a sense of warmth and mutual respect. My father believed that this history of profound fraternity between Jews and Muslims in Salé acted as a shield against the sectarian excesses experienced in other Moroccan cities during the first decades of the twentieth century. As for my parents and myself, we experienced many other stories, similar to this one, which have left deep marks in our memory.

While my father was, as a young man, a privileged witness to an exemplary page of the history of the relations between two communities, my mother, as a girl and later on as an adolescent, was taught needlework, sewing and embroidery in particular, by Saâda, a young Jewish woman. My mother, also a Slawi, had her own modest story to tell, one that concerned the unfortunate Saâda – an oxymoron, as *saâda* means 'fortunate' in Arabic – and that echoes the story of the friendship between Rabbi Raphael and Hadj Ali Aouad. The relationships between Jewish and Muslim men have undoubtedly determined many of the familial and emotional ties between Jewish and Muslim women in their daily lives, centered around domestic chores.

Saâda, well-known for her ability to perform tasks on many different fronts, happily provided the female members of great Slawi families with her invaluable and devoted help. It was Saâda who taught my mother the basics of household work, Saâda who taught her French, Saâda who helped her create one of the most important works in the life of a young Moroccan woman of yesterday: the bride's trousseau.

In the period immediately before her wedding, my mother's life was punctuated by Saâda's almost daily visits to her parents' home. A certain closeness and a feeling of mutual understanding grew between the two women, through literacy classes and the learning of sewing, embroidery, and especially crochet – my mother's favorite craft and the one in which she became an expert.

Saâda was so worthy and so brave. She was fatherless and her handicapped mother was bedridden. She seemed to enjoy the Muslim milieu and the tasty little dishes she loved to eat, unbeknown to her mother. Couscous and *harira*, a traditional soup, were her favorites. Since they had no telephone line at home, she would use her visits to my mother's to call her fiancé, again without her mother's knowledge, she being opposed

FIG. 41 Jew of Salé, 1940–43. Photograph by Jean Besancenot.

to Saâda's marriage to a goy (non-Jew). Needless to say, listening to the lovers' phone conversations was far more fascinating to my mother than learning how to sew or speak French. Saâda, who had been unlucky in love, lives today in Casablanca, after two failed marriages and a third one which turned out to be rather successful.

Sometimes, my mother would visit Saâda's mother in her home for a fitting, as the older woman would make her dresses. There, Mother loved to eat candy and sweets, such as quince *maâjoun*, or paste, of which she was particularly fond. Even now, she can still picture Saâda's mother sitting with her Singer sewing machine near the brazier where a meal was cooking, unable to move by herself. This brave old woman was also a healer. When my aunt was about to die of pneumonia, she saved her life with a magical brew made with honey and *hab-erchad*, or horseradish grains.

Saâda was also there when I was a young child: indeed my sisters and I owed to her

FIG. 42 Jews of Rabat, 1935–36. Photograph by
Jean Besancenot.

our most beautiful dresses. Her valuable and generous presence remained with us until
the early 1960s, when she left Salé for Casablanca, after her marriage and the death of
her poor mother. Less than a year ago, she sold her last properties in Salé's new *mellah*.
My mother still keeps a piece of embroidery made under Saâda's vigilant eye more than
fifty years ago. It is thanks to Saâda and her mother that my own mother entered the
modern world on her wedding day, wearing a Western-style wedding dress as well as
her traditional caftans. This was revolutionary in those days. Modernity was ushered
into the world of Muslim women thanks to Jewish women, who would open windows
onto the West for those women locked in golden cages.

Other Jewish women gave their valuable help to great Slawi families: mattress-
makers like the famous Yamna and Shamla, so well remembered by my mother and
grandmother; women selling lace, or pearls and jewelry, like 'Aicha the Jewess,' who
would go from door to door in the maze-like streets of the *medina*.

There were also many male mattress-makers and jewelers, as there was a great
tradition of expertise in those two professions among the Jewish community. Indeed, a
respectable bourgeois Moroccan home would trust only Jews with the manufacture of the
delicate apparel of the traditional sitting-room. To this day, numerous Moroccan-style

FIG. 43 Jewish Musicians, Morocco, 1930s–40s. Photograph by Flandrin.

sitting rooms have been upholstered by dexterous Jewish hands, or by Muslim apprentices to whom Jews have transmitted their skills. When working all day long in Muslim homes, Jewish men and women would bring their own pots to cook their meals, or would eat only eggs, boiled potatoes, black olives, dairy products, or fresh or dried fruit.

Jewish jewelers, who would, among other things, craft luxurious gold belts with diamonds and precious stones, were also an institution. It is still an enduring tradition in certain Moroccan families to have the future husband offer the bride one of these belts as a dowry. Even today, for a mattress-maker or a jeweler to be disciple of a *maâlem*, or Jewish master, or even the disciple of a *maâlem*'s disciple, is a great addition to his résumé.

There were also Jewish musicians who would perform at Muslim parties and ceremonies. My grandmother remembers those itinerant music players, with their lutes and violins scouring the narrow streets of the *medina* in search of celebrations to liven up. They used to ask the *moul al-faran*, the traditional Moroccan baker, where the parties were, as bread and *méchoui* (a meat dish) for celebrations are always cooked in public ovens. A baker boy would then take the musicians to the homes where the celebrations were taking place, and they would spontaneously brighten up the ceremony in exchange for a few coins.

When relations between the two communities began to become rather tense, and the first cracks appeared in this perfect harmony, Jews would be escorted by a Muslim friend from the *mellah* to the *medina*, to keep them from being stoned, mostly by children. My grandmother remembers that each time a Jewish woman came to her home, her nanny, Dada Al Yacout, formerly a black slave of the family, would have to walk them home.

The opposite trip, from the *medina* to the *mellah*, was mostly made by men, who liked to go to the Jewish neighborhood for its always festive atmosphere, to drink *mahia* – a kind of brandy made with dried dates or figs – for its relative sexual freedom, and, mostly, for its women. The *mellah* was often cursed and likened to a whorehouse by many Muslim wives who lost their husbands there. My mother remembers the early days of her marriage, when my father was so mesmerized by Jewish ways that she had trouble breaking the spell.

Romantic relationships between Jewish women and Muslim men form one of the most interesting and revealing chapters in the history of the relations between Jews and Muslims, but also one of the most concealed. Although rather rare, mixed marriages generally went smoothly. Jewish wives had to convert to Islam, and some of them even went on pilgrimage to Muslim holy places, a trip known as a *hadj* in Arabic.

A whole other chapter ought to be devoted to the secret love affairs between women from the *mellah* and men from the *medina*; indeed, they deserve to be treated individually. I can vouch only for the exemplary story of Abderrahmane, one of my relatives, and Perla. Their affair began in Salé in the 1940s and resurfaced only a few months ago, after fifty years of silence and separation.

When Moroccan theater was in its infancy, the young, beautiful, Jewish Perla was friends with a group of Slawi art-lovers, who created an itinerant theatre company. Perla, indeed a rare pearl at a time when men had to dress up to play women's parts, greatly contributed to the birth of the Moroccan theater. My uncle, who was a member of the company, remembers her remarkable performance in the play *Between Two Flames*, by the Moroccan playwright Ahmed Sefiani. Abderrahmane had to teach Perla how to pronounce Arabic without her typically Judeo-Arabic accent. He composed verses in her honor and then solemnly recited them to her. In the 1950s, when Abderrahmane was sent to New York as a diplomat, Perla, by then a talented pianist, went with him, and was hired by the New York Philharmonic Orchestra. She took Leila Farida as a stage name and settled in New York, where she still lives.

Back in Morocco after a few years in the United States, Abderrahmane married and founded a family. He had lost track of Perla until recently. Only a few months ago, she called her old Slawi friend, who is now over ninety years old. Unable to speak to him because of his deteriorated health, Perla spoke to his wife to inquire about him. I find this story of love, separation, and missed opportunities deeply moving.

Preceded by a climate of tension and suspicion, which continued under the French Protectorate, the slow but irreversible exodus of Jews from Morocco was accelerated by the creation of the State of Israel in 1948, the departure of the French in 1956, the death of King Mohammed V in 1961, and, most notably, by the Six Day War in 1967. It was only much later that the past could be revisited, and we could come to terms with the pain caused by hasty departures that felt like betrayals, and the often definitive breaking-off of relationships. The pain was as great for those who stayed as for those who left.

There were unmistakable portents of the break-up: prolonged absences, rumors of Zionist calls to the Moroccan people. It was often after the fact that we understood these warning signs, as certain Moroccan Jews led truly double lives. There was, for instance, a certain Isaac Halioua, whose father traded in tea, and who was a childhood friend and classmate of my uncle Ahmed Aouad at the College des Orangers in Rabat. During the years 1942–44, young Isaac started to miss classes, saying that he had been called for military service in Spain since he had obtained Spanish citizenship. A photograph of himself in uniform was shown to prove it. Moreover, an important change in his eating habits had occurred. When he went to see his friend Ahmed, he would not share meals with him anymore; rather, he would bring along his own food, or would eat only eggs and bread, and drink only tea. When my uncle teased him, saying he had become a rabbi, Isaac replied that maturity had taken him back to the right path. Later on, he continued to be politically active for the Moroccan cause, as a member of the National Movement, Al Haraka Al Quaoumia, led by Hassan El Ouazzani, which became the Democratic Party for Independence; he was also vice-president of Salé's sports club, whose team, founded and presided over by Ahmed Aouad, was in those days half-Jewish, half-Muslim. (Further events have shed more light on the seeming incompatibility of Zionist activism with Jewish Moroccan nationalism.) And yet the friendship between the two men remained strong, until one Sunday in 1961 or perhaps 1962. On that day, Isaac, who knew that my uncle and his wife were away on a trip, went to their home as usual to take their children out. He bought them candy and also a tricycle for my cousin, then brought them back home and promised to come back soon. But he never came back; my uncle never saw him again. Much later, we learned he was in Israel.

Many others left Morocco in a similar fashion. Although they had been planning to leave for years, they would always depart in great secrecy, without telling even their closest Muslim friends. It was rumored that many of them took their house keys when they left.

A time of breaking off friendships had come. Silence, doubts – sometimes unfounded – and rumors ignited mutual suspicion. Were the fears of the Moroccan Jewish community grounded in reality? International events and the Arab-Israeli conflict had certainly created anxiety, and fears for the future. But domestically, there was no real threat. There was some tension, leading to clashes and occasionally bloody incidents – easily settled – but there was neither a major impulse of hatred nor any kind of deliberate persecution. We should never forget King Mohammed V's fierce opposition to the enforcement of the French Vichy regime's anti-Semitic laws. When the Vichy government asked the King to count the Jews and take an inventory of their assets, Mohammed V famously replied: "We have no Jews in Morocco, only Moroccan citizens." Protection of Jews is part of a generous tradition inherited from the 'Alawid kings in conformity with the Muslim principle of *dhimma*. This principle, derived from the Koran, establishes the special status of Jews and Christians – the People of the Book – in Muslim lands, and is grounded on mutual respect and freedom of religion.

But fear and outside pressure were eventually stronger than tolerance. We should also note that Mohammed V and Hassan II after him, who both demonstrated a kind and enlightened attitude towards Jews, never prevented them from leaving, unlike

FIG. 44 Girls' School, Salé, c. 1950

other Arab or Muslim heads of state. Yet Jews faced another dilemma: they could either stay in what had been their own country for over two thousand years, but live in fear, or they could depart for seemingly safer and more welcoming lands – France, Canada, South America, and, of course, Israel. Ironically, adaptation was most difficult in the land of Zion. Most of them left with great pain, and for some it was truly a forced exile.

In the mid-1960s, rumors of the events shaking the relations between the two communities came to me less strongly thanks to my great friendship with Esther. But I could hardly imagine the consequences of the Jews' mass exodus. Moreover, it was difficult to know exactly what was going on as the topic seemed rather taboo. With our families and at the French school, Esther and I lived in a kind of cocoon, miraculously protected from the storm outside. In Rabat, a city more cosmopolitan, more European than Salé, and at the French school, where Jews, Muslims, and Christians lived together in perfect harmony, I became even more tolerant than my family had implicitly taught me to be.

How could I even imagine the dramatic upheavals undermining the relations between Jews and Muslims? At the Lycée de Jeunes Filles – the Girls' High School – in Rabat, most of my friends were Jewish. My Arabic teacher was a Jew named Mr. Cohen.

Esther had a Muslim boyfriend. Her brother was, and still is, close friends with a Muslim. At home, my brother often had his Jewish friends over, and he also visited them in the new *mellah*, sometimes even staying overnight. David, my hairdresser, was also Jewish. Good old David would even come to our home to do everyone's hair. And my father even trusted him with a delicate mission: cutting his daughters' first braids! David owned a hair salon in town and had been among my father's first hairdressers. Azuelos, my mother's jeweler, whose children still own stores in Rabat, was Jewish too.

But I especially remember when I was invited to Esther's on Saturdays to eat *skhina*, a divine traditional meal for Sabbath lunch. Before we ate, Monsieur Bitton would perform ritual prayers over the wine and bread. I will never forget Madame Bitton's sublime *skhina*! It was a feast made with lamb, eggs, potatoes, crushed wheat, chick peas, and rice, and it would have been simmering since Friday afternoon. It was so rich that I felt a kind of mellow haze for the rest of the afternoon, further aggravated by the effect of delicious sweets prepared by the magic hand of Esther's mother. Fortunately, we drank mint tea every time friends or relatives popped in, which would slowly pull me out of my ecstatic reverie. Oddly enough, to this day I have not rediscovered anywhere the magic taste of Madame Bitton's tea. Thanks to Jewish Moroccan cookbooks, I have prepared for myself some of those sweets, in order to sample once again those delicious flavors I used to share with Esther. But I have never dared to try to reproduce Madame Bitton's unforgettable *skhina*.

When Esther left for college in France after graduating from high school, her parents stayed in Morocco: she most likely intended to return. Indeed, I left a year later for the same reasons. Even now, after she has lived abroad for thirty years, I still wonder whether Esther really means to leave Morocco behind for good. She decided to take on French citizenship only recently and is still thinking now about coming back to her native country. Such a dilemma haunts, I suppose, all those who experience the difficulties of a dual identity, both geographical and cultural.

In my travels, I have had the opportunity to meet with members of the Jewish Moroccan diaspora, and I have seen how faithful they remain to their Moroccan origins. I will not forget the warmth of my meeting with North African Jews in Caracas in 1987. I need not say how moved I was when I saw how strongly Moroccan these men and women still felt after twenty or thirty years. For an outsider, such loyalty to one's Moroccan roots, and the profound brotherly feeling among Moroccans – probably unique in all of the Judeo-Muslim world – are difficult to understand. Indeed, they seem to resurface with national events, such as King Hassan's recent death. The transmission of that attachment to new generations of Jews who have never lived in Morocco is also remarkable. This should be seen not as an idealized nostalgia, but as a kind of mutual loyalty, the result of a fundamentally happy common history, despite the recent travails. And indeed, many fates have diverged and then miraculously joined again. There have been many such providential reunions.

Are the most unexpected meetings determined by fate, or are they pure coincidence? Because my childhood and adolescence were predominantly influenced by the profound friendship between Jews and Muslims, I have always looked forward to reunions, to reviving old bonds or initiating new ones.

Reading – and meeting authors – has provided an invaluable opportunity to experience this remarkable convergence. Indeed, both reading and writing are antidotes to oblivion. The work of Haïm Zafrani, Edmond Amran El Maleh, or Pol Serge Kakon somehow helps us bring closure to the difficult times between the two communities. As for me, the sudden communication breakdown has left me eager for explanations. Although the search could be endless, I turn to literature to find some light. Ami Bouganim's stories, especially *Le Cri de l'arbre* and *Entre vents et marées*, have most helped me heal open wounds, perhaps because the author and I are from the same generation.

In spite of the differences between their ages, these authors all started publishing their stories and essays in the 1980s, as if one could only talk about those often happy, but also sometimes painful events, with the help of time and distance. Indeed, writing implies standing back from, rather than instantly reacting to, events. While they have gone back to explore a common history that was alternately dark and bright, they have also shed light on misty or evasive memories. Oddly enough, Souiri people (inhabitants of Essaouira) wrote short stories that provide deep lessons. Indeed, Essaouira was undoubtedly the place where relationships between Jews and Muslims in Morocco were most intense and eventful. Rediscovering Essaouira, with the help of its literature and thanks to the cultural events of the city, and also because of the strong will of one of its greatest sons, has been a wonderful experience for me, like a revelation.

Essaouira – formerly Mogador – is a city faithful to its diverse origins, a mystical place that carries people on its wings and makes them fly on the ocean with their dreams and desires. Rocked by the magic breeze of trade winds, touched by a kind of supernatural grace, Essaouira creates enduring bonds with those who love it. Even with its problems of poverty and its geographic isolation, this city still displays signs of its magnificent past, thanks to the values of its inhabitants and the contributions of foreigners, especially artists, who have embraced it and cherished it. Indeed, being Souiri is not a simple question of belonging to the city where one was born, or which has adopted you, but rather means a fraternal relationship with others, a deeply humanist and festive vision of the world. This generous and welcoming city unites people with its sense of shared culture and is also a perfect example of artistic creativity through cultural diversity and cross-fertilization.

Essaouira-Mogador reminds me of another, similar place, al-Andalus, where diverse cultural, religious, and ethnic communities lived together in great harmony. It was a land of encounters and dialogue. Values such as tolerance, warmth, and the generous welcoming of outsiders made of multireligious Spain a model of successful religious, cultural, intellectual, and scientific integration.

Al-Andalus, an Arcadia for everyone, has transmitted to both East and West an incomparable heritage, thanks to extraordinary cultural middlemen such as Averroes (Ibn Rushd) and Maimonides. These multi-faceted geniuses gave birth to a universal culture. The modernity of their thought is a constant source of amazement to me. At the meeting point of three cultures and three religions, they embody the intense and extraordinary pages Jews and Muslims have written together. The parallel lives of these two great men from Cordoba, both doctors, legal counsels, and enlightened Aristotelians, who lived at the same time and probably never met, were equally

FIG. 45 Interior of the Cordoba Synagogue, built 1314–15

unpredictable: they were both wanderers, and both found refuge in Morocco when intolerance burst out.

In Spain, Jews and Muslims experienced the same bliss, followed by the same tragic exile. After 1492 and 1609, the *megorashim* and the *moriscoes* went south of the Mediterranean, looking for more welcoming lands. Rabat and Salé were among the exiles' destinations.

Aren't we, Jews and Muslims alike, wanderers in exile, together with Abraham, Moses, and Muhammad? And is not the founding moment in Judaism the passage of Abraham to the other shore – *ivri*, or 'Hebrew,' means 'those who have crossed the river' – and in Islam, Muhammad's exile from Mecca to Medina, a voyage also called *Hijra*? In other words, we have all traveled to the other shore, in search of new lands, of somewhere else. And so have the Slawis who, like my family and myself, settled on the left bank of the Bu-Regreg, and so have the Jews: like Esther, they crossed the Mediterranean Sea to the other shore.

We need to learn how to cross bridges, so that the traces of our common paths in time and space are not eradicated forever. We could, for example, dwell on the extraordinary gardens of Mogador or al-Andalus, where echoes of a shared memory still resonate strongly. Or we could follow the enchanted paths of poetry, be it in literature, music, architecture, or gastronomy, and keep them in our memories and in those of the generations yet to come – eventually, loose ties will tighten once again. The most accomplished integration and the most enduring harmony between the two communities have occurred particularly in the field of shared emotions. For instance, several magnificent poetic compositions, all bilingual, immediately come to mind: the *matrûz* is truly a piece of musical 'embroidery' in both Arabic and Hebrew, inherited from the Andalusian period.

Indeed, despite the ups and downs, this remarkable shared history did not come to an end with the departure of the Jews, unlike in other countries. It is resuming with a serene strength, now that things have calmed down, and the ice, as it were, is broken. As in a long and tempestuous love story, there was a serious crisis, leading to the lovers' rift. After sulking for a while, they strive to get back together without really knowing how to. Torn between mutual attraction and fear, they each hide their feelings behind their pride.

Being Moroccan is like being a multifaceted mirror: Moroccan identity, whether Jewish or Muslim, cannot be complete without including each other.

Personally, I carry with me the strong bond of friendship I enjoy with Esther. It has never been challenged either by the different paths we chose for ourselves or by geographic distance. I would like to borrow the words of José Saramago as an emblem of this privileged relationship:

We live in places, but we inhabit memories.

Opposite

FIG. 46 Torah Ark, Synagogue of Rich, High Atlas, 1998. Photograph by Rose-Lynn Fisher.

CUSTOMS OF THE
JEWS OF MOROCCO

HARVEY E. GOLDBERG

FIG. 47 Veneration, *hillulah* of Rabbi David u-Moshe, 1998. Photograph by Rose-Lynn Fisher.

The customs of the Jews of Morocco express the special conditions of their life in that country, and also provide an opportunity to understand the dynamics of Jewish customs in general. Historians have pointed to various sources of Jewish practices common in Morocco. Some originated in Spain, while others were influenced by local Arab and Berber culture.[1] Jews in Morocco absorbed these influences, but were also the shapers of customs and cultural patterns that later had an impact upon Jews elsewhere.

This diversity of origin can be seen in the spoken terms for traditional Moroccan customs, and in other aspects of language. The preparations for a wedding often entailed the construction of a *talamon*, a throne on which the bride, and later the couple, were seated during various phases of the ceremony.[2] This term derives from Judeo-Spanish, the language spoken by Jews who arrived in Morocco from Spain at the end of the fifteenth century. Another feature of weddings derived from Spain, and preserved for centuries, is the use of a large elaborate wedding gown (see fig. 86, p. 135; cat. nos. 146–49) that became known by an Arabic term: *el-keswa el-kbîra*, or the 'Grand Costume.'[3] Arabic words were also attached to matters of eminently Jewish content. For example, a printed prayer book, an item not easy to acquire in some of the remote rural communities, was known as a *mishaf*, the term applied to a printed Koran.[4] Beyond classifying the various features of Moroccan culture according to their origins, it is important to appreciate how customs crystallized in local contexts.

Berber linguistic influence appears in some family names. This probably reflects the fact that in rural areas Jews lived under the protection of tribal leaders and, at times, came to be known by the name of a Berber-speaking patron. An example of this influence is the prefix 'O' or 'U' in a name, which means 'the son of,' as in the name Ohana. There also exist equivalent Berber and Arabic/Hebrew variants, such as the name Ohayun, echoed by Ben Hayun. A legendary sainted rabbi, buried in the Atlas in Agouim and still revered in Israel today, is known as Rabbi David u-Moshe (perhaps more consistently spelled David Umoshe).[5] This sounds strange to a modern Hebrew speaker, who understands the 'u-' as 'and,' and perceives the name as the puzzling 'Rabbi David and Moshe.' It is correctly understood, however, as 'David, the son of Moshe.' The name does not necessarily make this rabbinic figure more Berber in character than other Jews. In English, prefixes such as 'Mac' are preserved over the generations without there necessarily being any contemporary affinity with their origin in Scotland.

FIG. 48 A traditional school (*ḥeder*) in Casablanca, 1949

Other influences on Jewish life came from central and eastern Europe. In the twentieth century, the Yiddish term *ḥeder* began to be used in Morocco to designate the school where young boys learned to read Hebrew, the Torah, and to recite prayers (see fig. 48).[6] This institution had long existed in Morocco, where it was usually known as the *sla*, the word for a synagogue, in which schools for elementary education were located. A Yiddish term that had previously reached North Africa was *yahrtzeit*, referring to the anniversary of the death of a relative. It was pronounced *yarsyat* in Morocco, and undoubtedly arrived there through written texts, such as the *Shulḥan Arukh*, into which it was incorporated when that sixteenth-century code of law was accepted as definitive in the Ashkenazi world. These examples highlight the interconnectedness of the traditional Jewish world, even as it was divided into regions and local variants.

FIG. 49 Amuletic dagger, Marrakesh, late 19th century; see cat. no. 172

The last example also shows that an important source of Moroccan terminology was the Hebrew and Aramaic texts of rabbinic culture, although Jews in Morocco generally use Sephardic reworkings of Hebrew terms and phrases. For example, the basic Hebrew designation for the 'covenant of circumcision' is *brit milah*. In Yiddish, the everyday expression for the ritual became *bris*, while Sephardic (including Moroccan) tradition chose the second term for vernacular speech and ordinarily refers to the ceremony as *milah*. In some instances, the two traditions selected a single term from several biblical options. Ashkenazi Jews refer to the cabinet in a synagogue in which the Torah Scrolls are housed as the *aron kodesh* (the biblical 'holy ark' that held the tablets of the Covenant), while Sephardic Jews commonly refer to it as the *heikhal*, one of the designations for the ancient Jerusalem Temple. It is also common to find the same Hebrew word or concept at the root of terminology that takes on different local forms. An example is the Moroccan Sabbath stew called *skhina*, made from mixed potatoes, rice, red meat, intestines stuffed with chopped meat and wheat, and whole eggs. Because it is not permitted to light a fire on the Sabbath, Jewish communities developed dishes that could be prepared on Friday afternoon and kept warm until Saturday on a steady flame, lit before the Sabbath. In the Talmud, such a dish is generically known as *ḥamin*, from the Hebrew word for 'warm.' The Moroccan word *skhina* also comes from an Arabic linguistic stem meaning 'warm'; it is a precise linguistic parallel to the Ashkenazi word for a Sabbath stew, *cholent*, a Yiddish term that evolved from an ancient Romance word that likewise meant 'warm,' like the contemporary French *chaleur* ('heat'). Thus, one might call *skhina* 'Moroccan *cholent*,' or refer to *cholent* as 'Ashkenazi *skhina*.'

In other instances of the evolution of local Jewish languages, Hebrew and local terms may combine. In Meknes, the 'bar mitzvah boy' was known as *mul a-tefillin*.[7] The first word means 'master' in Arabic, and the phrase as a whole indicates that the young man has reached the stage of donning *tefillin*, or phylacteries, during daily morning prayer. The expression also indicates that an important part of the ritual transition of becoming bar mitzvah took place not only on the Sabbath, but also on weekdays, when putting on *tefillin* is obligatory.[8]

These linguistic examples also show the extensive internal diversity of Moroccan Jewry, which stems, first of all, from geography. The cities of the northern coast were always exposed to Spanish influence, and even developed their own version of Judeo-Spanish, known as Haquitiá.[9] The religious influence of the Spanish exiles, or the *megorashim*, reached the interior of the country as well. At the same time, many local Jews, the *toshavim*, were tenacious in holding onto their own traditions. An account from the late seventeenth century states that Sephardic practices had spread everywhere except to Tafilalet and its environs in the southeast.[10] The exception is significant. A considerable portion of Moroccan Jewry lived in very small communities along the routes crossing the Atlas and penetrating the south. There, they were in close contact with their immediate neighbors and their cultures, either Arabic- or Berber-speaking. In the major cities of the interior – Fez, Meknes, and Marrakesh – rabbinic tradition was preserved and cultivated, but there were important differences between the practices and beliefs of the élite that embodied that tradition, and those of the minimally literate or illiterate members of the community, whose exposure to classical textual culture was indirect.[11]

A good example of Jewish diversity, placed in historical perspective, is the practice of polygamy. Marrying more than one woman is permitted by the Bible. Rabbinic culture viewed monogamy as both the norm and the ideal, but rabbis were reluctant explicitly to forbid what was permitted by scripture. Polygamy thus remained a possibility for Jews until the Middle Ages. In the Rhineland, amid a monogamous Christian culture, Ashkenazi Jews instituted a ban on polygamy that did not apply to the Jews of Spain. Most Spanish Jews lived initially in a Muslim environment and only later came under heavy Christian influence with the *Reconquista*. Sephardic rabbis used other means to discourage polygamy, for example by stipulating in a marriage contract (*ketubbah*) that a man was not allowed to take a second wife unless his first wife consented to it. This option, and other rules reflecting the status of women, for example in matters of inheritance, were part of the tradition brought to Morocco by Sephardic rabbis, and were among those practices that, as stated, spread everywhere except to the far south.[12] In some regions of Morocco, and elsewhere in North Africa, the possibility of marrying more than one woman remained. At the beginning of the nineteenth century, a Jew from Italy wanting to take a second wife could sail to Tripoli, where it would be permitted by the rabbis, under certain conditions.[13] Both in Libya and southern Morocco, there were isolated instances of polygymous marriages throughout the twentieth century.

The religious norms and practices imposed by the rabbis often underwent processes of localization. One instance is the development of a Sephardic ceremony for naming newborn girls, while boys were given their names at the time of circumcision. The celebration of the birth of a girl had a formal Hebrew designation, *zeved ha-bat*, 'the gift of a daughter.'[14] The word for 'gift,' *zeved*, appears in Genesis 30:20, when Leah names her last male child Zevulun. The following verse mentions the birth of her daughter, Dinah. After the movement to Morocco, the *zeved ha-bat* celebration was often referred to in Arabic as *tsemya* – 'name-giving' – while the Hebrew term was preserved as well.[15] When Jews from Morocco emigrated to Israel, they continued the practice. Because they stressed the Hebrew name of the ceremony, Moroccan Jews sometimes served as the model for other ethnic groups in Israel who wished to create appropriate name-giving celebrations for baby daughters.

Bar mitzvah provides another example of localization. We have already seen that the Moroccan term for the ceremony referred to *tefillin*. The marking of religious majority was closely linked to aspects of social maturity. Among the songs sung at bar mitzvah celebrations were those indicating that a youngster was prepared to begin working and help his family. A rabbinic ordinance (*taqannah*) from eighteenth-century Meknes forbids artisans from taking on young apprentices before they have reached bar mitzvah.[16] Bar mitzvah was also the occasion for a youngster to begin smoking cigarettes with his circle of friends.[17]

The age of bar mitzvah varied. It could be celebrated whenever a boy was capable of reading the prayers and blessings correctly, or of publicly presenting a Torah lesson – a *drashah* – that he had memorized. This variability, in fact, reflects historical reality, before the age of bar mitzvah was standardized to thirteen in Europe at the end of the Middle Ages. Because the regular celebration of bar mitzvah evolved only late in Jewish history, rabbis in Europe had to justify the fact that the festive meal

FIG. 50 Collective bar mitzvah,
Atlas Mountains, 1950s

accompanying it deserved the status of a *se'udat mitzvah*, a meal marking the
fulfillment of a commandment.[18] This process of justification still continued in
Morocco in the twentieth century. Rabbi Joseph Messas pointed to the content of the
piyyutim – religious poetry – sung at these meals, which transmitted the values of
Torah. He claimed that this edifying musical custom, which was a central feature of
Jewish culture in Morocco, qualified the occasion for inclusion in the category of
se'udat mitzvah.[19]

Just as the celebration of bar mitzvah entails the interweaving of an individual life
and a particular family with the community, so Moroccan Jews developed other
constellations of customs around milestones in the life cycle, in which these
milestones were marked by practices and symbols of general Jewish significance. Two
examples concern the festival of Shavuot, which in rabbinic tradition marks the giving
of the Torah. A ceremony reported from the Todgha valley in the south took place the
day before Shavuot. A young boy, who had not yet begun to study, was coupled with a
girl his age whom their respective parents had decided he would eventually marry.
They would take part in a miniature, symbolic, wedding ceremony. After returning
from morning prayers, men would gather at the 'groom's' home, where the synagogue
schoolteacher would trace, on a board the letters of the Hebrew alphabet in honey.
The child would be instructed to lick the letters, while he was told: "Thus, the words
of the Torah will be sweet to your taste."[20] The letter-licking rite, known in connection
with Shavuot in other parts of the Jewish world,[21] and the small-scale wedding are
expressions of the metaphor that links the receipt of the Torah by the people of Israel
to the image of God taking the Israelites as His bride.

The second custom connected to Shavuot is linked to the end of life. Jewish law
forbids the discarding or destroying of religious texts, or of any writing in which the
name of God appears. For this reason, old prayer books, Torah Scrolls, and other
religious books are stored away and eventually buried in a cemetery in a manner
similar to the internment of a human being. Occasionally, the death of a scholar was

seized upon as an appropriate occasion to bury the books that had been amassed in the communal store of worn-out texts (the *genizah*). In Morocco, the day following Shavuot was often selected as an apposite time for such book burials.[22]

Sometimes local customs developed that had their own logic, but that were opposed by the rabbis. An example is provided in the life of Rabbi Messas. Like other Moroccan rabbis, he sometimes served communities in Algeria, where French rule, established in 1830, had greatly weakened local rabbinic authority. Rabbi Messas reported the following incident in Tlemcen in Western Algeria. An unfortunate family experienced two deaths in one year. Its members would not allow the corpse to be removed from the house for ritual washing until they had slaughtered a rooster and spread its blood on the entranceway. Messas understood that this was a gesture intended to keep death from the doorstep, but could not condone it. At the same time, he was aware that people do not easily abandon customs that are deeply meaningful to them. His solution was to recommend that instead of slaughtering the fowl, the family perform the ceremony of *kapparot*, waving the bird around their head while stating that the bird is a substitute 'sacrifice' and atones for their sins. The fowl could then be donated to a poor family.[23] The *kapparot* ceremony, which originated in Europe, was derived from traditional practices on the eve of the Day of Atonement.[24] Its selection by Messas is particularly interesting because it, too, was originally a folk practice upon which the rabbis frowned, although ultimately they were forced to accept it, and Hebrew phrases were formulated to define its meaning. Thus, a 'compromise' custom that evolved in Ashkenaz several centuries ago was creatively utilized to meet another situation in North Africa that required negotiation between popular practice and rabbinic authority.

Moroccan rabbis, when writing about the practices and institutions of their communities, employed the concepts and language which characterized rabbinic discourse everywhere. The reality behind their formulations, however, was rooted in the specifics of Moroccan life. Communal documents, for example, draw upon rabbinic terminology and refer to *shiv'ah to'vei ha'ir* (the seven notables of the city) reaching a decision. In fact, such decisions did not stem from an established body responsible for formulating and executing policies. Rather, issues were dealt with on an ad hoc basis, reflecting an ethos of individual initiative rather than fully institutionalized communal life.[25]

This can be illustrated by an incident at the beginning of the nineteenth century that involved a ritual slaughterer (a *shoḥet*; see fig. 52). As the Passover season approached, members of the Jewish community induced him to carry out his slaughtering closer to the main market, which was a convenient location for them. He did so, but the Muslim butchers then complained to the urban authorities that he was competing with them. Even though he specialized in kosher meat, and Muslim rules for slaughtering were different from rabbinic rules, it was common for Muslims to buy meat from Jewish butchers that, after slaughtering, had been declared ritually-unfit for use by Jews. The authorities accepted this complaint and fined the *shoḥet*. He, in turn, sought a rabbinic judgment that the community should reimburse him the amount of the fine, for it was they who had encouraged him to move closer to the market. The decision, however, was that the community had no obligation to

FIG. 51 Rabbi Ifergan, the spiritual leader of the Jewish community in Oufrane, Anti-Atlas, March 1955. Photograph by Elias Harrus.

FIG. 52 Jews by the stall of a kosher butcher, Demnat, April 1958. Photograph by Alfred Goldenberg.

טבא וכמזלא יאי ובנטשיא מעליא ובשנת

והצלחה מוצא אשה מצא טוב
ויפיק רצון מיי

כרב ל על

91

Previous page

FIG. 53 Wedding Contract with *ḥamsa*, Larache, February 18, 1891; see cat. no. 105

FIG. 54 Jewish cemetery, Tetuan, March 1999. Photograph by Yvette Raby.

pay because the slaughterer had moved of his own free will, and not as their employee.

The importance of the individual within Moroccan Jewish life may also be observed in the existence of private synagogues. A person with the skills of a *ḥazan*, which meant someone who could lead the prayers and read from the Torah, might set aside a room in his home and make it into a synagogue. He would then enjoy the income that the synagogue generated from donations or from the auctioning off of the privilege of 'going up' to recite the blessings over the reading of the Torah. In North Africa this was called the sale of *mitzvot*, which was parallel to the auction of *aliyot* in Ashkenazi synagogues. From these funds, the owner of a synagogue could cover running expenses, and keep a surplus for himself. He would be helped by his wife, or other women in the family, who would clean the room, fill the lamps with oil, and make sure there were fragrant leaves available for the evening service at the close of the Sabbath, so that when leaving the synagogue people could make a blessing over them. Other

FIG. 55 Cemetery and tomb of Rabbi David u-Moshe at the *hillulah* compound in Timzrit, near Agouim, High Atlas, 1998. Photograph by Rose-Lynn Fisher.

women in the neighborhood might join in carrying out these tasks, even though they were not related to the owner, in order to gain the merit of a *mitzvah*. Synagogues could also be bought and sold. The privatization of synagogues was a development of the eighteenth century that took place in spite of rabbinic objections to the arrangement.

Personal initiative was also demonstrated by the membership of voluntary associations that combined religious and social purposes. An association – *ḥebra* – would focus on tasks such as finding spouses for orphans, providing for the poor so they could celebrate Passover with some degree of ease, or visiting the sick. Often, the name of the *ḥebra* did not directly describe its function, but was derived from a revered rabbi or other sainted figure from Jewish tradition. Thus, the association named for Elijah the Prophet dealt with matters surrounding the circumcision ceremony. Members of these associations, aside from carrying out their defined tasks, normally met on a weekly basis to read from classic texts.[26]

The most important *ḥebra* was the one associated with death and burial. In Jewish communities everywhere, there is a special association of individuals concerned with funerals, often known as the *ḥevra kaddisha*. Such *ḥebrot* existed in the smallest communities of Morocco, even if there were no other voluntary associations. It was always known as *ḥebrat rebbi shim'on* – 'the society of Rabbi Simeon.'[27] Rabbi Simeon bar Yoḥai was a second-century mishnaic sage who is considered the author of the book of the Zohar, the central tract of Jewish mysticism. The connection with Rabbi Simeon lay in the study activities of the association, which often took place on Thursday or Saturday nights. Normally they read from the *Idra*, the section of the Zohar that describes the death of bar Yoḥai. The prominence of Rabbi Simeon bar Yoḥai and of the Zohar among the Jews of Morocco is related to another feature of their religious lives: pilgrimages. Pilgrimages were one form of devotion to venerated *tzaddikim* (saintly rabbis).[28]

While Moroccan Jews recognized certain living rabbis as having special merit, it was the graves of *tzaddikim* that were especially prominent in their beliefs and religious practices. People hoped for the intercession of a *tzaddik* when they prayed for health, prosperity, or a successful match for their children. Even after their death, *tzaddikim* could be petitioned for personal requests at the places where they were buried, and it was believed that they could perform miracles for the benefit of their devotees.

Every local community had at least one *tzaddik* in or near its cemetery.[29] There were also regional *tzaddikim*, and a few, like Rabbi Amran ben Diwan of Ouezzane or Rabbi David u-Moshe, who attracted pilgrims from all over the country. In those cases, their graves were transformed into tombs, around which large buildings sprang up. A *tzaddik*, of any scale, could be visited by an individual at any time in order to pray or to fulfill a vow made as part of an earlier prayer. Visits were a way of paying homage to the *tzaddik*, as was the lighting of a candle by his tomb. There also were times when large numbers of people made pilgrimages to his grave. This took the form of a celebration known as a *hillulah*.

A local *hillulah* would bring together the whole community. People would visit the graveside, light candles, pray, sing hymns in honor of the *tzaddik*, give alms to the poor, and share a festive meal that involved the slaughter of animals. The occasion combined solemnity and festivity. It was a unifying experience that is often recalled with the phrase that 'men, women' and children all participated. The event had egalitarian overtones, marking it off from daily existence, in which people were separated by formal social distances.

Tzaddikim were important to women, who often invoked the name of a *tzaddik* in everyday life, one of the ways whereby wives, mothers, and grandmothers ensured the health and safety of the members of their families. During a *hillulah*, which is neither enjoined nor closely regulated by rabbinic rules, women could, in principle,

do everything that men did. It was customary for women not to approach a grave or a tomb side by side with men, and to refrain from visiting a *tzaddik*'s tomb when they were menstruating, but women were not barred from approaching the grave of a *tzaddik* at other times, or from lighting candles there in his honor. This code of behavior was substantially different from that which obtained in the synagogue, where central ritual roles were not available to women.

FIG. 59 Broadsheet of Rabbi Ḥayyim Pinto, Ashdod, first half of the 20th century; see cat. no. 115

FIG. 59 Broadsheet of Rabbi Ḥayyim Pinto, Ashdod, first half of the 20th century; see cat. no. 115

This ritual expression of relative equality related not only to women, but also gave greater religious recognition to the individual than is normally expressed in the synagogue. Standard synagogue life is rule-bound and highly structured. It also entails status markers: seating arrangements and the allotment of ritual honors separated the learned from the ordinary Jew, the wealthy from the poor. In contrast, a North African *hillulah*, whether it was to a faraway shrine or to the local cemetery, was not so encumbered by complex requirements and prohibitions. It was a congenial setting for individual men and women of humble social station to express their religious desires and personal wishes. The distinct presence of a *tzaddik* in a cemetery was a metaphor for individual distinction, allowing a person to feel that he or she might merit special attention.[30]

The *tzaddikim* functioned as important intermediaries for Moroccan Jews, just as there were sainted individuals, often termed *marabouts*, who were important in the lives of Moroccan Muslims.[31] Students of religion explain the significance of sainted individuals for the adherents of monotheistic traditions as follows: saints satisfy a need to fill the gap between men and an infinite God. It is believed that through his special merit, the *tzaddik* can relate to ordinary individuals on the one hand, and to the All-Powerful on the other.[32]

This religious pattern must also be understood against the background of Moroccan social life, in which intermediaries were an ever-present feature of daily interaction. An ordinary city-dweller, Muslim or Jew, assumed he could approach an important urban official only with the aid of a go-between whose status was higher than his own. In rural areas, far from the central government, Jews depended on local strongmen for their safety and ability to travel around the countryside as merchants and craftsmen. The local reality, that everyone was dependent on a patron more powerful than he, reinforced the religious notion of protection by patron saints.[33] One of the *tzaddikim*'s central tasks, in Jewish eyes, was to protect Jews from wanton Muslims who might exploit their vulnerability. Jews thus partially absorbed the notions of the culture in which they participated, as well as putting their own interpretation on it.

The idea that some people are 'holier,' or 'closer to God,' violates a strict monotheistic perspective, which views all people as equal in the sight of the Creator. Mystical tradition, however, provided the basis for assuming that some people are closer to God than rank-and-file believers. Jewish notions of sainthood have been shaped by the Kabbalah, and in particular by the image of Rabbi Simeon bar Yoḥai in the Zohar. Rabbi Simeon is considered the prototype of a *tzaddik*, which lends legitimacy to the existence of *tzaddikim* in Morocco in general.

The connection between bar Yoḥai and the *tzaddikim* in Morocco is apparent in various ways.[34] Moroccan *hillulah*s are smaller versions of the mass *hillulah* around the putative grave of Rabbi Simeon at Meron in the Galilee, which takes place in Israel every year at Lag B'Omer, the thirty-third day after the first day of Passover. The day of a *hillulah* is technically the date on which a saint died. Mystical understanding, however, converts that date to a happy occasion, even a symbolic 'wedding,' because it marks the reunion of a soul with its divine source. Often, the date of a local *hillulah* in Morocco was Lag B'Omer, suggesting that the link to bar Yoḥai overrode individual biographies.

FIG. 61 Interior of the Dahan Synagogue, Fez

The connection between the tradition of bar Yoḥai and the local *tzaddikim* is underlined by the text of the Zohar. For example, the term *hillulah*, which is associated with weddings in talmudic literature, appears in the Zohar in connection with the death of bar Yoḥai. The common Arabic term for 'cemetery' among Jews in Morocco, *me'arah* (derived from the Hebrew word for 'cave'), also appears in the Zohar, in reference to bar Yoḥai's burial place. To understand how this esoteric text and the traditions growing up around it played a role in everyday practice, even among people barely capable of reading it or understanding its contents, we must examine in detail the uses to which the book of the Zohar was put in southern Morocco.

The small communities of the south were obviously linked to wider Jewish tradition, but direct access to sacred texts was at times limited. The synagogue would normally have a number of printed Bibles (*ḥumashim*), which included translations of and commentaries on the Pentateuch, and a few liturgical collections. The central texts in the synagogue, however, were the Torah scroll, housed in the *heikhal*, and a set or sets of the Zohar.

The Torah scroll was '*the* book' in the synagogue, as the term *sefer* implies. It is essentially the presence of a Torah scroll that turns a room or building into a synagogue. It was a major communal event when a new Torah scroll was purchased by a person or a family for use by the community. Often the scroll would be kept at the home of the donor for a while, awaiting the ceremony that would transfer it to the synagogue. When the proper time arrived for the public presentation of a *sefer*, a procession would take place in which men walked slowly, singing and chanting, from the home of the donor to the synagogue. Eager to gain religious merit, different men would take turns at carrying the *sefer*. Women followed behind, contributing to the festivity with their ululations. These events could also include a *drashah*, and a festive meal for all the participants, provided by the donor.

The Jews of southern Morocco engaged in a similar round of ceremonies when a new set of the Zohar was brought to their communities. The Zohar does not have to be inscribed on parchment, but can be printed, and is ritually read in its printed form. This difference notwithstanding, the reverence offered the Zohar mirrors the honor bestowed upon the Torah scrolls. Among its other virtues, the Zohar allowed those who could not afford to pay for a scribe to write out a Torah scroll to contribute to communal life. A printed set of the Zohar costs much less than a *sefer*. When a new set reached a village, it was also a time for celebration.

The Zohar thus received treatment similar to that of a Torah scroll. It was placed in a specially prepared container during the procession, and people took turns carrying it, amid religious chanting. The Zohar also had a fixed place in the synagogue, in the *heikhal* or on a special shelf near it. There were also times, such as at the end of the Sabbath, when the Zohar would be taken from the *heikhal*, or its special shelf, and treated like a Torah taken out for reading during a service.

There was a major difference, however, between the treatment of the Torah scroll and that of the Zohar. Once brought into the synagogue, the Torah scroll was never removed from it, except when it was buried after it was no longer fit for ritual reading. In contrast to the Torah, the Zohar could be carried from the synagogue to individual homes, 'reside' in them for a few days, and then be returned to the synagogue. Standard occasions for 'visits' by the Zohar, and ritual reading from it, were the visitation of a difficult illness, the anniversary of the death of a relative, or the celebration on the night before a circumcision. The presence of the Zohar in the house was supposed to have a beneficial effect on an ill person or to protect the newborn, but it was also felt that keeping the books in the house for too long was not prudent. Usually they would be returned to the synagogue after several days. Every transfer of the Zohar from the synagogue or back again required a formal procession with hymns and all the signs of respect due to this venerated book.

Although this was an overall similarity in attitudes toward the Torah and the Zohar, the two differed in their sacrality. The Zohar was more accessible, even in terms of its purchase price, and could be brought into the lives of individuals at times of personal crisis. The Torah remained remote, in its own place. People could make personal requests in the presence of the Torah scroll in the synagogue, but they would have to come to the scroll in the *heikhal*; the Torah would not come to them. From this point of view, the Zohar was of lower status than the Torah, even though they were both objects of veneration, and the Zohar appears to have had a more immediate appeal to the rank-and-file Jew.

The logic of these rituals around books is directly derived from the rationale behind *tzaddikim* and pilgrimages, outlined above. Just as a *tzaddik* is a more accessible figure than the awesome One God, so the Zohar is more accessible, more 'user-

Opposite

FIG. 62 Torah Finials dedicated in memory of Simon Kastiel, Meknes, c. 1900; see cat. no. 12

FIG. 63 Jews on a pilgrimage in the 1930s to the tomb of Ulad Zemmur (the sons of Zemmur), seven brothers from a Sephardic family who were buried in a single tomb. Photograph by Moses Dloznazuski.

friendly,' than the Torah. Jewish mysticism supplied the theory that certain individuals, while remaining as human as everyone else, are blessed with a particular closeness to God. The Jews of Morocco took that logic one step further. Reluctant to be overly familiar with the Torah, the direct word of God, they were more comfortable with, yet still reverent toward, the Zohar, and could bring it into their individual lives.

Understanding *hillulah*s, and the importance of the Zohar among Moroccan Jews, entails paying attention to the Muslim environment in which they lived. In another celebration, for which Moroccan Jews have become well-known in Israel, relations with Muslim neighbors were one of the major features. The mutual involvement of Jews and Muslims was central to the *mimouna* festival in the spring, directly after Passover.

The *mimouna* was celebrated both within the home and in public spaces.[35] Immediately after Passover ended, at dark, an elaborate and attractive table would be set, containing many colorful sweets and milk, and featuring quickly prepared crepes known as *mufleta*. The table would be decorated with flowers, orange blossoms, and stalks of green barley. The last were also wrapped around lamps, clocks, and mirrors. As important was what did not appear on the *mimouna* table. Coffee was not allowed, and neither was meat, although fish was included. Each family made these arrangements for an 'open house,' while people also spent time out in the street of the Jewish quarter, visiting one another's homes to enjoy the food and gay atmosphere.[36]

When meeting someone in the street or in their home, the standard greeting and blessing was *Terbḥu u-tsa'du* – "May you profit and be happy." Often, upon entering a house, a person would be struck with a handful of green stalks as they were greeted. This might entail children striking their parents. This gesture was one of several that hinted at a reversal of status. Another entailed Jews dressing up in Muslim garb. In some instances, Jews borrowed clothes from Muslim neighbors. Muslims were linked to the celebration in other ways as well. They were often ready at the entrance to the *mellah*, the Jewish quarter, precisely as Passover ended, to sell the Jews greenery, or wheat from which to prepare the *mufleta*.[37] In the small communities of the countryside, where Jews were in daily contact with nearby Muslims, the greenery might be brought to Jewish homes as a neighborly gift.

Another part of the *mimouna* took place the day after Passover. Jews would go out to picnic and enjoy nature. Many would try to find streams or ponds, or to spend some time in the shade of trees. Often, this involved walking through the gardens of Muslims, who seemed to welcome the presence of Jews on that day. The overall atmosphere was that of a springtime 'new year' that exuded a sense of gaiety, spontaneity, and well-being.

The *mimouna*, taking place immediately after Passover, corresponds in time to what Jewish sources call the *isru ḥag* (the day following a festival),[38] but essentially has no textual basis either in general Jewish or regional North African literature. It is obviously a version of a Mediterranean springtime celebration, but Moroccan Jews have tried to assign to it a Jewish character. It is claimed that the word *mimouna* is connected to the Hebrew *emuna* ('faith') and that it refers to the fact that the Jews continue to believe that they will be redeemed from exile. This is folk etymology, for the Arabic word *mimouna* has a straightforward meaning in Morocco: 'good fortune.'

FIG. 64 *Mimouna* in Israel, 1970s

Further examination of the celebration's symbolism and social context, however, reveals that this folk etymology in fact encapsulates important aspects of the celebration's significance.

Three elements are brought together in the *mimouna*: a vernal new year, relations between Jews and Muslims, and reversal of status. These three things are interconnected in sometimes unexpected ways and through symbolic means that use elements of Jewish tradition.[39]

The blessing of the spring season is apparent in the greenery, the milk, and the fish, which point to reproduction and fecundity, while the absence of coffee is a mark of the repudiation of 'darkness.' What is somewhat surprising is that the Jews, who for the most part did not farm, were intimately involved in these ritual acknowledgments of the seasons. The Muslims seemed to feel that the Jewish celebration of a bountiful year was important. There was a tradition in Morocco, and elsewhere in North Africa, whereby during the festival of Shavuot, six weeks after the *mimouna*, Jews would splash water everywhere.[40] Muslim onlookers encouraged this practice, seeing it as a positive sign for the coming year. Muslims probably felt similarly indulgent toward the visits to their gardens by Jews on the day of the *mimouna*.[41]

The involvement of Muslims in the festivities, whether by selling greens or lending clothes, is surprising, particularly to those familiar with the often tense relationship

101

between Jews and Gentiles due to the religious differences between them. The *mimouna* stands in stark contrast to the previous week of Passover, where contact with Muslims was minimal, particularly in regard to anything having to do with food. From this perspective, and from several others, the *mimouna* is replete with signs of status reversal.

During the *mimouna*, many things take place that invert the normal routine of Moroccan Jewish life. Jews may dress as Muslims; children may 'strike' their seniors. The preparation of the *mufleta* is also topsy-turvy: often the crepe is placed on the surface of an upside-down frying pan. These inversions fit into a pattern that has been interpreted as symbolizing the 'power of the weak.'[42] In various ritual settings, it is the weak group that is viewed as representing general human morality, and as having a special closeness to the earth and the forces of fertility that affect all humankind. Such groups are often assigned ritual roles by the politically dominant majority. The 'closeness to nature' expressed by Jews was thus encouraged by Muslims, but how did the Jews make sense of this? Before answering this question, it is necessary to describe further the place of the Jews in Moroccan society.

Again, small communities concentrated in the rural south give us a clue to widespread patterns among all of Morocco's Jews. In these communities the economic lives of Jews and Muslims were deeply intertwined. Jewish peddlers and craftsmen plied the countryside, trading with Muslim villagers or providing them with services such as tinsmithing, shoemaking, carpentry, or saddlery. Often, Jews were away from home for days and even weeks at a time. On such occasions, they would be given lodging by Muslims. Jews would not eat full meals with Muslims, because of the rules of *kashrut* (ritual dietary laws), but might drink tea with them, or even eat their home-baked bread. Jewish traders and craftsmen were a common sight in the Moroccan countryside.[43]

At Passover time, all this changed. Signs of the disappearance or isolation of the Jews began as Passover approached. In some mountain villages, the Jews would arrange to rent the village mill, which would be powered by water running through the local wadi, for several weeks before Passover. There, they would carefully grind and examine the wheat for Passover, and no Muslim could come near the milling grounds. When the holiday itself arrived, Jews were hardly to be seen. Turned in upon themselves during the nights of the *seder*, and enclosed within the synagogue, contact was at an ebb and commensuality was inconceivable. It is easy to surmise that this drastic separation cultivated a query among Muslims: "What are the Jews, who normally are with us all the time, plotting among themselves?"

The suspicion that can be imputed to the Muslim majority is not without grounding in Jewish sources. Passover is, above all, a celebration of the historical exodus from Egypt, the redemption of the Children of Israel, and the punishment visited upon the Egyptians, who refused to acknowledge God's existence made manifest through his special relationship with Israel. Beyond that, Passover also celebrates future redemption, the end of exile, and the messianic return of the Jewish people to their land. A talmudic passage states that just as the Children of Israel were redeemed from Egypt in the Hebrew month of Nisan, so their future redemption will also take place in Nisan. This link is highlighted in the synagogue during the last days of Passover. On the seventh day of the festival, Moses' Song of Exultation at having crossed the Red Sea (Exodus 15) is read, followed on the eighth day by one of Isaiah's messianic visions (Isaiah 10:32–12:6). By the end of Passover, Jews are celebrating not only their past redemption, but also their hope of extricating themselves from their present exile.

The contrast between these messianic hopes and the reality of being a weak and tolerated minority, a contrast more clear than ever at the conclusion of Passover, forms the background of the *mimouna* celebration, which reintegrates the Jews into the local social, cultural, and even ecological milieu. It merges symbolic acts of status reversal, hope for an eventual redemption from subservience, and an indication of commonality and mutuality with the wider population. These gestures, expressing contradictory sentiments, are relevant to the local Moroccan setting, and also echo the ambivalence and moral complexity found in rabbinic tradition. A talmudic legend relating to Moses' song of exultation expresses this complexity thus:

When the Egyptians were drowning in the sea, the ministering angels sought to sing Moses' song of exultation before the Holy One, Blessed be He, but He said to them: "The work of My hands are drowning in the sea – and you are singing the song of exultation?"

Although few Moroccan Jews would have been aware of this legend,[44] it seems to encapsulate the ambivalence of the end of the Passover season – consisting as it did of a deep attachment to the historically based aspirations for the salvation of Israel, as well as a recognition of the humanity of Israel's oppressors. The role of the *mimouna* is to overcome this ambivalence, combining the leave-taking of Passover with a recognition of the mutual engagement of Jews and non-Jews. The absence of meat from the *mimouna* table is, perhaps, reminiscent of life in the Garden of Eden, before humans slaughtered animals, and portends a future idyllic state in the World to Come.

An indication of the ambivalence underlying the *mimouna*, even as it served to re-cement the bonds linking Jews to Muslims in everyday life, may be seen in a *piyyut* (hymn) that was sung in the synagogue in the Tafilalet region on the night of the *mimouna*. Based on an acrostic, the song was recited in a festive atmosphere, while the men drank *mahia* (raisin brandy). The first three lines convey the spirit of the twenty-two verses that follow, one for each letter of the Hebrew alphabet:

May light come to Israel, May a curse come to Ishmael
May a blessing come to Israel, May confusion come to Ishmael
May redemption come to Israel, May exile come to Ishmael

Each of these lines is followed by the refrain: "O day of joy, O day of joy, May the day of joy come, May it come, may it come, may it come." The researcher who recorded this verse and described its liturgical setting claims that this kind of direct expression of resentment was unusual, and should not be seen as contradicting the friendly relations that obtained between Jews and Muslims.[45] It is not important whether this kind of expression of hostility was typical, but that it points to ideas and sentiments that were entailed in the *mimouna* wherever it was celebrated, even as the festival symbolically overcame the ambivalence inherent in the socially inferior situation of the Jews. The *mimouna* linked the minority Jews with the Muslim majority, while anchoring Jewish existence in an established religious vision of redemption from exile.

The two forms of celebration that have been discussed at length, the *hillulah* and the *mimouna*, do not belong to the past. They continue in renewed and reshaped forms in France, Canada, and, of course, in Israel. There, from the 1960s onward, the Jews of Morocco became the largest group from one country until the recent Russian immigration. The establishment of shrines to *tzaddikim* has been prominent in Israel's development towns in the north and south of the country, where many Jews from Morocco settled from the mid-1950s through the mid-1960s. Some shrines are devoted to *tzaddikim* from Morocco, while others have been built up around rabbis who died in Israel.[46] Moroccan Jews feature prominently in celebrations that cross ethnic lines, such as the annual *hillulah* of Rabbi Simeon bar Yoḥai at Meron, which attracts well over 100,000 people. In these contexts, the rituals of the *hillulah* take on new meanings. Mothers pray for the well-being of their sons in the army, and for the safety of all of Israel's soldiers. Shrines to *tzaddikim* in the country's small towns engender a sense of local patriotism. Symbols from the past have helped strike roots in a new environment.

The *mimouna* has also found a second life in Israel.[47] There, the day of the *mimouna*, associated with picnicking, has taken on special significance. From the late 1960s, Moroccan Jews' practice of gathering together from the scattered parts of Israel to which they had moved began to snowball. In 1968, about ten thousand people came to the day-long celebration at the outskirts of Jerusalem; four years later, attendance reached eighty thousand, and the event took place in the Gan Sacher park, near the Knesset, in the middle of the city. It was as if the celebrants were reversing the policy of 'population dispersion' that had directed them to small towns in the north and the south. It was also a statement by Jews from Morocco that they no longer wished to be treated as new immigrants, but that they had 'arrived,' and had the right to display their culture in front of the rest of society.

As in Morocco, where the *mimouna* linked Muslims and Jews, the celebration evolved into a festival that created bridges between groups in contemporary Israel. It began to be supported and promoted by voluntary organizations and official bodies. Various immigrant groups were invited to attend and set up tents exhibiting aspects of their heritage. The *mimouna*, it might be said, has become Israel's festival of ethnicity. After a period in which government policy sought to make all immigrants conform to a standard Israeli model, society is now more comfortable with internal diversity. To understand the customs of the Jews of Morocco is to learn to appreciate a unique version of Jewish culture, and also to gain insight into the intricate dynamics of Israeli society today.

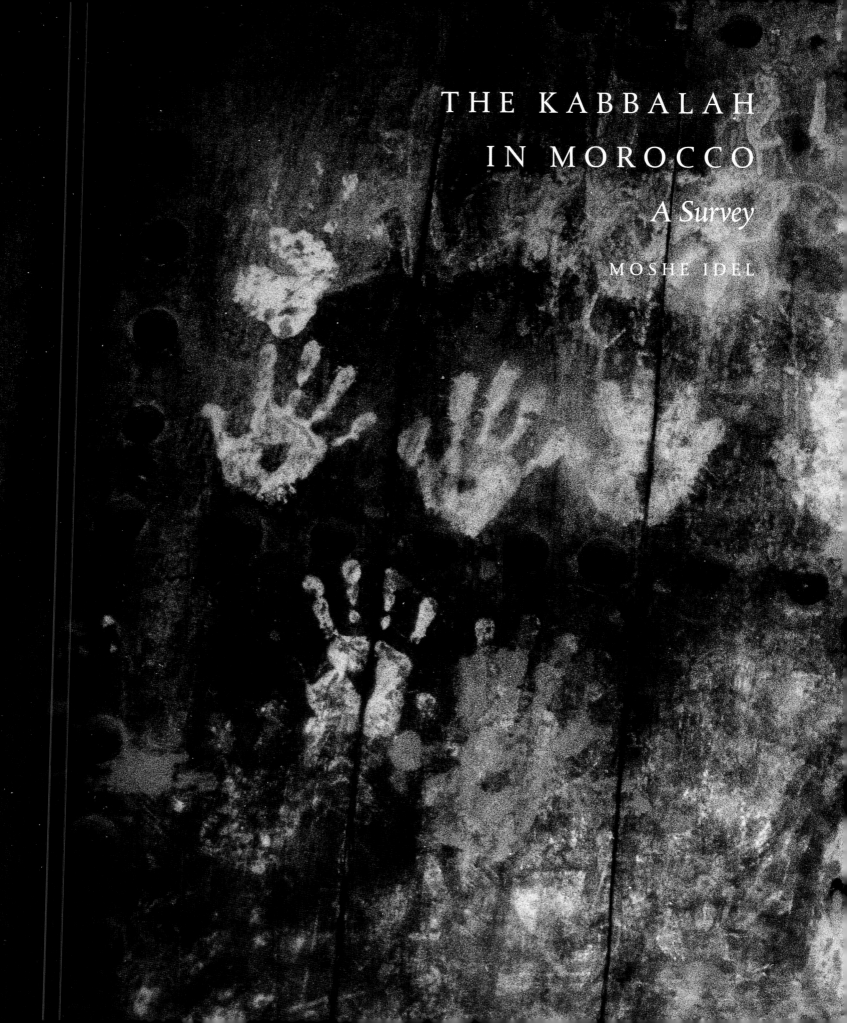

THE KABBALAH
IN MOROCCO

A Survey

MOSHE IDEL

Kabbalah and its Centers

Kabbalah is a variegated conglomerate of spiritual models, types of experiences, and modes of expressions that developed over the span of almost a millennium in different countries and continents. Although it stemmed from southern France at the end of the twelfth century and then flowered in Spain, some forms of this lore had developed outside the perimeter of the Iberian Peninsula prior to the end of the thirteenth century. This is apparently so in the case of the ecstatic Kabbalah of Abraham Abulafia, who produced most of his work in Italy, Sicily, and the Byzantine Empire, before disappearing around 1291. A book by one of his students, Nathan ben Se'adyah Harar, was composed, or at least copied, in Hebron in either 1289 or 1294. Forms of theosophical Kabbalah were already known in Rome in the 1280s, culminating with the kabbalistic writings of Menaḥem Recanati at the beginning of the fourteenth century. Other forms of Kabbalah were still known in Germany in the thirteenth century. However, it seems that contemporary with traditions of Kabbalah outside Spanish centers, there is also evidence of the existence of Kabbalah in Morocco, an issue discussed below. Before turning to this topic in more detail, however, let me address the importance of such a rapid and early diffusion of Kabbalah.

These expansions of Kabbalah did not merely develop concepts stemming from the Spanish centers of Cataluña or Castilla. The export into new places of forms of thought that had only begun to develop in Spain created syntheses that were less likely to have developed there. For example, Abraham Abulafia's ecstatic Kabbalah was banned by Shlomo ben Abraham ibn Adret, and its impact on Spanish Kabbalah was therefore negligible. In this case the controversy between two kabbalists created a schism in the history of Kabbalah. This was also the case with the influential writings of Menahem Recanati. A complex type of literature emerged in Byzantium at the beginning of the fourteenth century that produced a rich kabbalistic yield that had a great impact on the subsequent history of Kabbalah, although not in Spain. The story of Ashkenazi mystical lore and its synthesis with Kabbalah is not very different. Although there are significant traces of Ashkenazi esoteric theology in Spanish Kabbalah, the synthesis between kabbalistic theosophy and the thought of Ḥasidei Ashkenaz did not affect Spanish Kabbalah. Legends exist about the impact of Eleazar of Worms on Nahmanides's involvement in practical Kabbalah, but they do not change the fact that only scant examples of Ashkenazi esoteric theology occur in Spanish Kabbalah. With the exception of Abraham Abulafia, whose influence on Spanish Kabbalah was quite small, the lore of Ḥasidei Ashkenaz did not shape the theosophy of Spanish kabbalists in any dramatic manner.

Substantially different, however, is the relationship between the forms Kabbalah took in Morocco in the thirteenth century and the subsequent history of some forms of Kabbalah in Spain and then elsewhere. The fact that each center of Kabbalah has its own history, starting from different cultural and phenomenological premises, that influenced the general history of Kabbalah in a specific manner, suggests a methodological approach that has not yet attracted the attention of scholars of the subject. Immersed in what can be called monolithic visions of the phenomenology of Kabbalah, and in the acceptance of a unilinear history of this lore, scholarship in this field has still to investigate the specifics of each center in order to understand the wide spectrum of kabbalistic literature; this diversity represents different approaches that sometimes reflect interactions with local cultures. A less centralized vision of the history and nature of Kabbalah will allow a better understanding of specific phenomena and centers, as well as of the more variegated picture of this lore as a whole. In the following discussion, the main point that I shall attempt to make is that Morocco was a kabbalist center not only in the sense that it played host to a long series of kabbalists, but also because it produced books that had influence outside its boundaries. In lieu of the conceptual and élite-oriented approach that characterizes modern Kabbalah scholarship, I would insist on the need also to address the sociological aspects of this lore, and to emphasize issues of reception, dissemination, and appropriation by larger audiences, if the history of ideas is not to remain the single lens through which kabbalistic themes may be analyzed.

A Thirteenth-Century Testimony to Kabbalah in Morocco?

Given the limitation of our historical knowledge, we are not in a position to discover the precise beginnings of Kabbalah. The earliest evidence in Morocco is a story the historical authenticity of which cannot be verified, but that will serve, at least, to establish Morocco as the place from which some form of occult knowledge, thought to be Kabbalah, was transmitted to Sicily and then to Provence. This anonymous kabbalist forged an epistle attributed to Hai Gaon:

This great sage, may God save him, from whom I received all this, testified about a sage from Marseilles, who came to Montpellier, and asserted that he had seen in Sicily a great Moroccan sage, who was intelligent and profound in the science of astronomy, that of the ancients and of the later sages, and was the chief physician of the king of Sicily, and was highly regarded in the eyes of the king and his ministers and great ones, like an angel of God. And he [the sage] told his disciples: "Be careful of the sect of the inquirers, and the sect of those who speculate." Moreover, this [Sicilian] sage showed the sages of Montpellier a passage from the books of the great Moroccan sage:[1] "Woe to whomever relies on his sharpness and inquiry, and whose head goes after his feet, and who leaves aside the secrets of the prophets and the sages of the Children of Israel, and indulges in the science of philosophy, which is [nothing more than] an illusion[2] and the science of sorcerers and diviners. Its foot is without a head and a brain . . . Woe to whomever speculates but did not receive [training in Kabbalah], who received but did not speculate, because both should be learnt from the mouth of the Rabbi, and by the eye and the heart." This is the end of the passage.[3]

This passage originated in a circle of kabbalists whose identity is vague, given their recurrent resort to pseudepigraphy. However, it seems plausible that it was written in the third quarter of the thirteenth century in Spain.[4] Already, then, there existed the image of a Moroccan figure who was involved in speculations very close to what we conceive of as Kabbalah: namely secrets of the prophets and rabbinic sages, and an emphasis on the importance of the transmission of knowledge. This sage was visualized as a *homo universalis*: in addition to being a religious paragon, he was conceived of as being very learned in astronomy and medicine, and a figure to be admired by the entire Christian high élite.

This is not exactly a legend recording or inventing a case of *translatio scientiae*, legions of which appear in the history of Kabbalah. It is more an imaginary story about the greatness of an individual than the history of a lore. Assuming its audience was acquainted with the existence of occult lore in Morocco, the anonymous kabbalist who composed the above passage invented a line of developments that takes in no less than three continents; the alleged Moroccan author of the epistle, the famous Hai Gaon of Babylonia, testifies that an unnamed North African figure transmitted some form of religious knowledge to Sicily, from where it was imparted to Provencal rabbis, namely those living at the very epicenter of the emergence of Kabbalah. Though not antagonistic to natural sciences, the Moroccan figure argues against a reliance on philosophical speculations, an issue that reflects tensions characteristic of the first third of the thirteenth century, when the first debates over Maimonides's books took place. It is also possible that the attempt to combine the need for a transmitted tradition with speculation is an answer to Nahmanides's insistence on the importance of the oral tradition in matters of esoteric knowledge, and his interdiction on speculation about Kabbalah.

Yehudah ben Nissim ibn Malka

Although the passage above represents more a cultural image than a historical event, it seems that the Spanish forger may have had a certain historical figure in mind: the mid-thirteenth century thinker Yehudah ben Nissim ibn Malka, who was, probably, an inhabitant of Fez, a city destined to host more kabbalists than any other city in the world except Safed. His writings – discovered by Georges Vajda, who published and analyzed them in a number of seminal studies – point to an interesting combination of medieval philosophy, astrology, and some elements of Kabbalah.[5] Although there are some late indications that his father, Nissim, was also a kabbalist, the sources are unreliable, as they depend on Moshe Botarel's *Commentary on Sefer Yetzirah*, a book replete with false quotes. Yehudah ben Nissim ibn Malka was the author of three small books composed in Arabic, and of a short astrological treatise extant in Hebrew.[6] This astrological-messianic document determines the floruit of this figure at the middle of the thirteenth century, rather than the fourteenth century as earlier scholars opined. Yehudah ibn Malka had an interesting theory of strict astrological determinism, which is unusual in medieval Jewish writings. Combining neo-Aristotelian theories of the metaphysical realm with a belief in the impact of the astral bodies on mundane events, he proposed a hierarchy of knowledge that put philosophy on top, the natural sciences afterwards, and astro-magic at the lowest point. The combination of these theories had a special impact on his theory of revelation, which may be one of the most important contributions to kabbalistic theories of prophecy, and which had a lasting impact on the Jewish theory of revelation. In his *Commentary on Sefer Yetzirah*, he testifies that:

I have seen with my own eyes a man who saw a power in the form of an angel while he was awake, who spoke with him and told him future things. The sage said: "Know that he sees nothing other than himself, for he sees himself front and back, as one who sees himself in a mirror, who sees nothing other than himself, and it appears as if it were something separate from your body, like you." In the same manner, he sees that power which guards his body and guides his soul, and then his soul sings and rejoices, distinguishes and sees.[7]

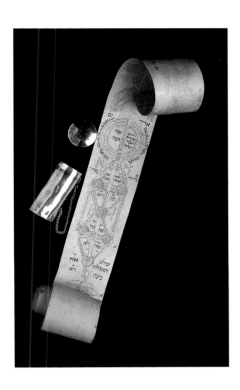

The astral aspect of the revelation, which reflects the impact of Muslim astromagical sources, is not the only explanation ibn Malka offers for this experience of self-revelation. Immediately after the above citation, ibn Malka offers an explanation that describes the process as a psychological one that takes place between three inner faculties:

And three powers overcome him: the first power is that which is intermediary between spirit and soul, and the power of memory and the power of imagination, and one power is that which imagines. And these three powers are compared to a mirror, as by virtue of the mixing of these powers the spirit is purified, and by the purification of the spirit, the third power is purified. But when the spirit apprehends the flux which pours out upon the soul, it will leave power to the power of speech, according to the flow which comes upon the soul, thus shall it influence the power of speech, and that itself is the angel which speaks to him and tells him of future things.[8]

The introduction of the inner faculties in order to describe the psychological mechanism of revelation is important as it internalizes the revelatory event, in terms uncharacteristic of the more objectivistic astral-magical systems. Therefore, a personal angelic guide of an astral nature reveals the future, by using the psychological organon of a certain person, an idea that would not seem especially surprising in the Middle Ages. However, what is of importance for the understanding of kabbalistic prophetology is the claim, recurrent in the book, that not only prophecy in general should be understood in an astral framework, but also Moses' prophecy. According to ibn Malka, the speech heard by Moses from the burning bush originated in Moses himself. The kabbalist resorts to gematria (the numerical equivalent of letters), which for the word *haSeneh* (the bush) yields 120, the number of years that Moses lived. Ibn Malka interprets Zechariah 4:1 in a similar manner, glossing "the angel who spoke to me" as meaning "from within me."[9]

The Hebrew term used by the translator of the original Arabic in order to describe the transmission of information is *heggid lo 'atidot*, which is used once, and then the term *maggid 'atidot* is used several times. In ibn Malka, there is already an anticipation of the later category of revelation that proliferated from the sixteenth century onward, the *maggid*, a personal guide or celestial angelic mentor. Shlomo Pines has already drawn attention to the affinity between some forms of Arabic astro-magic found in Abu-Aflah al-Syracusi's *Sefer ha-Tamar*, known in Spain in a Hebrew translation since the beginning of the fourteenth century, and later kabbalistic phenomena.[10] I propose a somewhat earlier date for the occurrence of such a phenomenon in Jewish occultism.[11] Yehudah ibn Malka should be seen as one of the first pioneers of a synthesis between astro-magic and kabbalistic elements, both as found in sefirotic Kabbalah and in the technique of combinations of letters. Important kabbalistic ideas that were prevalent in Spain, Italy, and Safed, like the concept of *heikhalot*, the astral bodies wherein the spirit dwell,[12] have affinities to the astral magic permeating the writings of Yehudah that point to the synthesis between Arabic philosophical magic and Jewish esotericism. The shift from an emphasis on the theosophical-theurgical to an emphasis on an astro-magical understanding of Kabbalah, based on Arabic sources, is quite conspicuous. The above passage is adduced not only for its phenomenological description of revelation, but also in order to argue that it

FIG. 66 Voleti after Wilhelm Gentz, *Prayers at Tomb of Rabbi Isaac ben Sheshet at Algiers,* oil on canvas, c. 1870; The Jewish Museum, New York, gift of Dr. Harry G. Friedman (F4176)

influenced the manner in which Kabbalah was later understood. Indeed, another figure who was active in North Africa during the fifteenth century was the Spanish-born Ephraim ben Israel al-Naqawah, whose tomb in Tlemcen became a site for pilgrimage. He wrote:

In the books of the sages, it is written of the zodiac signs that there are people who may see powers while awake, who will seem to them that they are bodies, and will speak with them and tell them future things. And they said the reason is that man receives the influx from supernal entities. And this thing will be strengthened in accordance with the structure of the constellation in the hour of their birth. And they explained, moreover, that the seer of those powers that appear to them in the likeness of bodies, does not see them without him, but all that they see is within them, just as he sees his form within a mirror or within something pure and transparent, where he indeed sees his form with his eyes.[13]

Interestingly enough, this passage made its way to Safed and is quoted verbatim by Ḥayyim Vital in his classic *Sha'arei Qedushah*.[14] Even if it is too early to determine, on the basis of extant material and the preliminary state of modern research on Kabbalah, the direct influence of Yehudah ben Nissim on later kabbalists in Morocco and elsewhere, it seems that it is possible to consider the tendency he represents as a shift toward astro-magic that changed the face of Kabbalah significantly, especially in fourteenth-century Spain and in late-fifteenth-century Italy, during the Renaissance. Jewish culture also served as a bridge between the Arabic world of thought and that of

FIG. 67 Amulet of Mess'udah, daughter of Ḥayyim, amulet against Lilith, amulet, Morocco, late 19th – early 20th century; see cat. nos. 35–37

Christian Europe. The magical reading of some of the aspects of Kabbalah that arose from the encounter between Arabic forms of magic and Jewish mysticism, characteristic of Moroccan Kabbalah in many of its phases, made its way to Florence, where, in the writings of Yoḥanan Alemanno, it reached its apogee. Christian Kabbalah, as formulated in the writings of Pico della Mirandola, one of the most important thinkers of the Italian Renaissance, reflects this astro-magical kabbalistic synthesis. In fact, Frances A. Yates's thesis that it was Pico della Mirandola who first created a synthesis between the Hermeticism he inherited from Marsilio Ficino's translations and writings and Jewish Kabbalah, does not take into consideration the earlier stages of the development of Kabbalah combined with talismanic views stemming from Hermetic sources that first appears in the writings of Yehudah ibn Malka. The main trends of thirteenth-century Spanish Kabbalah were not concerned with psychological and astrological explanations of prophecy or the Bible, preferring a much more theosophical-theurgical approach that remained dominant until the expulsion from Spain, and then influenced Kabbalah in Morocco.

Isaac ben Samuel of Acre

Related to Yehudah's books is the work of Isaac ben Samuel of Acre, an outstanding kabbalist who commented on Yehudah's commentary on the late Midrash *Pirqei de-Rabbi Eliezer*.[15] To a great extent, Isaac imposed a strong theosophical reading on the text he interpreted. Especially interesting is the strong affinity between this kabbalist's mystical experience and the one described above by Yehudah ibn Malka. Isaac contends that:

I, the young one, know and discern by a certain knowledge that I am not a prophet neither a son of a prophet, and I have not the holy spirit and I do not make use of the daughter of the voice, since I have not been vouchsafed them, and "I have not taken off my garment or washed my feet [Song of Songs 5:3]." Nevertheless, I call heaven and earth to witness – as the heavens are my witness and guarantor on high – that one day I was sitting and writing down a kabbalistic secret, when suddenly I saw the form of my self standing in front of me and my self disappeared from me.[16]

It is plausible, as has been pointed out recently by scholars, that Isaac of Acre reached North Africa, where he died.[17] In any case, some of his writings are extant in the form of North African Kabbalistic manuscripts,[18] and one of them, his *Commentary on Sefer Yetzirah*, is known solely from a copy made by an early sixteenth-century kabbalist in North Africa.[19] Together with excerpts from his own writings, kabbalistic traditions connected to Isaac's contemporary kabbalists Joseph ben Shalom Ashkenazi and David ben Yehudah heḤasid are found in his works. They constitute the first substantial kabbalistic material to reach North Africa, which greatly contributed to the configuration of later developments of Kabbalah in this region.

A legend adduced by Abraham Azulai, who copied it from an earlier source (Moses Cordovero's commentary on the Zohar), asserts that the Dra' valley was the source of the Zohar, which eventually came to Spain. This tradition stems from a no longer extant book by Isaac of Acre, and it may explain why this kabbalist came to North Africa.[20] This legend should be juxtaposed with the testimony about the Moroccan

sage who was active in Sicily, discussed above. In both cases, Morocco was believed to host early kabbalistic lore; both cases concern texts written in Aramaic, as in another short passage attributed to Yehudah ibn Malka.[21]

What happened to the study of Kabbalah in Morocco during the fourteenth and most of the fifteenth centuries is not clear. We have no reliable evidence of the development of independent schools there, which might have continued and elaborated the views of earlier kabbalists. Interestingly, as far as most of the fourteenth century is concerned, the lack of evidence regarding Kabbalah in Morocco does not differ dramatically from the lack of evidence in Spain, Israel, Ashkenaz, and Italy. Nevertheless, according to both direct and indirect evidence, it seems that before the expulsion of the Jews from the Iberian Peninsula, Moroccan kabbalists were already known outside the Maghreb, as was recently shown.[22]

Interestingly enough, both the pseudepigraphical epistle that mentions the secrets of the prophets and the passages from Yehudah and Isaac betray an interest in prophecy, which seems to characterize some of the discussions found later in Moroccan Kabbalah, especially that of the south, in the Dra' valley, as will be seen below.

The Expulsion from Spain and the Moroccan Kabbalistic Center

There can be no doubt that the decisive event that changed the history of Kabbalah in Morocco, just as it had an impact on the development of Kabbalah in general, was the expulsion of the Jews from Spain and Portugal at the end of the fifteenth century. Basically, the Spanish kabbalists followed two main trajectories: the northern or European one, and the southern or North African one. In some important cases, the final destination of kabbalists was neither Europe nor Africa, but the Land of Israel, which played host to the most important developments in sixteenth-century Kabbalah. Even in cases where kabbalists stayed for short periods on their way to the Land of Israel, I believe that the impact of even short contacts with the indigenous cultures shaped, to a certain extent, the formulations of the Spanish kabbalists. Groups of Spanish Jews, including some kabbalists, arrived suddenly on the northern shore of Morocco and enriched dramatically the knowledge and the impact of Kabbalah there. To enumerate just the most important of the expellees, let me mention Yehudah Ḥayyat, Abraham Sabba', Shimon Lavi, Abraham Adrutiel, Joseph ben Moses al-Ashqar, and Yehudah Hallewah. The impact on Kabbalah was more decisive than it was in the thirteenth century: not only ideas in their formative phase were involved, but also an entire literature, which articulated complex systems formulated by authors who had become well-known, and whose books, in some cases, enjoyed some degree of general recognition. The expulsion meant not only the uprooting of an entire community, but also the export of an elaborate and variegated culture. This strong Spanish culture, with Kabbalah as one of its major attainment, arrived in the various cities of Morocco in one huge wave, which changed substantially the high culture of Moroccan Jewry. The arrival of the kabbalists from Spain was accompanied by the arrival of Kabbalistic writings, and there can be no doubt that some of the manuscripts preserved or copied in Morocco are of great importance for the understanding of the history of Spanish Kabbalah. Several

FIG. 69 *Ḥamsas*, door of a synagogue in the *mellah* of M'Hamid, Dra' valley, 1998. Photograph by Rose-Lynn Fisher.

relatively early kabbalistic manuscripts preserved in Morocco – often found in private collections and not previously used for the analysis of Spanish Kabbalah – shed important light on the history of Kabbalah in late thirteenth-century Castille. For example, the manuscript printed by Jacob Toledano in Casablanca in 1930 under the title *Sefer haMalkhut* contains kabbalistic fragments and treatises stemming from late-thirteenth- and early-fourteenth-century Spain that otherwise appear in exceptionally few manuscripts.[23]

The most visible and most profound change evident in Moroccan post-expulsion Kabbalah consisted of the adoption of the book of the Zohar as the major text of Kabbalah and the transformation of this book into a canonical work. Ibn Malka and Isaac of Acre were the two major kabbalists active in North Africa before the end of the fifteenth century, and their writings do not display any particular affinity with the mythical worldview of the Zohar, but are more concerned with ecstatic experiences and talismanic magic: so the Zoharic ways of thought with their theosophical-theurgical propensities became the dominant trends only in the sixteenth century. However, this process of canonization reflects the growing importance of the Zohar earlier in Spain, and in order to understand it better it is necessary to inspect the nature of the lore of the first generation of expelled kabbalists. They all embraced forms of Kabbalah strongly influenced by the Zohar. That is why there is a strong affinity between the Moroccan kabbalist center and the Safedian one: it was only in these two places that kabbalistic literature cohered so strongly around the Zohar. A comparison with other centers of Kabbalah, such as Jerusalem at the beginning of the sixteenth century, or Italy, demonstrates the kinship between trends in Morocco and in Safed. Given the present state of studies in kabbalistic literature, it is difficult to conceptualize the main lines of development in any kabbalistic center, and thus the following discussion is rather preliminary. Some developments in Kabbalah in Morocco since the early sixteenth century have recently attracted the attention of scholars who have described in detail for the first time several kabbalists and schools, facilitating the first delineation of the main lines of development: these scholars include Moshe Hallamish,[24] Haïm Zafrani,[25] Dan Manor,[26] Rachel Elior,[27] and Elie Moyal.[28]

Morocco – The Southern Trajectory of Kabbalah: Four Examples

North Africa, especially Fez, was a major Jewish center that attracted many expellees. The closest state to Spain and Portugal, and the first to which the *megorashim* arrived in considerable numbers, Morocco was destined to host the earliest significant expatriate center of Spanish Kabbalah. There were two main trajectories after the expulsion, not only geographically but also culturally: the northern trajectory took the expellees through both Christian and Muslim – basically Turkish – culture, while the southern one passed through cities and areas that were predominantly Islamic.[29] Eminent among the centers created immediately after the expulsion was Fez.

The first example of a kabbalist who visited the city for a short period, and then left for another center, is Yehudah Ḥayyat. Sometime during the winter of 1492–93, he left Lisbon, together with his family and some two hundred other people. Because of the plague that was widespread among the passengers, the boat wandered for four months, and was finally forced to anchor in Malaga because it was not welcome in any other port. Finally, the boat was robbed by Basques. The Christian authorities or, according to another version, the priests convinced hundreds of the expellees to convert. Some of the others, including Ḥayyat's wife, died. The boat was detained in Malaga for two months and then allowed to leave. Ḥayyat arrived in Fez, where a Muslim acquaintance of the kabbalist initiated a libel, the precise nature of which is not clear. Ḥayyat was rescued by the Jews, to whom he gave two hundred books in return for the ransom. After a short stay in Fez, in the most inhuman conditions, in the autumn of 1493, he left for Naples, and then proceeded to Venice, where he was very well-received by the 'noble' Spanish refugees. The arrival of so many manuscripts in Morocco, the majority apparently kabbalistic, is a vital component of the southern trajectory of Kabbalah.

Another important figure who represents the southern trajectory was Yehudah Hallewah. A descendent of an important Jewish family from Spain – whose most eminent member was Baḥya ben Asher Hallewah of the late thirteenth century – Yehudah was, presumably, an exile from the Iberian Peninsula, who arrived and stayed in Fez for an extended period, then left for Safed, where he lived for some years

FIG. 70 Tomb of Soleika Hachuel (1817–34), Jewish cemetery in the *mellah* of Fez, 1995. Photograph by Rose-Lynn Fisher.

before 1545. There he composed one of the first ethical-kabbalistic books written in Safed, *Sefer Tzafnat Pa'aneaḥ*, a text that was intended to guide the Jewish inhabitants of the city to righteous behavior by emphasizing its consequences in the life to come. This strategy of guidance was the only option in a community whose leading figures had lost their authority. Hallewah contrasted Safed with the more organized Jewish way of life in Fez. This comparison testifies to the degree of cohesion characteristic of this Moroccan Sephardic community.[30]

An interesting account found in Hallewah's book concerns the transmigration of the soul of a kabbalist active in Spain in the generation prior to the exile to North Africa. Hallewah tells a story he heard, apparently while in Fez, about Joseph della Reina's soul, which entered the body of a gentile woman as a punishment for Joseph's sinful life. A Jewish magician, probably a Moroccan one, was asked to exorcize his spirit.[31] This is the first case of possession recorded by a kabbalist in a kabbalistic book, a generation before the surge of interest in the topic, better known under the later name of the *dibbuq*. A story told in Safed records an event that took place in North Africa and had as its main protagonist a Spanish kabbalist. This is an emblematic example of the importance of the North African trajectory of Spanish Kabbalah, which had an impact on the new center of Kabbalah in Safed from its beginning.

Hallewah's book, like most of the other books composed at the end of the sixteenth and the beginning of the seventeenth centuries, discussed in the next paragraph, displays strong eclectic tendencies, which rely on pre-expulsion Spanish Kabbalah and on a few later developments, as is the case with the writings of another exile, Meir ibn Gabbai. Judged by the criterion of conceptual innovation, only rarely can writings composed in Morocco be conceived of as important. However, if the criterion for importance is the role played in the life of the Jewish community, there can be no doubt that Kabbalah in Morocco became part of Moroccan Jewish ritual on a large scale.

On the southern shores of the Mediterranean Sea, in cities such as Tlemcen and Fez, exiles from Castilla and Granada brought a variety of kabbalistic books and even compiled a series of anthologies that reflect the status and nature of Kabbalah in Spain better than any speculation; this is obvious from a perusal of the kabbalistic works of Joseph ben Moses al-Ashqar and Abraham ben Shlomo Adrutiel. In Tripoli, now Libya, one of the exiles, Shimon ben Lavi, formerly an inhabitant of Fez, composed one of the most important and original commentaries on the Zohar, *Ketem Paz*, which relies on a long series of Spanish sources. These North African kabbalists shared a belief in the centrality of the Zohar, something that remained decisive for the subsequent culture of their Jewish communities. The ritualistic study of the parts of the Zohar became popular in large segments of the Jewish North African population, this phenomenon being one of the first instances of the broad dissemination of the Kabbalah beyond the élite.[32]

Part of the post-expulsion literature was composed in order to record religious traditions that had circulated only in restricted circles, perhaps orally, long before the expulsion, and that Jewish authors were afraid might be lost owing to the vicissitudes of exile. Indeed, this seems to be the case with Adrutiel's kabbalistic work *Avnei Zikkaron*, or Monuments of Remembrance. As Scholem pointed out, several earlier sources were copied verbatim in this treatise.[33]

To a great extent, this is also the case in the lengthy *Tsafenat Pa'aneah* by Joseph ben Moses al-Ashqar. This, the most important and most kabbalistically oriented of his many writings, was written in 1529 in Tlemcen. In its literary form mainly a kabbalistic interpretation of the Mishnah, this voluminous text allows an understanding of the kabbalistic manuscripts in the possession of North African kabbalists on the one hand, and, from the literary point of view, of the interpretive-conservative attitude that emerged among the expelled kabbalists in this period on the other. From the point of view of sources, al-Ashqar's thought was influenced mainly by Castilian Kabbalah of the end of the thirteenth and beginning of the fourteenth centuries.[34] An interest in a variety of magical theories and practices is also quite evident.

The Kabbalists at Dra': A Circle of Late-Sixteenth- and Early-Seventeenth-Century Kabbalists

Some of the exiled kabbalists moved to the south of Morocco, to towns in the provinces of Sous and Dra', where two main circles of kabbalists emerged during the sixteenth century. It was mostly in this area that a more complex Kabbalah appeared that continued Spanish trends similar to those found in Gikatilla's earlier writings, in Abraham of Granada's *Sefer Berit Menuhah* and in *Sefer haMeshiv*. The best-known southern kabbalist was David haLevi, the author of *Sefer haMalkhut* and *Kesef Tzaruf*, who seems to have been the main figure in a small circle that included two other kabbalists. This text is based upon a detailed theory of combinations of letters which is basically independent of the techniques of ecstatic Kabbalah. This book, the entire text of which has been printed only recently, had been commented upon by Abraham ben Esquira Mas'ud in a book entitled *Ginzei haMelekh*.[35] A student of haLevi, Mordekhai Buzaglo, wrote a lengthy and difficult kabbalistic book entitled *Ma'ayanot Hokhmah*.[36] This earlier circle was less concerned with ritualistic Kabbalah, gravitating instead around a theosophical-magical conception of language and combinations of letters.[37]

Later on, another circle of kabbalists arose in southern Morocco, one that was basically concerned with mystical interpretations of the ritual and canonical texts. Unlike the earlier circle, described above, the Zohar played a much more central role among the members of the later group. One of the most important treatises from this circle is Moshe ben Maimon Elbaz's voluminous *Sefer Heikhal haKodesh*, printed in Amsterdam in 1653 by the press of Emmanuel Benveniste at the insistence of Jacob Sasportas, who wrote an opening poem. Glosses were added by Aharon Siboni of Salé. This work is a lengthy commentary on Jewish liturgy, the composition of which began in 1575 in Taroudant and was finished, after many vicissitudes, in around 1603. It was the most influential book composed in this circle, which included other kabbalists, Elbaz's students. Elbaz also composed a commentary on the twenty-two

FIG. 71 Synagogue, *mellah* of Amzrou, Zagora, Dra' valley, 1998. Photograph by Rose-Lynn Fisher.

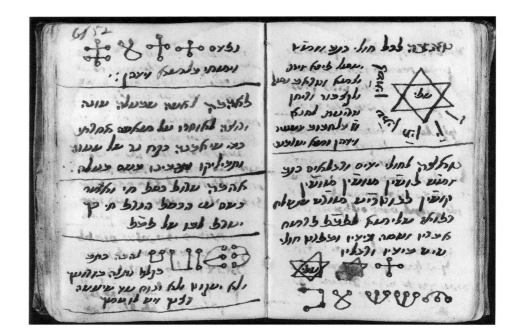

letters of the Hebrew alphabet and a commentary on the Passover Haggadah.

His disciples also adopted the interpretive mode and commented on canonical Jewish texts. Yehudah ben Hunain wrote a lengthy and rather original commentary on the Six Hundred and Thirteen Commandments, entitled *'Etz Ḥayyim*, which has been printed, and a Book of the Light, *Sefer ha'Or*, that is still in manuscript.[38] Another student, Isaac ben Abraham haKohen, wrote a commentary on the ten *Sefirot* entitled *Ginnat Beitan*.[39] A younger kabbalist from this circle, Jacob Ifargan, wrote a lengthy commentary on the Torah entitled *Minḥah Ḥadashah*, and a commentary on the Treatise 'Avot entitled *Peraḥ Shushan*.[40] It seems that these four kabbalists agreed upon a division of labor that produced complementary commentaries on the most significant portions of Jewish ritual. However, the interpretive enterprise amounted to an organization of earlier traditions according to the subject matter of the interpreted text, rather than according to any overarching theosophical-theurgical or magical systems, as was the case with Safedian Kabbalah, or according to more experiential-ecstatic concepts, as was the case with Polish Hasidism. The kabbalistic sources which inform their writings are rather similar: their views tend to stem from David ben Yehudah heḤasid's books concerning the ten supernal *Sefirot* that are higher than the 'regular' *Sefirot*, and from other kabbalistic concepts found in Abraham Adrutiel's and Joseph al-Ashqar's books, written a century beforehand in the north of Morocco. The conspicuous absence of the theosophical innovations in the vibrant Safedian center, which had already declined in importance when the southern group began to be active, is something to be emphasized. Though southern Moroccan kabbalists had been interested in Safedian kabbalistic customs, they were less receptive to the general systemic schemes of either Cordovero or Luria. Needless to say, later kabbalists from this group relied on the work of the earlier members, contributing to a certain conceptual homogeneity.

Moroccan Kabbalists in the Sixteenth and Seventeenth Centuries in the Land of Israel

Hallewah was not the only Moroccan kabbalist to arrive in Safed. In the period immediately following his stay there – he later left for Syria – other Moroccan kabbalists arrived to join the circle of Isaac Luria's students. The best-known is Joseph ibn Tabul, who seems to have been one of the most reliable transmitters of Lurianic Kabbalah. Abraham haLevi Berukhim, Suliman ben Ohana, Massud Azulai Ma'aravi Sagi-Nahor, and Ḥayyim Ma'aravi also played important roles among Luria's followers. Ḥayyim Vital, whose writings are one of the major sources for information concerning Moroccan kabbalists, mentions a certain David Ma'aravi, an expert in incantations to spirits, who initiated a disciple, Yehoshua' Bum. Abraham ben Shlomo 'Alon, who came from Dra' to Safed via Egypt. The arrival of these kabbalists in Safed and their activities there contributed to its special ambiance as a place where a variety of kabbalists encountered and cooperated with one another. If we assume that such a significant number of individuals arriving in one place over rather a short period of time could have influenced the spiritual processes going on there, then we may surmise such an influence on Safed, although, for the time being, it is difficult to assess its precise nature, despite the conspicuous manner in which Yehudah ibn Malka's passage had an impact on Ḥayyim Vital. In many cases, we learn of the names and activities of Moroccan Kabbalists in Safed from books dealing with occult events – reports of dreams in the case of Vital, and wondrous stories related to Luria and Abraham haLevi Berukhin – and much less from independent works, or even quotes from lost books. It is possible to formulate the significance of the arrival of the numerous Moroccan kabbalists, at least those who stayed for a lengthy period, as an exchange between the two most important centers of Spanish Kabbalah in the aftermath of the expulsion.

The most lasting contributions to the dissemination of Safedian forms of Kabbalah are due to members of the Azulai family, especially Abraham ben Mordekhai Azulai (1570–1644). Born in Fez to a well-known family that had arrived there after the expulsion from Spain and that included kabbalists in other parts of Morocco, he emigrated in 1619 to the Land of Israel, where he was active in Jerusalem and Hebron. His kabbalistic thought is strongly influenced by Moshe Cordovero's Kabbalah and books, especially his *Hesed le'Avraham*, which played a lengthy role in the dissemination of the thought of the Safedian kabbalists in eastern Europe.[41] Abraham Azulai's commentaries on the book of Zohar demonstrate the vital impact of Cordoverian Kabbalah, still powerful many decades after the emergence of the Lurianic system.

Interestingly enough, other Cordoverian treatises, such as Abraham Galanti's commentaries on the Zohar, *Zoharei Ḥammah* and *Yeraḥ Yaqar*, were known in Morocco. The manuscript of the latter commentary had been brought to Fez by none other than Elisha' Ashkenazi, the father of the famous Nathan of Gaza, the leading Sabbatean figure who was immersed in Lurianic Kabbalah. This manuscript attracted the admiration of several Sabbatean kabbalists in Morocco.[42]

FIG. 73 Frontispiece Sabbatai Zevi, *Tikkun Qeri'ah leKol Lailah veYom,* Amsterdam, 1666; The Library of The Jewish Theological Seminary of America, New York (RB97: 20a)

Sabbateanism in Morocco

Sabbateanism is the comprehensive messianic movement that emerged in the mid-seventeenth century and was centered around Sabbatai Tzevi's claim to be the Messiah. Like his prophet, Nathan of Gaza, Tzevi was a kabbalist, although of a different persuasion. The movement had a huge influence in numerous centers of Jewish culture, Morocco being one of the most important.

Indeed, Morocco is one of the regions where the acceptance and the impact of Sabbateanism among Jews, both élite and humble, was, apparently, immediate and widespread. Starting in the sixth decade of the seventeenth century, during a period of political and social instability in the life of the Moroccan Jewish communities that was due to the wars of Ghaylan, Sabbatai Tzevi's messianic role was easily accepted by a series of Jewish religious figures. It is known – despite the fact that the documentation has been destroyed – that both Tzevi and Nathan of Gaza corresponded with Moroccan rabbis. It seems that even one of the fiercest critics of Sabbateanism, Jacob Sasportas, a kabbalist who belonged to one of the noblest families of Moroccan Jewry, and who was active in various Jewish communities in Morocco and Europe, displayed some moderate sympathy at the earliest stage of the emergence of this messianic movement. Indeed, Moroccan communities contributed both a very fervent reception to the movement, and also its most vehement opposition. Apart from Sasportas,[43] it was Jacob Hagiz, a Moroccan figure active in Jerusalem, in whose *yeshiva* Nathan of Gaza and his son Moses studied, who attacked Sabbateanism at its inception.[44] However, their critiques, and other, less significant ones, do not represent the general mood in Morocco, where the reception was, rather, warm, immediate, and pervasive. One of the reasons for the persistence of Sabbateanism may have been the impact of the prolonged presence of Elisha' Ḥayyim Ashkenazi, Nathan of Gaza's father, in Salé and Meknes, where he established a *yeshiva* and was profoundly admired.

The most specific Moroccan contribution to Sabbateanism came somewhat later, in the 1790s, when a young and allegedly not well-instructed person named Joseph ibn Tzur proclaimed himself the Messiah ben Joseph, Sabbatai Tzevi having been recognized as the Messiah ben David, and revealed kabbalistic secrets learned from a *maggid*, or angelic mentor. Unlike later developments in the Ottoman Empire and Europe, where Sabbateanism in its different forms inspired conversions to Islam and Christianity, there was no apostasy in Morocco, a fact that may account for the longer and more peaceful persistence of Sabbatean beliefs.

Ḥayyim ben 'Attar, 1696–1743

In the post-Sabbatean period, Moroccan figures contributed to the expansion of Kabbalah in three different centers: in the Land of Israel, in Italy, and in London. Because of the various problems in their homeland, kabbalists from Morocco emigrated and wrote influential books abroad.

The most important commentary on the Torah, and the most influential book written by a seminal Moroccan figure on matters of spirituality, is Ḥayyim ben 'Attar's *'Or ha-Ḥayyim*. Born in Salé to a family of kabbalists, ben 'Attar left for Italy, where he stayed for a few years in order to publish his books, and then proceeded to Jerusalem, where he established an advanced *yeshiva*.

In a story attributed to Israel Ba'al Shem Tov (the Besht) by Yitzḥak Aiziq Teḥiel Yehudah Safrin of Komarno, the founder of Hasidism reported his intention to meet an important kabbalist who came from Morocco and was dwelling for a while in Jerusalem, namely Ḥayyim ben 'Attar. This meeting was supposed to unify the spiritual capacity of the Besht, namely his spirit (*ruaḥ*), which derived from the spirit of David and was found in the world of Emanation, with the soul of the kabbalist (*nefesh*), which stemmed from the lower ontological level, designated as the soul of David in the world of Emanation. When such a conjunction between the soul and the spirit took place, two higher spiritual capacities would descend, the higher soul (*neshamah*), and an even higher capacity (*yeḥidah*), and the true redemption (*hage'ulah ha'amitit*) would emerge. Such an encounter was conditioned by the Besht's envisioning "his image [and] resemblance" in the supernal world, with all its limbs.[45] The Besht, however, did not see his heels (*'aqevav*), and thus his attempt to meet the Moroccan sage failed. This story is a reinterpretation of the Lurianic understanding of the heels of the Messiah, as dealing with the Supernal Anthropos, in anthropological terms, namely by assuming that the messianic process does not depend on external theosophical processes but rather on the perfection of the individual. Being able to encounter one's perfected nature facilitates the messianic enterprise, which in this context was the joint effort of the Hasidic master and the kabbalistic saint. In one of these traditions, which apparently served as an important source for the rabbi of Komarno's discussion above, the Besht describes ben 'Attar as possessing a spark of the Messiah.[46] Last but not least, in the *yeshiva* he founded in Jerusalem, ben 'Attar was one of the teachers of the famous Ḥyda (Ḥayyim Yosef David Azulai), himself the descendant of a Moroccan kabbalist, Abraham Azulai.

Shalom Buzaglo, 1700–1780

Lurianic Kabbalah made its first inroads among Moroccan kabbalists at the beginning of the seventeenth century, as is evident from Elbaz's *Heikhal haShem*. However, a much greater acquaintance with this form of Kabbalah is evident from the writings of Abraham ben Musa and his son Moshe.[47] One of the most learned and productive kabbalists to start his career on Moroccan soil was Shalom Buzaglo. A student of Abraham Azulai of Marrakesh, he left Morocco because of persecution and spent his creative period in London, where he died. There he wrote his important commentaries on the Zohar, *Miqdash Melekh*, which was immediately printed in London and Amsterdam, and which had a substantial impact on some Hasidic circles, which also reprinted them. Buzaglo's books constitute one of the most authoritative Lurianic commentaries on the Zohar, and certainly the most influential. Together with Lavi's *Ketem Paz*, Buzaglo's seminal commentaries represent the deep immersion of Moroccan communities in a life shaped by interest in the Zohar.[48]

The high stature of this kabbalist can be deduced from the fact that both Jonathan Eibeschuetz and his rival Jacob Emden attempted to claim him as a fellow thinker, but Buzaglo hesitated to take a clear stand on the issue of Eibeschuetz's belief in Sabbateanism.

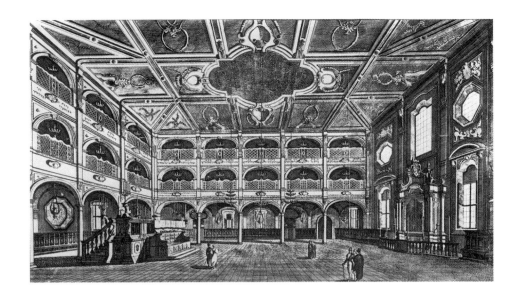

FIG. 74 Interior of the synagogue of Livorno, before 1938

The Livornese Center

Another extension of Moroccan Kabbalah is to be found in the Livornese Jewish community. Descendents of North African communities, some of those in Livorno who wrote about Kabbalah were nourished by material stemming from Morocco. Moroccan and Livornese relatives exchanged information about Sabbateanism in the mid-seventeenth century. Jacob Sasportas, mentioned above, served as spiritual leader of the Livornese Jewish community for several years. Ḥayyim ben 'Attar's 'Or haḤayyim was printed here for the first time in 1742. So was Shimon Lavi's voluminous Ketem Paz, in 1795. Later on, a Livornese printing house published a collection of kabbalistic material under the title Ma'or vaShemesh in 1839. The printer, Yehudah Qoriat, and his nephew, the famous kabbalistic thinker Elijah ben Amozeg (then no more than a precocious youngster who had already written a poetic introduction to this collection), were the first publishers of material that reflects the development of Kabbalah in Morocco. This accounts for its particular approach to the nature of Kabbalah, as well as its debt to Cordoverian treatises. For example, the collection includes a long kabbalistic poem dealing with the ten Sefirot by the Moroccan Aharon ben Joseph ibn Ivgi, accompanied by a commentary that he taught his friends, Mas'ud Tabib, Sa'id Barukh Bitton, and Mas'ud Mordekhai Bitton.[49] This work displays some interesting affinities with the manner in which Kabbalah was expounded in Adrutiel's 'Avnei Zikkaron,[50] and in the Dra' circle of kabbalists. Moreover, a substantial passage from David haLevi's Sefer haMalkhut that was apparently written at Dra' was printed in Livorno.[51]

However, the course of ben Amozeg's thought was destined to take another path, one that interpreted Kabbalah more as universalistic lore in the spirit of some forms of Italian Kabbalah, but also related it to nineteenth-century idealistic philosophy.[52]

Perhaps the last major enterprise in the field of publication of Moroccan kabbalistic material was the reprinting of Buzaglo's Miqdash Melekh in 1858.

Makhluf ben Isaac Amsalem, 1837–1928

One of the most interesting cases in the entire history of kabbalistic literature, in which Kabbalah was combined with astrology and alchemy, was found in the writings of Makhluf Amsalen. Following Muslim alchemical traditions and some Jewish propensities in Morocco to combine Kabbalah and alchemy,[53] Amsalem formulated the most detailed and articulated synthesis of these lores, writing in both Hebrew and Judeo-Arabic. The majority of his writings are still in manuscript.[54] Amsalem was active as an alchemist and physician at the court of the Sultan Mulai al-Hasan, after which he moved to Tangier. In his last years he emigrated to Jerusalem, where he died.[55] The first part of his most important book, *Tappuḥei Zahav beMaskkiyyot Kesef*, was first printed in Jerusalem in 1978.

Some Concluding Remarks

The writings of most Moroccan kabbalists do not display much conceptual innovation. Judged from this point of view, they had no major influence on the development of Kabbalah. This intellectual perspective is, however, only one possible approach to research on Kabbalah. A more sociologically-oriented view would consider the impact of kabbalistic themes on rituals and beliefs. In this regard, kabbalistic literature was an important factor shaping the religious life of Moroccan Jewry, in a manner reminiscent of the impact of Hasidism on some communities in eastern Europe. The permeation of Moroccan poetry with kabbalistic themes is unmatched in other centers where Kabbalah developed. It is emblematic that the most famous kabbalistic text composed in North Africa is Lavi's song describing the high status of the author of the Zohar, Simeon bar Yoḥai.[56] While the east-European Hasidic understanding of Kabbalah was strongly mediated by Safedian systems of

FIG. 76 Portraits of Tzadikim in a home in Rabat, 1995. Photograph by Rose-Lynn Fisher.

thought, this was less the case in Morocco. But, as with Polish Hasidism, Moroccan families produced lines of accomplished kabbalists, as was the case in the Azulai, Serrero, ben ʿAttar, or Abuḥatsira families. Again, like the later Hasidic masters, Moroccan Kabbalists were seen as more than spiritual masters: they were considered capable of wondrous deeds, which might be called magical. These figures' tombs often became, like the tombs of ancient Jewish figures around Safed, and of the Hasidic masters in Podolia and Galicia, sites for pilgrimage, although there may be various explanations for this similarity. Moroccan Jewry may have been influenced by local popular religiosity, in the form of Maraboutism.[57] It is possible, however, that a common source lay in the form of the Safedian custom of visiting the tombs of the ancient greats who were buried around Safed. Therefore, the main achievement of Kabbalah in Morocco lies more in informing the daily life of the common people than in developing original systems of thought characteristic of élites. In Morocco itself, more eclectic and reproductive modes were dominant, which emerged from the ritualization of communal life, including the ritual perusal of the Zohar. This communal, ritualistic propensity was combined with the deep interest in magic characteristic of so many of the Moroccan kabbalists, a phenomenon again reminiscent of Polish Hasidism.

However, unlike Hasidism, which produced almost all its fundamental literature within eastern Europe, the vast majority of the most original and most influential kabbalistic writings composed by Moroccan kabbalists was produced outside Morocco, in Safed, Jerusalem, or Hebron, or in European cities. This is the case with Hallewah, ibn Tabul, Abraham Azulai, Sasportas, Shalom Buzaglo, ben ʿAttar, and ben Amozeg, to mention only the most illustrious names. This radiation of kabbalistic erudition rendered premodern Morocco a center. It was self-contained and addressed ritualistic aspects of Kabbalah, rather than developments taking place outside. David haReuveni's activities, the emergence of Safedian Kabbalah, and Sabbateanism were absorbed and sometimes deeply internalized in Moroccan Kabbalah. Morocco produced a series of leading figures who participated vigorously in some of the most crucial enterprises that characterized the history of Kabbalah.

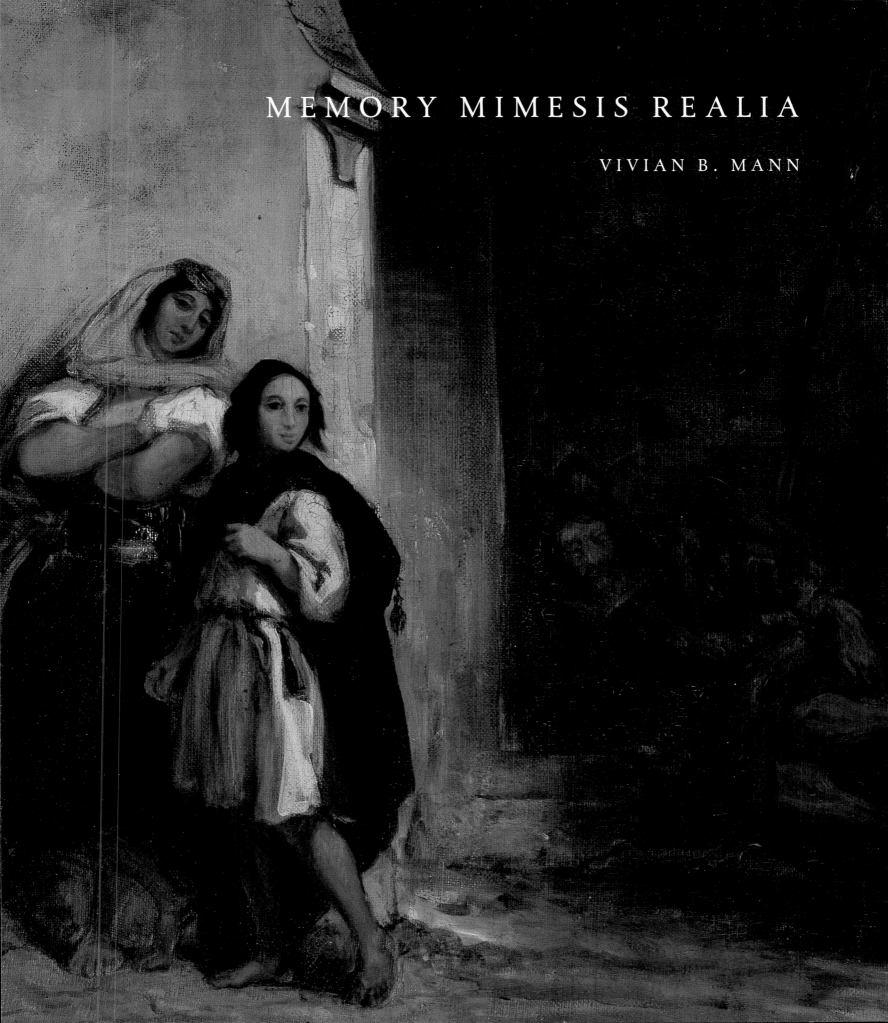

MEMORY MIMESIS REALIA

VIVIAN B. MANN

Figurative art of a secular nature, recording the deeds of rulers and the lives of the people, was produced in many Muslim countries. But, in the far west of the Islamic world, in Morocco, Muslim artists and patrons and most of their Jewish colleagues seem to have adhered to iconoclastic orthodoxy (although a paucity of medieval remains, aside from architecture, makes an absolute judgment impossible). How, then, can the appearance of the Morocco of the past and visual memory be remembered and preserved? Through texts and oral history, certainly, but these are often minimal in their descriptions of costumes and objects, and the spatial contexts in which they were used. We read them and hunger for more detail.

Some of the Islamic art and architecture of Morocco from the Middle Ages and the centuries following remains, affording glimpses of the grandeur that once existed. The same is not true of Moroccan Jewish art and architecture. Synagogues were usually less substantial than mosques: many were the humble work of carpenters, rather than architects (fig. 61, p. 97). The monumental mud-built synagogues in the south, devoid of their congregants, are in a deteriorated state (fig. 71, p. 117). Rare, too, are works of Jewish ceremonial art or personal artifacts that predate the eighteenth century. Those who owned antique metalwork seem to have melted it down in order to fabricate new pieces, rather than conserving and repairing that which was old. This practice may reflect the religious customs of the majority, since Islam requires few ceremonial objects and eschews the cult of relics, with its inherent preservationist tendency, that was so important to Christianity. Nor did the Roman and the later Renaissance tradition of collecting works of art and thereby saving them penetrate North Africa prior to the modern period.

Only outside developments served to make Moroccan history and memory visible. Although a few foreigners who had visited Morocco in the eighteenth century created images of its inhabitants,[1] it was only in the early nineteenth century that interest in Morocco became more widespread among French artists. For them this portion of the Orient was part of France's overseas empire, and, therefore, more accessible.[2] This artistic development began as an offshoot of political events, namely the French annexation of Algeria in 1830, the problems of which resulted, two years later, in Count Charles de Mornay's expedition to Tangier to negotiate a non-intervention treaty with the government of Moulay Abderrahman. De Mornay invited the artist Eugène Delacroix (1798–1863) to join his entourage. After the French arrived in Tangier in February, the Moroccans temporized, leaving Delacroix time to observe the people and the landscape of northern Morocco.

Unlike the voyages abroad that were undertaken by artists to study classical art, Delacroix's trip to Morocco was a confrontation with a living civilization that was unknown to Europeans. He constantly stated in his notebooks how different North Africa was from Europe: how Morocco was the paradigm of "a lost, true classicism" characterized by the ideal of noble simplicity.[3] "They are closer to nature in a thousand ways: their dress, the form of their shoes. And so beauty has a share in everything that they make. As for us, in our corsets, our tight shoes, our ridiculous pinching clothes, we are pitiful . . ."[4] Perhaps owing to his concept of the noble Moroccan, many of Delacroix's compositions, such as *A Street in Meknes* (cat. no. 90), are classical compositions, possessing a sense of gravitas and timelessness, despite the

127

inclusion of observed, ethnographic detail. The artist used stylistic elements that had previously been employed for religious and historical paintings to render the daily life of Morocco, transforming the quotidian into the archetypal.

Although Delacroix painted a wide range of subjects, Muslim women are absent from his works, due to their seclusion in accordance with Islamic custom. But no such religious strictures pertained to Jewish women, who became the focus of many paintings by Delacroix and those artists who followed him to North Africa (fig. 77, p. 127; fig. 78; fig. 15, p. 40; cat. nos. 92–96).

Nous passons notre temps à parcourir la ville [he wrote] *... de precautions interdisait la visite "des maisons de Maures ... l'intérieur des maisons juives ... offraient en dédommagement le caprice et la grâce du génie moresque ... et les femmes que nous y rencontrons n'en étaient pas le moindre ornement. Ces femmes sont à la foies belles et jolies et leurs habits ont une certaine dignité qui n'exclut ni la grâce ni la coquetterie.*[5]

The depiction of Jewish women was due to positive factors as well: the relationships that linked a painter like Delacroix to the dragoman Abraham Benchimol, employed by the French Consulate in Tangier, who served as guide, mentor, and host to the artist; and the fact that foreigners were often housed in the *mellah*. William Lemprière, a French army physician who journeyed through Morocco in 1789, stayed exclusively in the homes of Jews.[6] The oeuvres of the Orientalists who painted scenes of Morocco are, therefore, particularly rich in depictions of Jewish life. Nevertheless, the Jewish women depicted are atypical of Moroccan society as a whole. Delacroix's Jewish women – serene, attractive, and comfortable – are similar to those of other Orientalist painters, a myth that mirrors the artist's ideal of the exotic East.[7] A much more erotic view of Jewish women appears in the works of Charles-Émile Vernet-Lecomte (1821–1900): for example, the *Femme Juive de Tanger* (fig. 78; cat. no. 96). Patent eroticism is a familiar strain in the paintings of Orientalists.

Delacroix filled seven notebooks with sketches and descriptions of Morocco.[8] More than a third of these record Jewish life in Tangier and Meknes, including not only observations of Abraham Benchimol's immediate family, but also depictions of his extended family and of prominent Jews in the two cities. His notations record the constraints on Jewish life in Morocco, but also marvel at the unity of the community and the closeness of family ties: "*Le Juif retrouve une patrie sous son toit au milieu de sa famille*" (A Jew finds his country under his roof, in the midst of his family).[9] Delacroix also painted watercolors, including several of the Benchimol family (fig. 77, p. 127; cat. nos. 92, 94), which he later presented to Count de Mornay at the end of their journey. Back in Paris, Delacroix used the notebook sketches as the basis for oil paintings, which were shown in various Parisian Salons. His canvas of a Jewish wedding, *La Noce juive au Maroc*, was a center of attention at the Salon of 1841. Smaller compositions were produced to satisfy the demands of patrons (cat. no. 94).[10] His stay in Morocco, although only six months in duration, furnished Delacroix with subjects for the next three decades of his career, although by the 1850s his compositions were less anchored in the reality of his journey twenty years before, and became more imaginary.[11] Delacroix's Moroccan experience was also significant for its influence on other painters who were inspired to follow his path southward.[12] After Delacroix

Opposite

FIG. 78 Charles-Émile Vernet-Lecomte, *Femme Juive de Tanger*, Paris, 1886; see cat. no. 96

130

FIG. 79 *Jeune femme Juive de Tanger*, Tangier, c. 1920; see cat. no. 122

FIG. 80 Edmé-Alexis-Alfred Dehodencq. *Jewish Festival in Tetuan*, Paris, c. 1858; see cat. no. 97

came Charles-Émile Vernet-Lecomte (1821–1900), Edmé-Alexis-Alfred Dehodencq (1822–1882), Francisco Lameyer y Berenguer (1825–1877), Théo van Rysselberghe (1862–1926), Raymond Crétot-Duval (1895–1986), and others.

Another French artist whose oeuvre includes many depictions of the Jewish community was Alfred Dehodencq, who journeyed to Morocco in 1853 and stayed until 1864, the longest stay among the first group of European artists to work in Morocco. While sketching Muslims in public was risky, no such danger attended Dehodencq's depicting Jews. Some of the artist's works refer to historical events. He sketched and painted the martyrdom of Soleika Hachuel (1817–1834), a beautiful Jew of Tangier who was accused of reciting the Muslim declaration of faith and then of refusing to abjure Judaism. She was executed in Fez and buried in its Jewish cemetery, where her tomb became a focus of pilgrimages and a locus of miracles.[13] The painting was destroyed under mysterious circumstances the night after it was finished in 1860, nineteen years after Dehodencq's first stay in Morocco; only the preparatory sketches remain, in the collection of the Israel Museum.[14] They reveal a somber, strong, sometimes caustic rendering of this subject, true also of other Jewish themes in Dehodencq's oeuvre, a reflection of his awareness of the humiliations suffered by this minority in Morocco. His vision of Jewish life was darker than Delacroix's, perhaps because Dehodencq spent many more years in Morocco (cat. no. 97). Even his paintings of Muslims are marked by "strident and brutal colors with a heavy use of black."[15]

Once Orientalist artists created their paintings, black-and-white versions appeared in popular European journals and newspapers, thereby disseminating images of a foreign and exotic way of life to a wider European public.[16] The same was true for photographs of Morocco, the first of which were taken as late as 1859–60, partly because Morocco lay outside the itinerary of the Grand Tour, which was elsewhere a major stimulus to photography.[17] As was the case for European painters, photographers found Jewish subjects more compliant about having their pictures taken, while their Muslim neighbors saw photography as an invasion of their integrity and their faith. The same model was often dressed in different costumes or placed in various surroundings. Photographs subsequently appeared in the popular press and were reproduced on postcards, both avenues of wide circulation, which served to make the exotic Orient more familiar to Europeans (fig. 79, cat. no. 122).[18] Although Morocco lacked an indigenous artistic tradition for the depiction of people and events, owing to religious restrictions, the opening of the country to Europe and her painters and photographers allowed for a visual understanding of Morocco outside her borders. The works of these European artists evoke a culture never before recorded, and provide a context for understanding the artistic creations of the Moroccans themselves.

In Muslim lands, the principal art forms are metalwork, jewelry, textiles, calligraphy, and ceramics. In the West, these genres had been disparagingly termed the minor or decorative arts, but they are the *major* forms of Islamic art, into which Muslims and Jews poured their artistic energies. As Hanns Swarzenski convincingly demonstrated for the metalwork and manuscripts of the Western Middle Ages,[19] small size is no barrier to beauty, monumentality, or technical excellence. The creation of metalwork and jewelry in Morocco was largely the work of Jews. Some writers have cited the koranic

FIG. 81 Earrings, Meknes, 19th century;
see cat. no. 55

FIG. 82 Ceremonial dagger, Essaouira, 1912; see
cat. no. 9

prohibition against taking usury (Sura 2:198), which could apply to metalsmithing if
residual materials were left to the artist, as the reason for Muslim avoidance of the art
and Jewish dominance of it. This rationale appears in one of the earliest descriptions of
Jewish life in Morocco, Leo Africanus' *Description de L'Afrique*, published in Lyons in
1556.[20] Leo wrote that most of the goldsmiths of Fez were Jewish; they worked in the
new part of Fez and sold their wares in the old, Muslim section.[21] (cat. no. 68) But the
Koran contains no prohibition against working with metals, and lists "bracelets of gold"
as one of the rewards of Paradise.[22] In the *ḥadith* (Muslim traditions), however, the
profession of metalsmithing is viewed negatively: its practitioners are accused of being
liars, counterfeiters, and swindlers. Rather than any outright prohibition, it may have
been the Islamic disdain for metalworking that discouraged Muslims from becoming
practitioners of the art. The Jews of Arab lands filled a lacuna left by the Muslims, just
as their coreligionists elsewhere in the Diaspora filled marginal professions that were
avoided by the majority.[23] This interpretation of the dominant role of Jews as
metalsmiths and jewelers in Morocco is reflected in the events of the twentieth century.
Muslims trained with Jewish artisans and then replaced them, following the emigration
of the majority of the Jewish community in the 1950s and 1960s.

The related profession of trading in precious metals and stones was another Jewish
occupation associated with goldsmithing. Prior to the discovery of the Americas, the
Jews of pre-Saharan Morocco engaged in the gold trade, the paths of which lay
through the desert to southern Africa. The making of jewelry and metalwork is a
natural outgrowth of such trade, and it is not surprising, therefore, to find gold
jewelry made by the Jews of the Tafilalet region, the technical composition and design
of which reflect that which was made in the south of the continent (fig. 84, fig. 13,
p. 37; cat. nos. 82, 84–86).

Paths of conquest and migration likewise influenced the jewelry and metalwork of
northern and central Morocco. In areas once under Byzantine control, like Greater

FIG. 83 *Cache-matelas brodé* (embroidered mattress cover or *'arid*), Tetuan and Chefchaouen, 18th century; see cat. no. 168

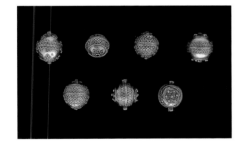

FIG. 84 Gold beads, Akka, pre-Sahara, early 20th century; see cat. no. 85

Syria, older forms and techniques continued to be used in jewelry and metalwork made after the Islamic conquest.[24] These included crescent-shaped earrings, filigree, openwork, biconical beads for necklaces, and motifs such as birds, which were then carried westward by victorious armies or sent as gifts throughout the Islamic world. During the Fatimid period (979–1171), one of the most creative periods for the making of jewelry, new types and motifs appeared in Egypt and Syria, where many ateliers were located. One example is the eagle with spread wings, which was later a popular motif in the art of Morocco as a pendant or as part of a bridal crown (cat. no. 52). Knowledge of eastern models came to Morocco directly, or indirectly from Spain, following the expulsions of the Jews and the Muslims that began in the late fifteenth century. Fatimid jewelry was imitated in Spain, and examples of openwork, filigree, champlevé enamel, and basket-shaped earrings are extant.[25] Another type of Moroccan jewelry, the hoop earring with pierced spherical stones (cat. nos. 57–58), reflects jewelry known to have been worn by Jews in Spain.[26]

The Muslim artists of medieval Spain had also excelled in the weaving of silk in complex compositions and varied colors. Even following the *Reconquista*, Mudejar silks were considered to be *objets de luxe* by the highest echelons of Christian society. Kings and queens buried in the royal pantheon of Santa María la Real de Huelgas in Burgos are clothed in Mudejar textiles.[27] But it is possible that some of these fabrics were made by Jews. A responsum of Rabbi Solomon ben Abraham Adret (c. 1235–1310) answers the question of whether it was proper for Jewish women in Toledo to weave silk textiles with designs that included crosses.[28] A number of known Spanish weaves might fit his description. During the Middle Ages, Jews also traded in textiles of

FIG. 85 Jean Besancenot, "Jewish City-Dweller,"
Costumes du Maroc, 1942

various sorts throughout the Maghreb, as is known from texts found in the Cairo Genizah.[29] Their multifaceted involvement with textile production in medieval Spain explains the emergence of Jews as weavers of textiles in Fez, one of the principal cities settled by those expelled from Iberia. The sashes and belts of Fez repeat Spanish medieval textile designs (cat. nos. 150–52), while larger cloths woven in Tetuan and Chefchouan incorporate designs executed in metallic threads, based on the same Spanish textiles or on similar designs on tile (fig. 83, p. 133; cat. no. 168). Another type of textile made by the Jews in Morocco is the red embroidery of Azemmour, a small coastal town that belonged to Portugal in the sixteenth century (cat. no. 170). As a result, peninsular influences were particularly strong in Azemmour and can be seen in compositions like the paired birds drinking from a krater, which derive from classical art.

The other textiles made and used by the Jews of Morocco in their homes are no different from those used by Muslims. Only the costumes show some deviation, often to indicate the lower status of *dhimmi* Jews.[30] *Djellaba* worn by Jewish men were of sober colors like black and blue;[31] and the *akhnif*, the dark, woolen, embroidered cape worn by males in Berber villages, was worn by Jewish men with the embroidery inside out (cat. no. 141). Jewish women's dress, worn largely in private spaces, was often outstanding, particularly the *keswa el-kbîra*, the elaborate and rich wedding costume worn by brides in the cities in which Sephardim settled. It consisted of a long skirt, a bodice, and a jacket, usually of silk velvet embroidered with gold metallic threads that parallel the materials from which Torah Mantles are made (cat. nos. 146–49) and lend a sense of ceremony to the costume.[32] The embroidery symbolizes aspects of marriage: concentric curves rising from the hem represent fertility, and golden circles on the waistcoat represent the sun or infinity (eternal life). The jacket has seven silver filigree buttons, signifying the seven blessings of the wedding ceremony that are repeated for an entire week at the close of festive meals.

The dressing of the bride is done by a woman knowledgeable in tradition. At various moments, Spanish sayings are recited by those assembled. When the family goes to bring the bride from her father's home to that of the bridegroom, they say: "*Daimos a la novia que por ella venimos. Si no nos la dan, a la ley volveremos.*" (Give us the bride because we are here for her. If you do not give her to us we will return to our holy studies.) After receiving his bride, the groom escorts her to a throne, where his mother awaits her daughter-in-law. Candles placed before the throne serve to illuminate and enlighten the bride in her new life. Following the owner's wedding, this costume is reserved for special occasions. The *keswa el-kbîra* (fig. 86; cat. nos. 146–49) was often described by foreign writers who were struck by its sumptuous beauty. J. Goulven, who wrote the following description in 1927, obviously observed the ceremony.

The bride has to remain motionless as a doll while the maids hand her the *ktef*, a kind of velvet chemise worn over the breast, and the *gonbaiz* which is a claret or green velvet corsage [bodice] embossed with gold stripes and silver buttons. She is then wrapped in a wide velvet skirt (*jelteta*) of the same color, which usually is richly ornamented with gold braid … There is a choice of two belts: the endema, the same colour as the dress, embroidered with gold thread and fastened with a silver clasp (*lezim*) or the *hezam*, a stiff, wide belt of gold embroidered velvet. Added to the

Opposite

FIG. 86 *El-keswa el-kbîra* (Grand Costume), Rabat, late 19th century; see cat. nos. 146, 164

FIG. 87 Hanukkah Lamp, Anti-Atlas, 17th–18th century (detail); see cat. no. 29

principal articles of this curious costume are silk stocking and gold embroidered slippers called *kheaya el kebira* or *baboutcha*. There remain now such details as the wide separate sleeves of white voile, *lekmam detsmira*, which are stitched to the shoulders in such a way that the remainder of the material floats bell shaped . . .[33]

Women wearing the *keswa el-kbîra* were painted and photographed by numerous European artists (fig. 79, p. 131; cat. no. 95). Jean Besancenot (1904–1992), who both photographed and painted watercolors of Moroccan costumes, published the watercolors in elaborate folios that included ten depictions of Jewish women wearing various regional costumes, including the *keswa el-kbîra*. The prevalence of these elaborate costumes in cities with Sephardi populations and the Spanish terminology used suggest that Spanish customs lie behind it, but the exact models are unclear.

Ceremonial textiles were another area of Jewish creativity. The synagogue service requires the use of a cloth on the Reader's Desk to provide a ritually clean place on which to lay the Torah Scroll,[34] just as the prayer rug provides a Muslim with a ritually clean space on which to pray. (Similar embroidered cloths are used to cover the tombs of venerated rabbis and Muslim saints.) Because of the height of the Reader's Desk, akin to that of the *minbar*, to which it is functionally related, it became customary to hang a silk velvet antependium, decorated with embroidered inscriptions and Jewish symbols (cat. no. 134, p. 172). Another commonly used synagogue textile is the mantle for the Torah scroll, which was made of unadorned fabric or of silk velvet, richly embroidered in gold metallic threads (cat. nos. 131, 132, p. 169). These are skirt-type mantles, known from manuscript illumination to have been characteristic of Spain.[35]

Many of the techniques, motifs, and compositions used to manufacture jewelry were adapted to the creation of ceremonial objects, particularly to the finials used to adorn the Torah scroll and the reader's desk. Because of the close relationship between jewelry and Judaica, finials can also be assigned to regional workshops. For example, tower-form finials, the ancestry of which lies in the ceremonial objects of Christian Spain, stem from cities whose population included large numbers of expellees. Those examples of this group with enamel inlay were made in Meknes, the jewelry of which boasts the same refined technique. Another regional type is the finial with repoussé ovals and lines, which mirrors fibulae from the Rif (cat. no. 13).[36] Since all of these works were made by Jews, the correspondences are not surprising.

Occasional details of Jewish metalwork provide unexpected glimpses of a turn to representational art. Inlaid or engraved on some metal objects are human forms that contradict the traditional aniconism of Moroccan art. The earliest is on a Hanukkah lamp of the seventeenth or eighteenth century that was made in the Anti-Atlas and is decorated with red enamel (figs. 87, 88; cat. no. 29). The form of the backplate of the lamp derives from those produced in medieval Spain: a series of horseshoe arches, below which is a framed panel. The major difference between the two types is the absence of a rose window and the presence of red enamel and an inscription on the Moroccan example. Near the top of the backplate is a scene that appears to be the Offering of Isaac, executed in champlevé. In the context of Moroccan art, the scene is an extraordinary intrusion; as a reflection of the Jewish art of Spain, the corpus of which includes biblical cycles in illuminated *haggadot*, its presence is explicable. The

FIG. 88 Hanukkah Lamp, Anti-Atlas, 17th–18th century; see cat. no. 29

enamel on the lamp imitates the two-dimensionality of painted representations. The schematic figures, without much interior detail, are comparable to those of the *Sister Hagaddah* (London, British Library, Or. 2884).[37] A similar lamp published in 1939 is abraded where the scene should be, suggesting its later removal.[38] The narrative manuscript illuminations comissioned by Spanish Jews may have served both as models and license for the two-dimensional enameled scenes created by Moroccan Jews.

Other human figures appear engraved on nineteenth- and twentieth-century ceremonial objects. A Torah Pointer has the head of a bearded male, accompanied by the abbreviation for the phrase "May his soul be bound up with the bonds of eternal life" (cat. no. 15). It is a strange inscription to be placed without reference to a name, but its memorial character is a link to the tombstones found in Jewish cemeteries such as those in Essaouira (and nearby Marrakesh), and in Safi, Mazagan, Azemmour, and Salé, with their carvings of human forms. All are coastal cities, and the presence of

FIG. 89 Hanukkah Lamp, Morocco, late 19th –
early 20th century; see cat. no. 31

anthropomorphic images may represent Phoenician influence, just as the *ḥamsa* (hand) form came to Morocco with the seafaring conquerors in the seventh century BCE.[39] Other instances of similar humanoid depictions are the set of oil holders on a northern Morocco Hanukkah lamp that dates from the end of the nineteenth or the beginning of the twentieth century (cat. no. 31), and figures on jewelry from the High Atlas.[40] Perhaps these late depictions of human forms by Jewish artists were stimulated by new contacts with the art of Europe in the work of artists such as Delacroix. It was the Jews who introduced Morocco to Delacroix, but it may have been Delacroix and his fellow artists who reinforced the forceful impact of figurative art, moving it beyond the cemetery and the amulet. The appearance of these new representations of human forms is another example of the change in orientation toward European culture that marked the life of Moroccan Jewry in the nineteenth and twentieth centuries.

CATALOG

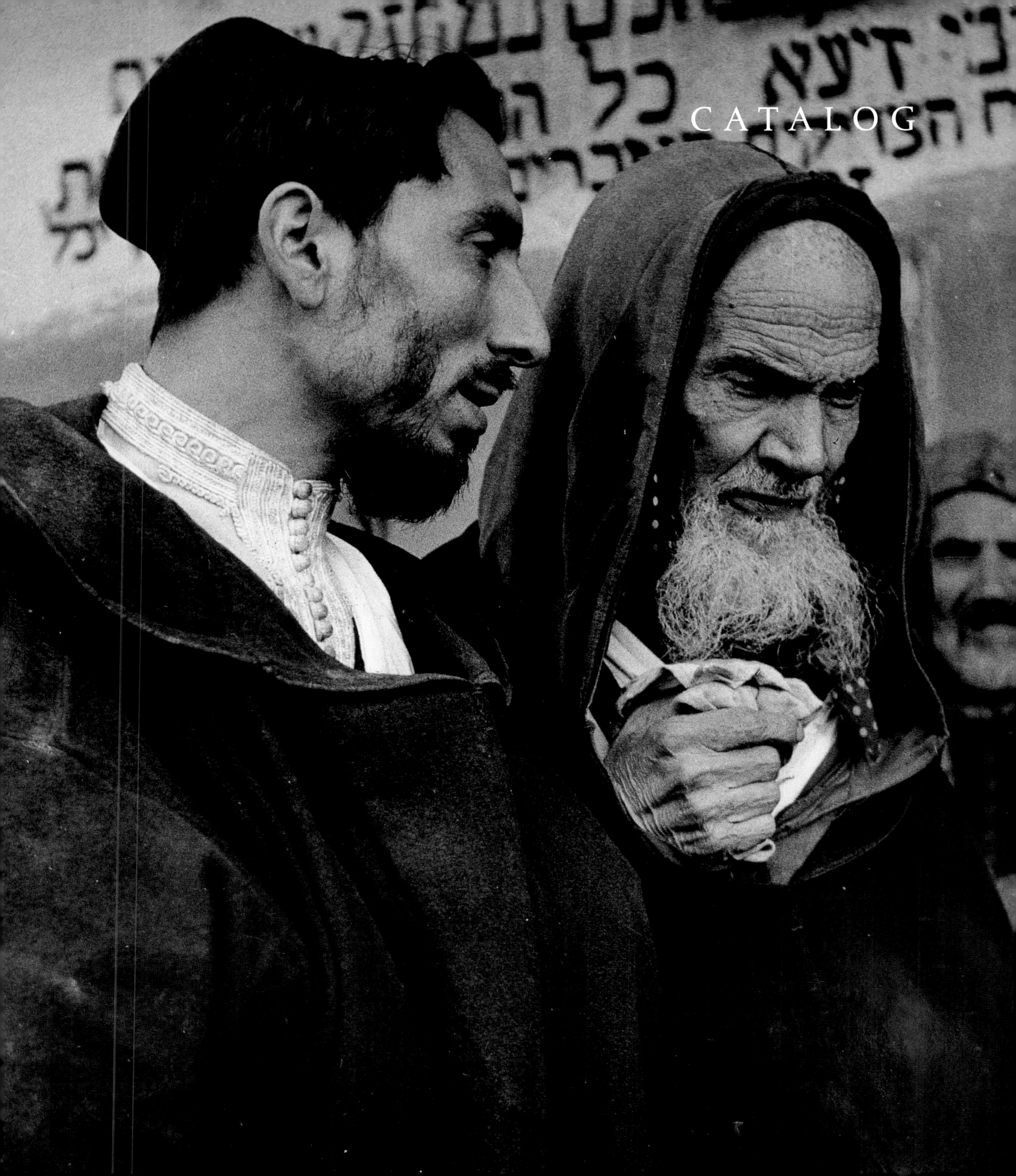

Unless otherwise noted by an author's initials, the entries on paintings were written by Maurice Arama, Paris; those on jewelry by Ivo Grammet, Essaouira. The remainder was written by Vivian B. Mann.

The city known today as Essaouira was called Mogador until 1765. It became known as Mogador again between 1912 and 1956, after which the name Essaouira was reinstated. For simplicity's sake, and because dates of objects are often approximate, the name Essaouira is used in all cases.

If no bibliography is cited, the object is unpublished.

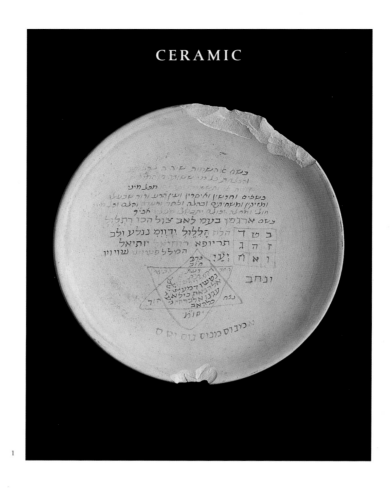

CERMIC

1

MANUSCRIPTS AND PRINTED BOOKS

1 Amuletic bowl

Morocco, 20th century
Ink on ceramic
6¾ × 1 in. (17 × 2.6 cm)
Collection of Dr. Paul Dahan

The original inscriptions, the ink of which has faded, were partially rewritten at a later date. They mention various evil forces, such as witchcraft and the evil eye, and calamities, injuries, and floods, against which "the Guardian of Israel," that is, God, will protect the owner.

Amuletic bowls with Aramaic inscriptions were used in the Near East, and Jewish examples from the fourth to the seventh century are extant.[1] They were used to 'capture' demons, to protect a home or an individual, or to inflict harm on someone. In Morocco, both Muslims and Jews used this type of magical device (see no. 8).

5

2 Torah Scroll

Morocco, 1885–86

Ink on parchment; wooden staves: stained and appliquéd with metal

Height 22¼ (plus 4¼ in. finial; 56.5 plus 10.8 cm)

Courtesy of The Library of The Jewish Theological Seminary of America, New York

Scroll 430

The tiered, architectural form of the staves is typical of Moroccan Torah scrolls.[2] The original mantle bears a silk plaque, embroidered with metallic gold threads in the shape of a Torah ark. Its inscription reads: "Holy to God is that which was dedicated by Meir the son of Abraham Hakohen for the elevation of the soul of Rabbi Reuben, the son of Joseph Hakohen, 5646[1885/86]."

This Torah Scroll and Mantle were acquired by an ethnographer who settled in Puerto Rico. His daughter donated the scroll to The Jewish Theological Seminary, and the mantle to The Jewish Museum (1998-23).

3 Fragment of the Zohar

Morocco, 18th century

Ink on paper

7⅞ × 5⅞ in. (19.5 × 15 cm)

Collection of Dr. Paul Dahan

The Zohar, the primary kabbalistic text, was long thought to have been written by the mishnaic authority Rabbi Simeon bar Yoḥai, who lived in the second century CE. Recent scholarship has suggested a later date and various authors. In Morocco, the book of the Zohar was venerated in unique ways that reflected the sanctity accorded the Torah Scroll.[3]

4 Tefilot Shonot (Various Prayers; fig. 72, p. 118)

Morocco, 19th century

Ink on paper

4¼ × 3 × ¾ in. (10.8 × 7.8 × 1.9 cm)

Courtesy of The Library of The Jewish Theological Seminary of America, New York

MS 4797

5 Sefer Abudarham

Printer: Samuel ben Isaac and Isaac ben Samuel

Fez, 1521

Printed on paper

11½ × 8½ × 1¾ in. (29.2 × 21.6 × 4.5 cm)

Courtesy of The Library of The Jewish Theological Seminary of America, New York

RB 1729;3

The title of this work derives from the name of its author, David ben Joseph Abudarham, who was active in Seville during the fourteenth century. His work explaining Jewish blessings and prayers for the whole year, together with a calendar and astronomical tables, was printed in Fez by two Portuguese natives, Samuel ben Isaac and his son, Isaac. It was the first book printed on the continent of Africa. Samuel and Isaac's press survived only six years, because of an embargo on paper imposed by the Portuguese government.

This copy is unpublished.

METALWORK

FOREIGN METALWORK

6 Lamp with menorah

Roman Empire, 4th–5th century CE

Bronze

5½ × 6 in. (14 × 15 cm)

Musée Archéologique, Rabat

Vol. 563

This bronze lamp was made to hang from chains that passed through three holes, one on top of the menorah and two at the opening of the well for oil. The presence of a defined base, together with the elongated form of the body and the unusually wide spout, suggest a date in the fourth or fifth centuries.[4] The presence of the menorah served as a symbol of religious identity, and may also indicate that this lamp was reserved for ceremonial purposes.

BIBLIOGRAPHY Goldenberg 1992, p. 53; Paris, Le Petit-Palais 1999, p. 115.

7 Candlesticks

Birmingham, England, 20th century

Copper alloy: cast and engraved

Height 17¼ in. (43.8 cm); base diameter 5½ in. (14 cm)

The Jewish Museum, New York

Purchased with funds given by the friends of Marjorie and Howard Berrent in honor of their twenty-fifth wedding anniversary

1993-202 a, b

Candlesticks such as these, made by various English firms, were used both in homes and on readers' desks in synagogues. This pair belonged to the Elmaleh family of Essaouira, who used them for Sabbaths, holy days, and other festive occasions. The original owner was the daughter or daughter-in-law of Rabbi Joseph Elmaleh (1809–66), who served as head of the rabbinic court in Essaouira, and as ambassador to the Austrian Empire.

CEREMONIAL ART

11

8 Amuletic bowl with Arabic inscription

Morocco, 18th–19th century
Copper alloy: cast and incised
2 × 7⅛ in. (5 × 15.5 cm)
Musée Batha de Fès, Fez
21.1064

9 Ceremonial dagger *(Khoumia)*

Essaouira, 1912
Silver: cast and engraved; wood; iron
16 × 2¾ in. (41 × 7 cm)
Musée Sidi Mohamed Ben Abdellah, Essaouira
A.46-1-33, N.81-1-36

Daggers like this one were used in rural areas to kill sheep, but were also a part of men's ceremonial regalia and status symbols. Its sheath is decorated with flowers, and its base with a palmette. The sheath is also furnished with rings, for the attachment of a leather shoulder strap. On the reverse is the name of the maker, and the date: *malem Mbarek Loum 1331* [1912]. The shape of the sword handle is known as a peacock's tail.

10 Powder horn

Essaouira (?), 19th century
Wild sheep horn; brass: cast, engraved and ajouré
14⅓ × 2¾ in. (36.5 × 7 cm)
Musée Sidi Mohamed Ben Abdellah, Essaouira
A.46-1-92, N.81-1-37

The sheep's horn is closed with a brass fitting at the large end, leaving a small spout for pouring the gunpowder at the other end, which is likewise fitted with a brass cover. All the brass is decorated with an engraved floral pattern, except the base of the large end, which is formed as an ajourée arcade and circles.

11 Torah Finials

Essaouira (?), 18th–19th century
Silver: cut, chased and gilt; velvet
13¾ × 3½ in. (35 × 8.9 cm)
Collection of Mr. and Mrs. A. Halpern

This pair of pierced, hexagonal finials is an extremely fine example

10

14

of a type popular in Fez, Tetuan, and Essaouira. The tower form probably derives from Spanish models, as does the ornament – pierced surfaces, foliate motifs, and horseshoe openings – and the engraving techniques. These characteristics appear later in Moroccan metalwork. The tall proportions of the horseshoe "windows" distinguish this pair from other pierced, tower-form finials. The shafts of both finials are inscribed with the name of the owner:

a) שמואל מטיטיהו [!] יצו ("Samuel Matityahu . . .")

b) שייך לשמואל מטיטיהו [!] ב״ר מסעוד ("... belongs to Samuel Matityahu . . . son of Mass'ud.") This phrase implies that Samuel owned the finials and lent them to the synagogue, or brought them from home on special occasions, practices known from the responsa literature.[5]

BIBLIOGRAPHY Weinstein 1985, fig. 98; New York, Yeshiva University Museum 1992, no. 323.

12 Torah Finials dedicated in memory of Simon Castiel (fig. 62, p. 99)

Meknes, c. 1900
Silver: cast, engraved, parcel gilt; enamel; velvet
10⅝ × 2⅛ in. (27 × 5.4 cm)
Gross Family Collection
No. 050.001.034

Metalwork from Meknes is distinguished by the incorporation of colorful cloisonné enameling,

here black, blue, and green. Many Meknes finials have shafts, the lengths of which are subdivided by thick gilt bosses, which may have had the practical function of allowing them to be held without damaging the enamel surfaces to either side. Similar bosses appear on a pair of finials in the Sir Isaac and Lady Edith Wolfson Museum of Jewish Art, Jerusalem, and another in the collection of Mr. and Mrs. A. Halpern.[6]

According to the inscription, these finials were dedicated in memory of Simon Castiel, son of Mordecai.

למנוחת הזקן הכשר/שמעון קסטייל
ב״ר מרדכי נע

13

13 Torah Finials

Rif, second quarter of the 20th century
Copper alloy: cast, hammered, repoussé, and gilt
Height 11 in. (28 cm); diameter 4⅜ in. (11 cm)
Collection of Dr. Paul Dahan

This pair of finials exemplifies a group of Torah ornaments, the decoration of which is closely related to jewelry worn by women.[7] Each finial is adorned with repoussé ovoid and bulbous forms, seen against a background of chiseled floral motifs. The same combination of elements can be seen on silver fibulae from the Rif area.[8]

14 Torah Finials from Thilin or Demnat

Thilin or Demnat, early 20th century
Copper alloy: cast and engraved
10⅖ in. (26 cm) and 10¾ in. (27 cm)
The Jewish Museum, New York
Gift from the collection of Professor Kurt A. Fischer
1998-24 a, b

The openwork form of these finials resembles both standards used by Muslims and the techiques of some forms of Moroccan jewelry (for example, nos. 56, 68).

15 Torah Pointer

Tetuan (?), 19th–20th century

Copper alloy: cast, silvered, and engraved

10¼ × 1 in (26 × 2.5 cm)

The Jewish Museum, New York

Purchased with funds given by the Judaica Acquisitions Fund

1997-166

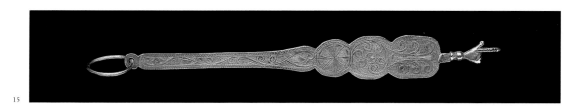

15

The flat form of the pointer is typical of Morocco. Its surface is decorated with engraved spiral designs that recall those on tombstones of the Jewish cemetery in Tetuan. A singular motif is the bearded face engraved on one side where the upper portion narrows into the shaft.

On the reverse are the initials תנצב׳ה, which stand for "May his soul be bound up with the bonds of eternal life," a phrase commonly found on tombstones.

BIBLIOGRAPHY *The Jewish Museum 1996–1998*, 1999, p. 24.

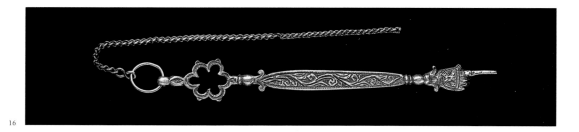

16

16 Torah Pointer

Morocco, 19th–20th century

Silver: cast, engraved, enamel, and parcel gilt

Length 7 in. (18 cm)

The Jewish Museum, New York

Purchased with funds given by the Judaica Acquisitions Fund

1997-165

17 *Tallit* Bag of Simon Coriat

Meknes, 20th century

Silver: ajouré and engraved; silk and cotton velvets; lining: cotton

7⅔ × 10½ in. (19.5 × 26.5 cm)

The Jewish Museum, New York

Gift of Dr. Harry G. Friedman

F 5666

Tallit Bags were given to young men at the age of thirteen when they became bar mitzvah and wore a prayer shawl for the first time. Examples with ajouré plaques suggest the wealth of their owners. That this *Tallit* Bag was made in Meknes is indicated by the name of the city inscribed on the Star of David at the center. The cutout inscriptions include quotations from the Bible on the back,[9] and the

17

18

19 Lamp hung on wall

Morocco, 20th century
Silver: cutout; glass: gilt
14⅔ × 14⅓ × 15½ in. (37 × 37 × 40 cm)
Collection of Dr. Paul Dahan

Like the hanging examples, wall lamps such as this one were memorials hung in synagogues or in saints' tombs. The gilt letters form a standardized inscription referring to the deceased, while the silver hanging device was cut with a personalized dedication:

[.;..בן אברהם למנוחת]

"For the repose of Abraham, son of . . ."

20 Hanging lamp

Essaouira, 1938
Silver; glass
32 × 9 in. (81.3 × 22.8 cm)
Collection of Mr. and Mrs. A. Halpern

This lamp is engraved with a memorial inscription in Hebrew and French:

לעלוי נשמת הנפטר במבחר ימיו/שארל
בשנאינו נלבע/קדש לק״ק ויתאלי מידגאר
[!] יום ב׳ ר״ח אדר א׳ שנת התרצב תנצב״ה

"For the elevation of the deceased, Charles Besnanou, who died in his prime, *Ch. Besnanou decedé 8–2–30*; dedicated to the Vitale Congregation Essaouira on Monday, the New Moon of the First Adar in the year 5692 [1932] . . ."

name of the owner, Simon, son of Maḥluf Coriat, on the front.
BIBLIOGRAPHY New York, The Jewish Museum 1977, no. 113.

18 *Tallit* Bag of Yaḥya Ohana

Morocco, early 20th century
Silver: ajouré and incised; velvet cardboard; wool
10 × 7½ in. (25.4 × 19 cm; excluding handle)
The Jewish Museum, New York
Gift of Mr. and Mrs. Albert List
JM 30-66

This bag is marked several times with the ram's head punch introduced after the establishment of the French Protectorate in 1912. "Yaḥya, son of Raphael Ohana," the name of the owner, is cut out of a silver panel on the front. Three nearly identical bags, but with different owner's names, are JM 31-66 in The Jewish Museum and nos. 157/75 and 157/206 in the Israel Museum, Jerusalem.

19

The form of the lamp is European, rather than Moroccan, and reflects Essaouira's role in European trade.

21 Hanging lamp

20th century
Silver: cut-out; glass
43 × 16 in. (109 × 40.6 cm)
Collection of Mr. and Mrs. A. Halpern

The form of this lamp, a silver holder for a glass oil container, is commonly found in Moroccan synagogues. The inscription cut out of the holder reads:

למנוחת הכה"צ חדרה תמך אם ה"ח הש
כהדר שם טוב/שני לחודש תשרי שנת
תרצ"ג לפ"ק תנצב"ה

"For the repose of the *kohen* (priest) . . . Shem-tov, the second day of the month of Tishrei [5]693" (October 2, 1932).

22 Hanging lamp holder

Morocco, 1906
Copper alloy: cast, cutout
Length 11 in. (28 cm); diameter 28¾ in. (73 cm)
The Jewish Museum, New York
Gift of Jane and Stuart Weitzman
1992-3

The cut-out dedicatory inscription on this holder reads:

למנו' נ'... שלום אדרע' נלב"ע ב' ש"ק ט'
סיון תרס"ו

"For the repose of the soul of . . . Shalom Edrehi who died on the holy Sabbath, the ninth of Sivan [5]666" (June 2, 1906).

23 Eternal Light

Essaouira, 1928
12 in. (30.5 cm)
Silver: cut-out; glass
The Jewish Museum, New York
Purchased with funds given by the Judaica Acquisitions Fund
1999-78

In its form, this Eternal Light is identical to other synagogue hanging lamps. Only the inscription reveals its specific purpose:

נר תמיד למנוחת נפש החכם השלם והכולל
ה"ר מאיר אברהם קוקוס ז"ל שניזלבע ליל
כ"א אדר ש' תרפ"ח תנצב"ה

"An Eternal Light for the repose of the perfect, erudite scholar Rabbi Meir Abraham Corcos of blessed memory, who died on 21 Adar [5]688" (March 13, 1928). Meir ben Abraham Corcos was made United States Consul in Essaouria in 1884. He was the author of a two-volume work on the laws of the Sabbath and Passover entitled *Ben Me'ir* that was published in 1912 and 1925. The glass lamp bears a generalized inscription: מנוחת המאור לעלוי נשמת הנפטר תנצב"ה "The lamp of the light for the elevation of the soul of the deceased . . ."

24 Synagogue chandelier

Morocco, 18th century
Copper alloy: cast and openworked; glass
Height 36⅔ in. (93 cm) width 19⅔ in. (50 cm)
Heichal Shlomo, The Sir Isaac and Lady Edith Wolfson Museum of Jewish Art, Jerusalem
No. 21/38-1510

Elaborate chandeliers for the synagogue are rarer than individual hanging lamps. This one includes openwork *ḥamsa* amulets suspended from the cross bars.
BIBLIOGRAPHY Muller-Lancet and Champault 1973, p. 44.

25 Glass for hanging lamp

Morocco, first half of the twentieth century
Glass
36⅔ × 19⅔ in. (93 × 50 cm)
Musée du Judaïsme Marocain de Casablanca
MHE 45.84

26 *Ḥamsa* for hanging lamp

Anti-Atlas, 18th–19th century
Copper alloy: engraved and ajouré; enamel
7½ in. × 4¾ in. (19 × 12 cm)
The Jewish Museum, New York
Gift of Dr. Harry Friedenwald
JM 14-47

20

21

22

23

In Morocco, hanging lamps were suspended from a *ḥamsa*-shaped hanger, which sometimes became separated from the lamp. This example has finely worked Moorish arches in the upper half, and an overlay of floral motifs elsewhere, the interstices of which are filled with the red enamel characteristic of works from the Anti-Atlas (see no. 29). The extended thumb is formed in the shape of a rooster's head.[10]

27 *Kandil*

Anti-Atlas, 19th century
Copper alloy
Height 16½ × 6½ (41. 9 × 16.5 cm)
Collection of Dr. Alfred Moldovan

A *kandil* is a lamp, once used in the home for Sabbaths and festivals, that was donated to the synagogue following the owner's death. This elaborate example is entirely covered with engraved ornament, even on the underside of the basin. Related examples are in the Musée dar Belghazi near Rabat; in the Eretz Israel Museum, Tel Aviv (no. MHE 5.95); and in the Ethnographic Museum, Stockholm.

28 *Kandil* for Issah

Morocco, 20th century
Copper alloy: engraved
6¼ × 5½ × 4¾ in. (17 × 14 × 12 cm)
Collection of Dr. Paul Dahan

The inscription on this rather simply worked example reads:
למנוחת/עיסה בן ראללך/תנצב״ה
"For the repose of Issah the son of . . . M[ay] his s[oul] be b[ound up] with the [bonds] of l[ife]".

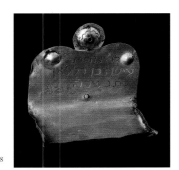

28

29 Hanukkah Lamp (figs. 87, 89, pp. 136–37)

Anti-Atlas, 17th–18th century
Brass: enameled
7¾ × 5¾ in. (19.7 × 14.6 cm)
The Jewish Museum, New York
Gift of Dr. Harry G. Friedman
F 3804

This is the earliest piece of Moroccan Judaica in The Jewish Museum's collection. The form of the lamp derives from those of the fourteenth century produced in northern Spain and southern France, and has the characteristic arcade of horseshoe-shaped arches above a rectangular frieze. The earlier triangular backplate has here been interpreted as birds and arabesques, resulting in a more open silhouette. Another change is the insertion of an inscription in the frieze: "The commandment is a lamp, The teaching is a light, And the way to life is the rebuke that disciplines" (Proverbs 6:23), a quotation that appears on the earliest known Hannukkah Lamp, that from Lyons in the Klagsbald Collection, Paris.[11]

The most remarkable change is the inclusion of an enameled *Offering of Isaac*, below the suspension ring. The schematic figures are similar to those in the *Sister Haggadah* (London, British Library, Or. 2884). A related lamp shows an abraded area below the ring, which may indicate that a similar scene was removed.[12]

30 Hanukkah Lamp

Anti-Atlas, 19th century
Copper alloy
13½ × 7½ in. (34.3 × 19 cm)
The Jewish Museum, New York
Gift of Dr. Harry G. Friedman
F 2974

The workmanship of this lamp is similar to that on the *kandil* (no. 27) and suggests the same origin and date.

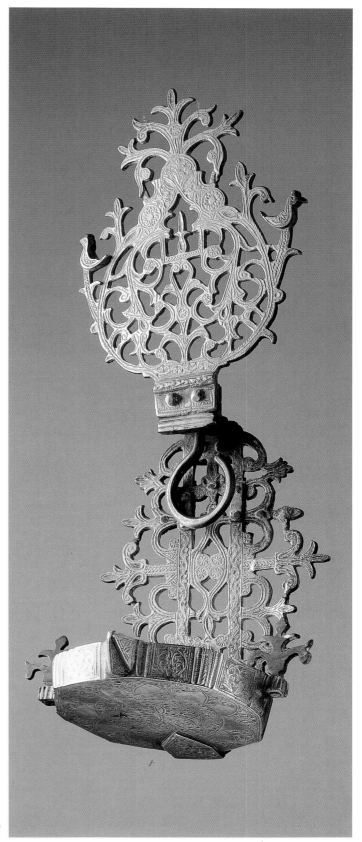

27

31 Hanukkah Lamp

Northern Morocco, late 19th – early 20th century

Silver: engraved; brass: cast

10¾ × 11¾ in. (27.6 × 30.2 cm)

The Jewish Museum, New York

Purchased with funds given by the Judaica Endowment Fund and the Nash Aussenberg Memorial Fund

1996-46

The gilt appliqués on this Hanukkah Lamp closely resemble those on bracelets made in northern Morocco, and suggest the same origin for this piece. An unusual feature is the flame-shaped, anthropomorphic forms behind each oil container. This is another example of the presence of figurative iconography in Moroccan Judaica, something never noted in the literature (see nos. 15, 29).

32 Hanukkah Lamp

Meknes, early 20th century

Silver: openwork and engraved

10 × 6¼ in. (25.4 × 15.9 cm)

The Jewish Museum, New York

Gift of Dr. Harry G. Friedman

F 5606

The workmanship and motifs on this lamp resemble those found on prayer-shawl bags hallmarked Meknes. In particular, a bag in the Israel Museum, Jerusalem (no. 157/73), is decorated with openwork tendrils of the type found on this Hanukkah lamp. The motif along the bottom panel is the same as that found on bracelets from the Zamour region, in which Meknes is located.

33 *Mezuzah* Cover of Mess'ud el-Carif

Morocco, 20th century

Silver: engraved and pierced

10¾ × 7 in. (27.6 × 17.8 cm)

The Jewish Museum, New York

Purchased with funds given by the Judaica Acquisitions Fund

1997-170

Moroccan Jews place the scrolls of their *mezuzot* under covers, rather than in closed containers as is the

Ashkenazi tradition. The aesthetic appeal of this cover is related to similarly formed Hanukkah lamps (no. 32) and prayer-shawl bags (nos. 17, 18).

34 Amulet

Morocco, 1861–62

Silver: engraved and gilt

3¼ × 3 in. (8 × 7.6 cm)

Collection of Rabbi and Mrs. M. Mitchell Serels

This unusual heart-shaped amulet is inscribed with the words "God Almighty," followed by the priestly blessing (Numbers 6:24–26) – "I hope for your salvation Lord" – and an individualized text: "May God give him life and peace, and fear of God, the youth Bitoul Ada, son of Y…, in the year 5622 [1861/2]."

35 Amulet of Mass'udah, daughter of Ḥayyim (fig. 67, p. 111)

Morocco, 19th–20th century

Silver over brass

2 × 1½ in. (5 × 3 cm)

The Jewish Museum, New York

Gift of Dr. Harry G. Friedman

F 4965

Apotropaic devices in the shape of a human hand appeared in the time of the Phoenicians, who reached Morocco in the ninth century BCE. They continue to be used by both Jews and Muslims. The hand-shaped amulets are called *ḥamsa* (i.e. five [fingers]) by Jews, and the Hand of Fatima [daughter of Muhammad] by Muslims. The name of the owner, Mess'udah, daughter of Ḥayyim, is inscribed on this *ḥamsa*.

36 Amulet against Lilith (fig. 67, p. 111)

Morocco, late 19th – early 20th century

Silver: engraved

1¾ × 1¼ in. (4.4 × 3.2 cm)

The Jewish Museum, New York

Gift of Dr. Harry Friedenwald

JM 29-47

All the texts are engraved on one side of this small amulet. Most are various names of God written in

30

32

33

34

cursive script: the tetragrammaton, Almighty, and *yoh. Paspasim* is engraved on the fourth finger: this is part of the twenty-two-letter name of God, the meaning of which is equivalent to Numbers 6:24–25, a passage promising God's protection.[13] This inscription and the remainder are engraved in block letters. Filling the pointer finger is *Zamarchad,* the name for the kingdom of Lilith, a demon believed to be particularly active during childbirth and immediately afterwards. Many amulets were created to thwart her dangerous effects. A name in block letters was written around the outer contour of the hand. All that is decipherable is:

...בן יוסף מנחם ....

"... Menaḥem Yosef ben . . ." He may have been the husband of the woman for whom the amulet was made to protect her against Lilith, but whose name is now effaced.

37 Amulet (fig. 67, p. 111)

Meknes, early 20th century
Silver: incised; enamel
2¼ × 1⅓ in. (5.7 × 3.5 cm)
The Jewish Museum, New York
Gift of Dr. Harry Friedenwald
JM 23-47

The use of enamel on this amulet is typical of metalwork produced in Meknes. The expressionistic outline of the thumb is unusual.

38 Amulet case

Tahala, c. 1900
Silver; enamel; glass; amethyst
2¼ × 2¼ in. (5.7 × 5.7 cm)
Collection of Ivo Grammet and Guido Bellinkx

Amulet cases such as these contained a paper inscribed with an apotropaic verse that protected against the evil eye. They were often worn on a necklace.[14]

39 Pendant amulet (*foulat khamsa*)

Morocco, 20th century
Silver: repoussé; glass stones
4½ × 5½ in. (12.2 × 10.3 cm)

Collection of Ivo Grammet and Guido Bellinkx

The quadrilobes of the amulet, together with its center, represent the number five, or *hamsa,* the name given to hand-shaped amulets with five fingers. The term *foulat* refers to the spaces left between the repoussé elements on the two plates composing the amulet. Occasionally, the raised portion of the amulets were set with glass stones, as here.

BIBLIOGRAPHY Grammet 1998, no. 494.

40 Pendant amulet (*foulat khamsa*)

Essaouira, 1910
Silver: filigree, gilt, stamped; gilt appliqués; glass stones
5¼ × 4¾ in. (14.4 × 12 cm)
Musée Sidi Mohamed Ben Abdellah, Essaouira
81-1-73

This elaborate amulet is composed of filigree. The five appliqués on the back symbolize its role as a *hamsa* amulet.

41 Filigree *hamsa*

Tangier (?), c. 1910
Gold: filigree
2½ × 1¾ in. (6.4 × 4.4 cm)
Collection of Juliette Halioua

42 *Hamsa* with floral motifs

Tangier, c. 1910
Gold: engraved, filigree
1¼ × 1¾ in. (3.1 × 4.5 cm)
Collection of Juliette Halioua

43 Boxes for colored inks and ash

Essaouira, early 20th century
Copper alloy: engraved
6 × 6 in. (15.2 × 15.2 cm) each
Collection of Dr. Michael M. Cernea

From residues in one box, it appears to have held colored inks used for decorating documents such as wedding contracts (nos. 104–07). The other held ash for drying the pen. The engraving on the top of the boxes is in the style of Essaouira, and includes motifs typical of its silversmiths, such as a fully opened flower set amid vegetation.

44 Charity box

Essaouira, 20th century
Metal; paper: printed
4 × 2⅜ in. (10 × 6 cm)
Musée du Judaïsme Marocain de Casablanca
98-19-06

All of the charity boxes exhibited are of the same simple form: a rectangle with a slit in the top to receive coins. This example was dedicated to Rabbi Ḥayyim Pinto of Essaouira (see no. 115).

45 Charity box

Essaouira, first half of the 20th century
Metal; paper: printed
4 × 2⅜ in. (10 × 6 cm)
Musée du Judaïsme Marocain de Casablanca
98-19-08

According to the printed inscription, the text was written and the box donated by Simon Wa'qnin, a scribe in Essaouira. It is dedicated to Rabbi Meir Ba'al haNes, the *tanna* (talmudic scholar) who established a *yeshiva* in Tiberias. Later rabbis named Meir have also been identified with the tomb on the outskirts of Tiberias depicted here, to which miracles are attributed. From the eighteenth century, emissaries from the Land of Israel who traveled throughout the Diaspora drew attention to the tomb of Rabbi Meir, so that collection boxes for its support were commonly found in Jewish homes throughout the world.

46 Charity box

20th century
Metal, paper: printed
5½ × 4⅓ × 1¾ in. (14 × 11 × 4.4 cm)
Musée du Judaïsme Marocain de Casablanca
98-19-10

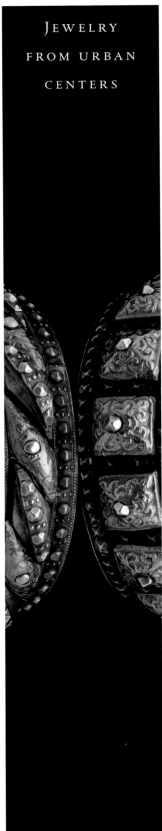

65

JEWELRY FROM URBAN CENTERS

48

47 Headdress (*soualef*)

Tetuan (?), 19th century
Cotton; silk velvet; gold metallic braid; pearls; precious stones; gold beads
12 × 5⅔ in. (30.4 × 14.4 cm)
Museum of New Mexico Collections in the Museum of International Folk Art, a unit of the Museum of New Mexico, Santa Fe
A.1955.86.757

The wearing of a headdress (*soualef*) by married Jewish women stems from the biblical statement that hair is nakedness (Babylonian Talmud Berakhot 24a). In Morocco, Jewish women fashioned an elaborate headdress out of superimposed scarves, on which were placed headbands (*ayyacha*) or diadems (*taj*), and braided silk threads. In Tetuan, women hung their braids on either side of the face, while in Fez, the braids were hung down the back.

This example represents the oldest type of headdress from urban centers in the north. Made of silk velvet and richly decorated with gold elements and semiprecious stones and pearls, they are used as frontals or as diadems on the head veil. Sometimes, two or more are placed above one another.

BIBLIOGRAPHY Chicago, DePaul University Gallery 2000, no. 31.

48 Headdress (*hiyout*)

Tetuan (?), late 19th century
Gold; pearls; precious stones; coins; silk
7 × 24½ × 10⅜ in. (18 × 62 × 27 cm)
Collection of Isabelle C. Denamur

The nostalgia for Spain felt by medieval Muslim and Jewish refugees who had settled in Morocco was not limited to literary expression, but was given concrete form in the preservation of Andalusian music and costume, and even keys to former homes on the Iberian Peninsula. The inclusion of a fourteenth-century Spanish coin in this bridal headdress, the equivalent of a precious stone, is likewise an expression of nostalgia and allegiance that testifies to the origin of the bride or groom's family. The row of gold crescents and the lack of braids suggest Muslim ownership (see no. 47).

49 Headdress (*hiyout*)

Tetuan, Tangier, or Rabat, 19th century
Seed pearls; precious stones
16¾ × 4¾ × 1 in. (43 × 12 × 2.6 cm)
Collection of Dr. Paul Dahan

The embroidering of the entire ground with small pearls in a diamond pattern is typical of headdresses made in Tetuan, Tangier, or Rabat.[15] This one incorporates pieces of jewelry on

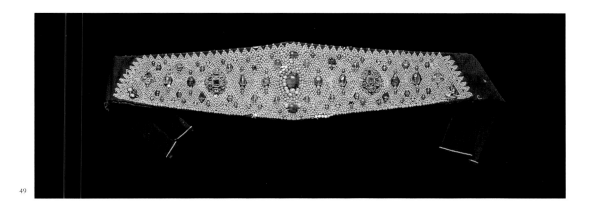

49

50

51

either side of the central emerald. The piece originates with a Jewish family in Tangier; a similar headdress is in a private collection in Paris.[16]

50 Headband (*khit er rih*)

Tetuan, early 19th century
Wool; cotton backing; gold; enamel; passamenterie; metal; thread
10 × 1¼ in. (25.5 × 3 cm)
Museum of New Mexico Collections in the Museum of International Folk Art, a unit of the Museum of New Mexico, Santa Fe
A.1955.86.706

Repoussé gold elements flank a central square embossed with a rosette of gold and precious stones. These are stitched to the headband, which is called *khit er rih* (literally, "the thread of the wind"). The pendant filigree elements would have been seen against the forehead of the wearer. Headbands of this type were inspired by Algerian and Ottoman models, and were largely fashioned in Tetuan.

51 Pendant from a headband (*tab'a*)

Meknes, 19th century
Gold; enamel; emeralds; rubies
Diameter 2⅛ in. (5.5 cm)
Museum of New Mexico Collections in the Museum of International Folk Art, a unit of the Museum of New Mexico, Santa Fe
A.1955.86.761

The *tab'a* is a disk-shaped pendant that was placed on the headband or suspended from it, to lie on the forehead. This example is made of solid gold, and decorated with precious stones and the typical red, green, and blue enamel of Meknes. The reverse is engraved in a pattern of floral elements and arabesques.
BIBLIOGRAPHY Chicago, DePaul University Gallery 2000, no. 29.

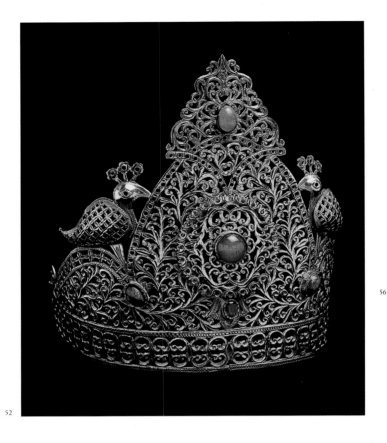

52

56

52 Bridal crown (*taj*)

Fez, c. 1920

Silver: engraved; emeralds; rubies

Height 7½ × 4¾ × 7⅛ in. (19 × 12 × 18 cm)

Collection of Dr. Paul Dahan

Silver openwork crowns decorated with precious stones became popular in the first quarter of the twentieth century, and were worn by both Muslim and Jewish brides. The bird motifs that surmount the crown are typical of examples made in Fez and Tetuan.

BIBILIOGRAPHY Rabaté and Goldenberg 1999, vol. 2, p. 83.

53 Ear pendants (*khras kbach*)

Tetuan, 19th century

Gold; pearls; emeralds; diamonds; rubies

8⅛ × 3⅝ in. (21 × 9 cm)

Israel Museum, Jerusalem

Gift of Mme. Esther Benazéraf-Ettedgui, Casablanca, 1965

At great occasions, Arab and Jewish women of Tangier and

Tetuan wore large, splendid ear pendants, as depicted in the painting by F. Lameyer y Berenguer (no. 95). This example is composed of three very elaborate elements. The big hollow rings with engraved patterns pass through the lobe or the hair above the ears. To balance their weight, the pendants are attached with a chain and hook at the headband. The front part of the ring is typical Tetuan openwork, embellished with precious stones and pearls.

BIBLIOGRAPHY Muller-Lancet and Champault 1986, no. 427.

54 Pair of ear pendants

Meknes, 19th century

Gold; emeralds; rubies; enamel

3⅞ in. (10 cm)

Museum of New Mexico Collections in the Museum of International Folk Art, a unit of the Museum of New Mexico, Santa Fe

No. A.1955.86.760a, b

Smaller ear pendants were for everyday wear. The obverses of this pair are decorated with semiprecious stones, while the reverse sides are of solid gold, embellished with floral engravings and green, blue, and red enamel inlays. The engravings and enamel are typical of Meknes jewelry.[17]

BIBLIOGRAPHY Chicago, DePaul University Gallery 2000, no. 28.

55 Earrings (fig. 81, p. 132)

Meknes, 19th century

Gold; enamels; emeralds

2⅜ × 1⅛ in. (6 × 3 cm)

Collection of Isabelle C. Denamur

56 Earrings

Tangier (?), 1900–25

Gold: openworked and chased

2 × 1 in. (5.4 × 2.6 cm)

Collection of Mrs. Sonia Azagury

These earrings represent a style that became popular in the early twentieth century.

57 Earrings of Grandma Toledano

Rif, late 19th – early 20th century

Silver: gilt; coral; emeralds

4¼ × 2¾ in. (11 × 7.2 cm)

Collection of Mrs. Sonia Azagury

This type was popularly called 'earring bracelets,' because of the large size of the circle.[18]

58 Earring

Rif, late 19th – early 20th century

Gold; coral; pearls

length 4¼ in. (10.8 cm); diameter 2¼ in. (5.7 cm)

The Jewish Museum, New York

Gift of Isaac Genack

JM 21-60

59 Necklace with seven pendants (*tazra*)

Meknes, 19th century

Silver: gilt, incised/engraved, pierced; coral beads; enamel

length 24¼ in. (61.5 cm)

Museum of New Mexico Collections in the Museum of International Folk Art, a unit of the Museum of New Mexico, Santa Fe

No. A.1955.86.637

The oldest and most remarkable *tazra* are composed of a strand with pearls and emeralds, and one or three rosette-shaped pendants filled with openwork arabesque patterns. This example from Fez is formed of trilobe floral elements set with precious stones, from which are suspended a crescent and a piriform pendant.

59

60

60 Pendant

Tetuan, 19th century
Gold; emeralds; rubies; pearls; amethyst
Height 3¼ in. (10 cm)
Collection of Isabelle C. Denamur

This oval-shaped necklace pendant was executed in the traditions of jewelers of the nineteenth century who worked in northern Moroccan centers such as Fez and Tetuan. The base is solid gold, engraved and openworked; the cabachons are set in stamped gold sheet; and there is an abundance of semiprecious stones and pearls.

61 Necklace (*lebba*)

Meknes, early 20th century
Silver: gilt; precious stones; silk
Length 27 in. (68.6 cm)
International Folk Art Foundation Collection in the Museum of International Folk Art, a unit of the Museum of New Mexico, Santa Fe
No. FA.1963.13.46

The *lebba*-type necklace was created in the early 1900s. It is actually a pectoral, composed of ten almond-shaped, hollow, ribbed, gold beads (*krakeb*), which alternate with nine similar pendants, each consisting of a trilobe form, a pendant, a circular element, and a crescent. The beads of a *lebba* can be smooth or filigree.

BIBLIOGRAPHY Chicago, DePaul University Gallery 2000, no. 30.

62

62 Necklace (*lebba*)

Meknes, late 19th–20th century
Silver: gilt; precious stones
17½ × 3½ in. (44.4 × 8.9 cm)
Collection of Mrs. Sonia Azagury
See no. 61

63 Hair ornament

Tangier, c. 1880
Gold: filigree; emeralds
3¾ × 2 in. (9.5 × 5 cm)
Collection of Mrs. Sonia Azagury

A Tangier provenance is inferred
from the history of this piece, and
from the evidence provided by the
portrait of Mme. Abraham Sicsu of
Tangier in the collection of Paul
Dahan, where the sitter is adorned
with a very similar ornament. Her
husband served as Consul-General

and Chargé d'affaires of Belgium
during the late nineteenth century
(see no. 99). Mme. Sicsu was
painted by Émile Wauters (Brussels,
1846 – Paris, 1933), a well-known
history painter and portraitist. In
1880, he traveled to Egypt, Spain,
and Morocco. During this trip,
Wauters must have sketched Mme
Sicsu's hair ornament.

64 Sun and moon bracelet
(*chems ou qmar*)

Meknes, 19th century
Silver; gold; enamel; fabric; répoussé
Height 1⅛ in. (2.8 cm); diameter 2½ in.
(6.5 cm)
Museum of New Mexico Collections in
the Museum of International Folk Art,
a unit of the Museum of New Mexico,
Santa Fe

A.1955.86.720

The 'sun and moon' bracelet
received its name from the
alternation of silver and gold, or
gilt, segments. These pieces were
cut from sheets of metal, then
hammered on a matrix, engraved,
and, sometimes, openworked. The
resulting raised forms were then
filled with a hot, black, resinous
paste. After cooling, the element
was riveted to a base of solid silver.
The most beautiful examples have
silver elements with enamel inlays.
The dark blue of the enamel on this
example indicates a Meknes origin.

65 Bracelet of Simḥah Pinto

Tangier (?), early 20th century
Silver and gilt silver
Diameter 2⅖ in. (6.6 cm); thickness ⅞ in.
(2.2 cm)
Collection of Mrs. Sonia Azagury

This 'sun and moon' bracelet
originally belonged to a native of
Tangier named Simḥah Pinto.

66 Bracelet with bird finial
(*mounida*)

Morocco, early 20th century
Silver: gilt
Height ⅞ in. (2.2 cm); diameter 2⅖ in.
(6 cm)
Museum of New Mexico Collections in
the Museum of International Folk Art, a
unit of the Museum of New Mexico,
Santa Fe

A.1955.86.697

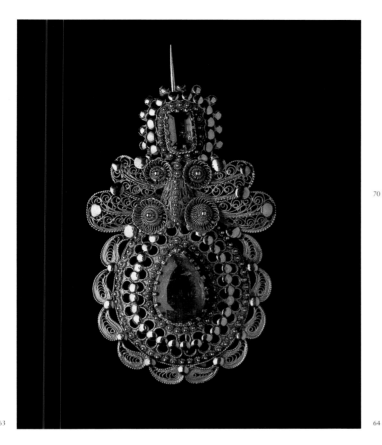

63

70

64

66

Bracelets of the *mounida* type were made in the same way as those called 'sun and moon': out of a gold sheet repousséd and filled with paste. Here, the repoussé elements are pyramidal in shape. A bird sits on the hinge finial. Similar birds are often found on Islamic metalwork as accents.[19]

67 Sun and moon bracelet

Tangier, early 20th century
Jeweler: Cascasi
Silver: gilt
3⅜ × ⅞ in. (8.6 × 2.2 cm)
Collection of Mrs. Sonia Azagury

68 Pierced bracelet (*deblij mkherram*)

Tangier, c. 1926
Gold: openworked and chiseled
Diameter 2½ in. (6.5 cm)
Collection of Juliette Halioua

Floral elements and arabesques form the openwork of this bracelet.

For similar earrings, see no. 56.

69 Ring (*khatem*)

Probably Fez, early 20th century
Gold; rubies; emeralds; diamonds
Diameter ½ in. (1.5 cm)
Museum of New Mexico Collections in the Museum of International Folk Art, a unit of the Museum of New Mexico, Santa Fe
A.1955.86.759

This type of ring is known as a 'bird's nest' (*khatem el ach*), because the upper face of the ring suggests a nest containing eggs (represented by the precious stones).
BIBLIOGRAPHY Chicago, DePaul University Gallery 2000, no. 27.

70 Ankle bracelets (*khlkhala*)

Safi, 19th century
Silver: inlaid with enamel; glass stone
3¾ × 2⅜ in. (9.5 × 6 cm) each

Museum of New Mexico Collections in the Museum of International Folk Art, a

unit of the Museum of New Mexico, Santa Fe
A.1955.1.343 a, b

This pair of anklets represents a type commonly found in Moroccan urban centers. Each is of one piece, smaller in the back, but larger at the rounded ends, with an

opening that slides over the ankles. This pair is decorated with an engraved pattern and riveted appliqués.
BIBLIOGRAPHY Chicago, DePaul University Gallery 2000, no. 25.

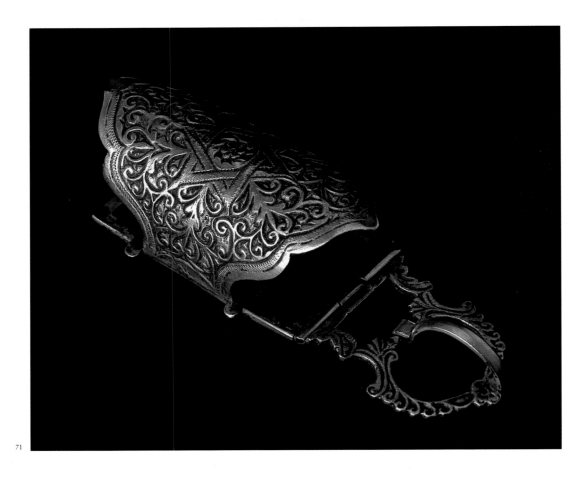

71

closing pin attached to a chain. The workmanship of this pair is very refined and includes engraved arabesques and floral patterns, as well as riveted appliqués. Birds are affixed to the hinges (see no. 66). They represent a popular type of Moroccan ornament.

74 Ankle bracelet

Essaouira, 1903
Silver: cast, gilt, and filigree; red cloth
3¾ × 2⅜ in. (9.5 × 6 cm)
Mark: Essaouira
Musée Sidi Mohamed Ben Abdellah, Essaouira
A.77.0.200
N.81-1-73

75 Molds for ankle bracelet, fibulae, and *ḥamsa* amulet

Essaouira, first half of the 20th century
Lead
Ankle bracelets: 5¾ × 2¼ in. (15 × 6 cm)
Turtle-shaped fibula: 3¾ × 2¼ in. (12 × 5.5 cm)
Ram's head fibula: 4⅔ × 3½ in. (12.4 × 9 cm)
Ḥamsa (amulet): 1¾ × ¾ in. (4.7 × 2 cm)
Musée Sidi Mohamed Ben Abdellah, Essaouira
81-1-125(d)
81-1-120(d)
81-1-120(c)
81-1-121

Matrices in the Essaouira Museum show the types of jewelry produced by the city's silversmiths. They used a horseshoe-shaped iron mold in two parts, each of which was filled with a wet mix of fine sand and clay from the Oued Ksob river. The matrix was then placed between the halves of the mold, and liquid silver poured in. Essaouira jewelry was sold locally and to the neighboring Chiadma and Haha peoples.

73

71 Belt buckle

Essaouira, 1832
Silver; gilt appliqués
2¼ × 6 × 1½ in. (5.7 × 15.2 × 3.8 cm)
Lent by The Minneapolis Institute of Arts, The Christina N. and Swan J. Turnblad Memorial Fund
91.141.8 a

Buckles of the *fekroun* or turtle type, like this one, are used at the end of a small belt called a *mdemma*. The buckle is decorated with finely engraved arabesque and floral patterns, and with gilt appliqué elements. The central appliqué is the typical Essaouira flower, while the two pigeons are a common motif. This buckle is richly worked and indicates the wealth of the owner; it was probably displayed on special occasions.

72 Belt Buckle with Star of David

Essaouira, 19th–20th century
Silver: gilt
5½ × 2¼ × 1½ in. (14 × 5.5 × 4 cm)
Collection of Dr. Paul Dahan

73 Ankle bracelets

Essaouira, 1832
Silver with gold-plated motifs
Height 2½ in. (6.4 cm); diameter 4 in. (10.2 cm)
Lent by The Minneapolis Institute of Arts, The Christina N. and Swan J. Turnblad Memorial Fund
91.141.8 b–c

Anklets from Essaouira were made in two parts, with a hinge and

76 Headdress (*mehdor*) from Tiznit

Tiznit, 20th century

Silver threads: coiled; enamels; coral; glass paste; silk; silk tafetta ribbon; coins; hair; cloth-covered base

Frontal 10⅝ × 7½ in. (27 × 19.1 cm); tie 42 in. (106 cm)

Collection of Mr. and Mrs. A. Halpern

Tiznit is the most southerly coastal city in which refugee Sephardim settled.[20] Most of the Jewish men of Tiznit and nearby Berber areas were silversmiths who specialized in enamel jewelry. Their women wore a unique metal headdress, the *mehdor*, that served to contain their natural hair, while allowing some false hair to be seen on the forehead. It was composed of interwoven coils of silver threads, enclosing animal hair to which rows of enamels and glass stones were added, separating the coils into distinct zones.[21] Two coins of the headdress are Maria Theresa Thalers, still in circulation in this area of Morocco when this head covering was made. A 1960 photograph taken in Ifrane, Anti-Atlas, shows a woman wearing such a *mehdor*.[22]

BIBLIOGRAPHY New York, Sotheby's 1986, no. 126; New York, Yeshiva University Museum 1992, no. 415.

77 Jewish woman's headdress

Dra' valley, late 19th century

Velvet; silver; glass stones; horsehair; cloth-covered base

8¾ × 10 in. (22.2 × 25.4 cm); braids 20½ in. (52 cm)

Collection of Linda Gross

This type of headdress is related to that of Tiznit (no. 76) in its material and basic conception, but its coils are not interwoven. The shape and addition of braids are distinctive elements of Dra' valley examples. A very similar example is in the Musée royal de l'Afrique centrale.[23]

78 Pair of fibulae (*tizerzai*) with pectoral

Ida ou Semlal, Anti-Atlas, late 19th – early 20th century

Silver: cast, engraved; cloisonné enamel; glass cabochons; coins

42 × 7¼ in. (106. × 18.4 cm)

The Jewish Museum, New York

Purchased with funds given in memory of Ruth Herzog by the Henry Herzog family and friends, and the Judaica Acquisitions Fund, New York

1999-58

In rural areas, Berber and Jewish women fasten their clothing with fibulae, each consisting of a pin and ring. The triangular fibula is decorated with enamel and engraved with a geometric pattern, as is the attachment area of the pin. The rings are decorated with glass stones. Two heavy silver chains with suspended coins link the fibulae. They are attached by a large circular bead in silver and enamel, called a *tagmout*.[24] The Jewish silversmiths who worked for the

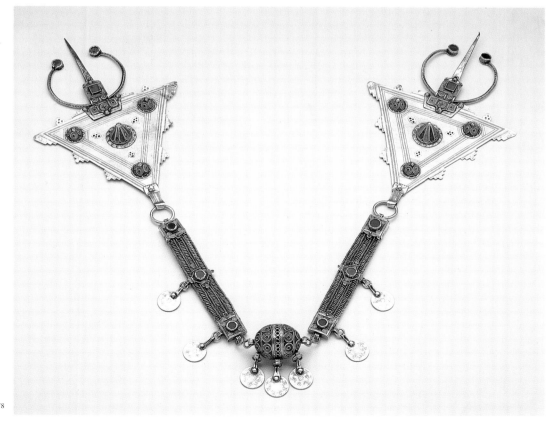

81

78

81

Berber Ida ou Semlal tribe who lived in villages in the western Anti-Atlas largely settled in Tiznit after the pacification of southern Morocco under the French Protectorate.

79 Pair of fibulae (*tizerzai*) with pectoral

Tamgrout or Talouine, late 19th – early 20th century
Silver: cast, filigree, granulated, and engraved; carnelian; leather
29½ × 4 in. (75 × 10.2 cm)
The Jewish Museum, New York
Purchased with funds given by the Judaica Acquisitions Fund
1999-61

The fibulae terminals are modeled on those from the Dra‘ region, while the filigree with inset cabuchons is typical of the work of Jewish silversmiths from the region of Talouine, which is the territory of the Aït Ouaoumsguit, a confederation of Berber tribes.[25]

80 Pair of fibulae (*tizerzai*)

Aït Baha, Chtouka people, western Anti-Atlas, late 19th – early 20th century
Silver: cast and engraved
9¼ × 4 in. (23.5 × 10.5 cm)
The Jewish Museum, New York
1999-60 a, b

These fibulae are designed as *ḥamsa*, amulets based on the number five. The four rays or lobes or circular patterns, together with the center, comprise the number five. The surfaces are engraved with floral patterns and arabesques. The fibulae are the work of a Jewish silversmith in Aït Baha.[26]

81 Bird medallion (*serdokh*)

Southern Morocco, early 20th century
Silver: cast, filigree, hammered; glass stones
4⅜ × 4⅜ × ⅝ in. (11 × 11 × 1.5 cm)
Collection of Dr. Paul Dahan

This central ornament was once attached to an openwork crown, like no. 52. Another detached bird ornament of similar shape, but lacking any filigree, is in a private collection.[27] A third example, in filigree, differs in showing a double-headed bird surmonted by a crown.[28]

The motif of the bird with spread wings is an heraldic emblem of Fatimid origin, and gold examples were produced by the jewelers of Tetuan. The use of silver for this work, the character of the filigree, and the stone setting suggest an origin in southern Morocco. It may have been produced by a Jewish silversmith from the Aït Ouaoumsguit.

BIBLIOGRAPHY Rabaté and Goldenberg 1999, vol. 2, p. 70

82 Disk for necklace (fig. 13, p. 37)

Tafilalet, pre-Sahara, early 20th century
Gold
Diameter 2⅛ in. (5.2 cm)
Collection of Ivo Grammet and Guido Bellinkx

In the Jewish-Berber communities of southern Morocco, silver, not gold, is commonly used for jewelry. Gold jewelry is found, however, in the Jewish communities in the Tafilalet and Akka. A necklace of gold disks like this one belonged to the traditional costume of the Jewish woman in the Tafilalet region.

The disks are made of two layers of gold wire wound in spirals around a horizontal tube so that an open center remains. The two layers are fixed together by transverse strips of gold that are twisted at the ends. Dots of gold decorate the front side of each disk. This technique is unknown elsewhere in Morocco, but is related to sub-Saharan Africa. The Tafilalet region has always been an important trade center, through which passed caravans connecting northern Morocco with sub-Saharan Africa. This trade was controlled by Jewish families, which explains the Saharan models for Jewish jewelry of the Tafilalet (see no. 84).

BIBLIOGRAPHY Grammet 1998, p. 595.

83 Necklace (fig. 14, p. 39)

Tafilalet, early 20th century
Silver; colored beads
Length 15¾ × 1⅝ in. (40 × 4 cm)
Collection of Dr. Paul Dahan

The silver disks of this necklace are technically similar to the gold example (no. 82).[29]

84 Cruciform pendant (*khmar*; fig. 13, p. 37)

Akka, pre-Sahara, early 20th century
Gold
1⅝ × 1¾ in. (4.1 × 4.4 cm)
Collection of Ivo Grammet and Guido Bellinkx

Cruciform pendants in gold became popular after the middle of the nineteenth century. This example, and the two following, were made using traditional Islamic techniques. An outline of each piece was cut on a sheet of gold, and the relief added. The surface was then decorated with small circles, which, together with granulation, were soldered to the surface. This technique spread to southwestern Morocco, where Tiznit became an important production center. From there, pieces were shipped all over the country.

For a short period, Akka became a center for the making of gold jewelry. By the end of the nineteenth century, Akka was an important stop on the caravan routes linking Essaouira and sub-Saharan Africa. Wealthy Jewish families, such as the Abizror, jewelers in Akka, controlled the trade with the south. They were the first Jews to reach Timbuktu, from which they exported gold dust to create gold jewelry and beads, and ostrich feathers for headdresses that were sent to England through Essaouira.

BIBLIOGRAPHY Grammet 1998, no. 594.

85 Gold beads (fig. 84, p. 133)

Akka, pre-Sahara, early 20th century
Gold with filigree and granulation
Diameters range from ⅝ to ⅞ in. (1.5–2 cm)
Collection of Ivo Grammet and Guido Bellinkx

Each bead is composed of two half-spheres that were hammered to shape on a matrix and then welded together. The main decoration consists of small circles soldered to the surface.

BIBLIOGRAPHY Grammet 1998, no. 592.

86 Cruciform pendant (*khmar*)

Akka, pre-Sahara, 1900–25
Gold
1⅝ × 1¾ in. (4.1 × 4.4 cm)
Collection of Ivo Grammet and Guido Bellinkx
See above, no. 84

87 Cruciform pendant (*khmar*)

Morocco, c. 1950
Gold
1⅜ × 1 in. (3.5 × 2.6 cm)
Collection of Juliette Halioua
See above, no. 84

88 Bracelet with high bosses

Ida ou Semlal, Anti-Atlas, late 19th – early 20th century
Silver: cast; granulation; cloisonné enamel; glass
Diameter 3⅞ in. (9.8 cm); width 2¼ in. (5.7 cm)
The Jewish Museum, New York
Purchased with funds given by the Judaica Acquisitions Fund
1999-59

This bracelet is formed of two half-cylinders; one encloses the hinge, the other, the closing pin. Geometric patterns of enamel cover the outer surface. The high bosses are characteristic of Jewish bracelets from Ida ou Semlal.

89 Ring

Ida ou Semlal, western Anti-Atlas Mountains, c. 1850
Silver: hammered and granulated; enamel; glass
Height 1⅜ × ⅜ in. (3.4 × 1 cm)
Collection of Anna Stern

A glass cabochon mounted on a platform is affixed to the disk of the ring. This type of jewelry was not only worn on the finger, but also served as a hair ornament or, when suspended on a leather band, as a necklace.[30]

PAINTING

95

90 *A Street in Meknes*

Eugène Delacroix (Charenton-St Maurice, 1798 – Paris, 1863)
Tangier (?), 1832
Oil on canvas
18¼ × 25¼ in. (46.3 × 64.5 cm)
Albright-Knox Art Gallery, Buffalo, New York
Elisabeth H. Gates and Charles W. Goodyear Funds, 1948

Early criticism ascribed less value to this small painting than to Delacroix's more monumental works. Delacroix was seen to have a limited vision, a view that diminished the message of fraternity expressed by the painting. Today, critical opinion regards *A Street in Meknes* as a serene and harmonious work, the transparent light of which illuminates a row of personal types that Delacroix had observed in Moroccan society: a distinguished native of the Rif in his white burnoose, an Arab, and a Jewish woman with her baby, who stands as if rejected at the extreme left, at the limit of the painting field.

Although Delacroix gave the painting its title, the lamp in the form of a pierced polygonal star is found in the Kasbah of Tangier. The Rifain appears as the guardian of the consulate in the same city in a watercolor, and in the painting *Marocains jouant aux echecs*,[31] while the woman leaning on the wall is the wife of the French consul, Abraham Benchimol (see no. 92). Delacroix's inclusion of the child removes any moral ambiguity from her presence on the street.

BIBLIOGRAPHY Paris, Institut du Monde Arabe 1994, pp. 190–91, there the older literature.

90

91

91 Fanatics of Tangier

Eugène Delacroix (Charenton-St
Maurice, 1798 – Paris, 1863)

Paris, 1837–38

Oil on canvas

38½ × 51½ in. (98 × 130.8 cm)

Lent by The Minneapolis Institute of
Arts

Bequest of Mr. Jerome Hill

73.42.3

Count Charles de Mornay, head of a
French mission to the King of
Morocco in 1832, included Eugène
Delacroix among his retinue. The
failure of Mornay's mission may
have occasioned the choice of this
subject, fanatics who engage in
contortions and dangerous acts.
The French pursuit of the
colonization of Algeria rekindled
differences between France and
Morocco, the government of which
lacked the power and will to close
its frontiers to Algerians. This
painting emphasized the antipathy
of Morocco toward Europeans.

The Aïssaouas reunited yearly at
the mausoleum of the founder of
their confraternity, Sis Aissa, in

Meknes. On the way, they marched
in processions through cities,
receiving donations and recruiting
neophytes. The processions
attracted curious onlookers, among
them Muslims and Jews of all ages,
many of whom mounted balconies
for a better view.

Since Delacroix had left Tangier
in June, and this procession took
place in August, he must have
worked from descriptions rather
than direct observation.

Another version of this subject is
in the Musée des Beaux-Arts,
Ontario, Canada.

VBM

BIBLIOGRAPHY Paris, Institut du
Monde Arable 1994–95, pl. 10; Lattre
1998, p. 13

92 Saâda, the Wife of Abraham Benchimol and Préciada, One of Their Daughters (fig. 77, p. 127)

Eugène Delacroix (Charenton-St
Maurice, 1798 – Paris, 1863)

Tangier, 1832

Watercolor over graphite

9 1/4 × 14 1/4 in. (48.9 × 36.2 cm)

Lent by The Metropolitan Museum of Art,

New York

Bequest of Walter C. Baker, 1971

1972.118.210

Delacroix gave de Mornay eighteen
watercolors he had painted in
Morocco. After the death of the
count, the suite of watercolors was
dispersed. Several are known to
have portrayed the family of
Abraham Benchimol, dragoman of
the French Consulate in Tangier.
Benchimol served Delacroix as
host, translator, guide, and adviser.

In this work, Benchimol's wife
Saâda, née Azencot, drapes the
head of their daughter as a sign of
her married status following her
wedding to a cousin, David
Azencot. Her vest, richly
embroidered with gold and silver
threads, and her jewelry are similar
to works described elsewhere in
this catalog (see no. 145).

SELECTED BIBLIOGRAPHY
Robaut 1885, p. 133, no. 500; Guiffrey
1909, p. 189, no. 9; Escholier 1927, opp.
p. 30; Virch 1926, no. 97; Alazard 1930,
opp. p. 38; Sérullaz 1963, no. 162; idem
1981, p. 62; Paris, Institut du Monde
Arabe 1994–95, pp. 178–79

93 A Jewish Woman of Tangier in Festive Costume (fig. 15, p. 40)

Eugène Delacroix (Charenton-St
Maurice, 1798 – Paris, 1863)

1832

Watercolor over graphite

8¾ × 5¾ in. (22.2 × 14.6 cm)

Private collection, Courtesy of Nathan A.
Bernstein, Fine Arts, New York

On Tuesday, 21 February 1832,
Delacroix attended a party on the
occasion of the wedding of the
daughter of Abraham Benchimol of
Tangier (see no. 92), and recorded it
in his travel notebook. The artist's
interest in the event is reflected in
his several versions of the eight
days of festivities.

BIBLIOGRAPHY New York, The
Metropolitan Museum of Art 1997, pp.
40, 115, 119, fig. 141, there the older
literature

94 La Juive d'Alger

Eugène Delacroix (Charenton-St
Maurice, 1798 – Paris, 1863)

Paris, c. 1833 (?)

Oil on canvas

18½ × 15½ in. (47.3 × 40 cm)

Collection of Samuel J. LeFrak

Although the Benchimol family
lived in Tangier, the misleading title
The Jewish Bride of Algiers was added
to an 1833 engraving of the painting
of a daughter's wedding. Two
versions of the subject exist;[32] this
one was shown at the Bordeaux
Salon in 1851. Their small format is
typical of works that Delacroix
made in the 1850s to satisfy the
demands of the bourgeoisie.

BIBLIOGRAPHY Kalder 1988,
pp. 12–14

95 La Mariage Juif à Tangier (pp. 6–7)

Francisco Lameyer y Berenguer (Puerto
de Santa Maria, 1825 – Madrid, 1877)

Madrid, 1875

Oil on canvas

58¾ × 82¾ in. (49.2 × 210.2 cm; framed)

Collection of Serge Berdugo

Although he had begun a military
career, a chance encounter in Rome
with a group of Spanish artists
impelled Lameyer to take up

painting. His works appeared in numerous Spanish publications and are today in the Prado, Madrid, and in the Calouste Gulbenkian Foundation in Lisbon.

Delacroix became a major influence, particularly his Oriental subjects, and Lameyer made numerous sketches after his works. Some of the figures in this painting recall those in Delacroix's *Jewish Wedding*. On the whole, Lameyer's treatment of the subject is more theatrical and more vividly colored. This work is a warm witness to an event that united Muslims and Jews.

BIBLIOGRAPHY Arama 1991, pp. 68–69; Goldenberg 1992, p. 238

96 *Femme Juive de Tanger* (fig. 78, p. 129)

Charles-Émile Vernet-Lecomte (Paris, 1821 – Paris, 1900)
Paris, 1868
Oil on canvas
48¾ × 35½ in (124 × 90 cm)
Private collection

Although he was born into a family of well-known artists, Lecomte's career has not been well documented. He showed his first Orientalist painting in the Salon of 1847, and seems to have traveled to the Orient c. 1850. A similar subject, entitled *The Oriental Beauty*, was auctioned in 1998.[33]

BIBLIOGRAPHY "Exotische Juden," *Ost und Ouest* 1901, p. 939; Goldenberg 1992, opposite p. 157

97 *Jewish Festival in Tetuan* (fig. 80, p. 130)

Edmé-Alexis-Alfred Dehodencq (Paris, 1822 – Paris, 1882)
Paris, c. 1858
Oil on canvas
63¾ × 52.6 in. (162 × 133.5 cm)
Musée d'Art et d'Histoire du Judaïsme, Paris
No. 95.13.1

98 *Entrance to the Mellah of Salé*

Raymond Crétot-Duval (Menton, 1895 – Bordeaux, 1986)
Morocco, 1925
Oil on canvas

95

18½ × 14½ in. (47 × 37 cm)
Private collection

Crétot-Duval was raised in an artistic home. His parents took him on a trip to Mauritius, Madagascar, Reunion, and Senegal, and upon their return, they encouraged him to apprentice himself as a cleaner of painted decorations in the Opera of Monte Carlo and in Parisian theaters. Under the tutelage of Leon Bakst, Cretot-Duval painted sets for the Ballets Russes.

In 1923, he returned to Tunis, Algiers, and Morocco. In Morocco, he was offered an atelier in which to work by a patron who was eager to have French artists capture the fertile images of Moroccan traditions, before the country was transformed under the influence of Western modernity. This painting is an example of Crétot-Duval's admiration for the urban architecture of Morocco, and his fascination with the way light played on the surfaces of buildings, varying with the time of day and with the season, and with the delicate colors of the structures. Weak figures in black, hunched, with concealed faces, drag themselves toward the

monumental arch of the gateway. Behind the fortress walls, a well of light announces the familiar cocoon of the *mellah*. The huge slabs of the architecture contrast with the daily life within.

Crétot-Duval showed in the Salons held in Paris; his works are in French museums and in those of North Africa.

BIBLIOGRAPHY Goldenberg 1992, p. 235.

99 *Portrait of Abraham Sicsu* (fig. 17; p. 43)

Théo van Rysselberghe (Ghent, 1862 – St Clair, Manche, 1926)
Tangier, c. 1880
Oil on canvas
34⅜ × 4⅜ × 2⅜ in. (88 × 11 × 6 cm)
Collection of Dr. Paul Dahan

Abraham Sicsu served as Belgium's Consul-General in Tangier, appointed to that post by the Duke of Brabant, later Leopold II, in 1862. The consul's home was a former Muslim palace with elaborate gardens known as La Villa de Belgique; there he entertained members of the Belgian royal family and visiting European artists. The works of artists who lived in Tangier

or whom Sicsu patronized hung from the villa's walls.

The consul helped visiting artists find lodging, studio space, models, and whatever else they required. Among those he assisted were Delacroix, Eugène Giraud, Louis Boulanger, Mariano Fortuny, and Théo van Rysselberghe. His portrait of Sicsu is astonishing in its classicism, given van Rysselberghe's involvement with the European avant garde. He and Octave Muse founded the *Cercle artistique des XX* and the *Libre Esthéthique*, and van Rysselberghe was the friend of writers such as André Gide. His association with progressive art movements continued until his death.

The viewer's gaze is drawn to Sicsu's dress, which symbolizes his assimilation of Western culture. The wearing of a fez and a large overcoat was popularized by teachers of the Alliance. For a Jew such as Sicsu to affect this dress, in a country in which the Islamic majority had forced Jews to wear different clothes and to go barefoot in the street as a sign of inferior status, was a privilege of his consular status. Van Rysselberghe also painted a portrait of Madame Sicsu, Doña Hadra.

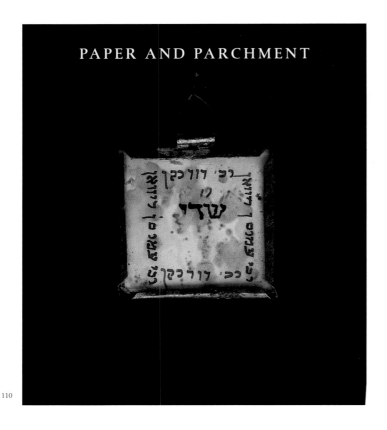

110

100 Menorah papercut (pp. 14–15)

Morocco, c. 1900
Paper: cutout and inscribed; metallic foil
17½ × 33½ in. (44.5 × 85.1 cm)
The Jewish Museum, New York
Purchased with funds given by the
Judaica Acquisitions Fund
1997-161

Only a few North African Jewish
papercuts are known among the
hundreds that were made
throughout the Jewish world
during the late nineteenth and early
twentieth centuries.[34] The Jewish
Museum's example appears to be a
smaller version of a composition in
the Wolfson Museum, Jerusalem,
which has similar motifs and style.
These motifs include arcades filled
with lamps, *hamsa*, architectural
niches, flora, and fauna. In
comparison with the larger
Wolfson papercut, the Jewish
Museum example appears
unfinished. It lacks the inscriptions
on the menorah and in the
cartouche beneath that are found

on the other work, and the swans
lack any detailing of the feathers.
The inscription on the right side is
from Genesis 28–29, a selection
from the blessing given by Isaac to
Jacob, and on the left is a passage
from Deuteronomy 7:14–16, which
likewise articulates blessings.

101 Blessings for reading the Torah from the Nahon Synagogue

Tangier, 1902
Ink on paper; copper alloy frame; iron
chain
Length (chain) 3½ in. (8.9 cm); plaque
4½ × 7 in. (11.4 × 17.8 cm)
Collection of Ami Sibony

This double-sided plaque bears the
blessings recited over a reading
from the Torah on one side, and the
prayer of thanksgiving for
deliverance from illness or danger
on the other.

102 *Shiviti* with Menorah

Morocco, 20th century

103

Ink on parchment
6¾ × 4⅜ in (17.2 × 11.1 cm); 16½ × 11 in.
(41.9 × 28 cm; matted)
Gross Family Collection
No. 027.012.017

A *shiviti* is a plaque inscribed with
the verse "I have set the Lord always
before me" (Psalms 16:8). It was
placed in the synagogue as a
reminder to the worshipper to
concentrate on his or her prayers.
Moroccan *shiviti* are decorated with
a large menorah or branched lamp-
stand inscribed with verses from
Psalms. Additional temple
furnishings depicted on this
example are: an altar, the flask of
oil, tongs, and a censer.

103 Wedding Contract from Sefrou

Sefrou, 18 Adar 5544[=1784]
Ink on paper
11⅝ × 7¾ in. (29.5 × 19.7 cm)
Gross Family Collection
No. 035.011.013

The text of this contract is unusual
in that it records a levirate marriage
in which Joseph, son of the late
Rabbi Joshua, the son of Rabbi
Aaron, took as his wife the widow
of his brother, Gracia, the daughter
of Rabbi Solomon, son of Rabbi
Maimon Abitbol. The signatures of
the witnesses at bottom form
baroque, interwoven designs, as on
Muslim contracts.

104

104 Wedding Contract from Meknes

Meknes, November 28, 1855
Ink, gouache, and gold paint on paper
22½ × 17¾ in. (57.2 × 45.1 cm)
Gross Family Collection
No. 035.011.010

This wedding contract is conceived as a segment of a building that frames the text. Each part is filled with varying patterns, unified by the same color scheme. At top, along the upper edge of the 'wall,' is a monumental inscription with expressions of good luck (*mazal tov*). In the windows below is a text that reads from right to left, offering the wish that the bride's home be like that of biblical women (see also no. 107). The contract is enclosed by a large horseshoe arch set between two rectangular pillars. It was written in Meknes on the eighteenth of Kislev in the year 5616 [November 28, 1855] for the marriage of Judah haLevi, son of Samuel haLevi, and Zaḥra, daughter of Isaac.

BIBLIOGRAPHY New York, Yeshiva University Museum 1992, no. 379.

105 Wedding Contract with ḥamsa (fig. 53, p. 91)

Larache, February 18, 1891
Watercolor and ink on paper
18 × 14 in. (45.7 × 35.6 cm)
Collection of Rabbi and Mrs. M. Mitchell Serels

The architectural frame of this contract is much looser and less structured than that which appears on no. 104. In place of architectural motifs, the columns are filled with flowers, and two fancifully colored ḥamsa take the place of capitals. The text celebrates the marriage of Abraham, son of Samuel, who was called Matitye, and Hadra, daughter of Simḥah.

106 Wedding Contract

Sijl Massa, February 22, 1928
Ink and paint on paper
20½ × 14¼ in. (52 × 36.9 cm)
Gross Family Collection
No. 035.011.018

This contract records the marriage of Joseph ben Abraham and Aziza, daughter of Jacob Malka. Above the written contract is a passage expressing the hope that the bride's home would be like those of Rachel and Leah and Tamar. Implements of the Temple in Jerusalem flank this passage, a reminder that a Jewish home is referred to in Hebrew as a small Temple.

The other decorative motifs display the same aesthetic seen on embroidery from the Tafilalet region (no. 142). Openwork patterns in which red, green, and yellow predominate contrast with a differently colored ground.[35] Here, the white of the paper forms rows of repeated motifs that alternate with colored rows. The guilloche pattern above the main text often appears as a border on embroidered clothing. A related but cruder *ketubbah*, from Erfoud in the Tafilalet, is in the Israel Museum, Jerusalem.[36]

107 Amulet for the protection of a traveler (fig. 65, p. 109)

Morocco, 19th century
Ink on parchment; silver case
3¾ × 1¾ × 1¾ in. (9.5 × 4.5 × 4.5 cm)
Collection of Dr. Paul Dahan

A portion of the scroll is inscribed with a tree-shaped diagram of the *Sefirot*, the ten Emanations or Principles of the *Ein-Sof* (the Infinite), one of the basic concepts of Kabbalah, Jewish mysticism. The common translation for the names of the *Sefirot* are: crown, wisdom, intelligence, greatness or love, power or judgment, beauty or compassion, lasting endurance, majesty, and righteous one. When rolled in its case, this amulet could be worn on the belt of a traveler to afford him protection.[37] The case is inscribed in Hebrew "the holy tree,"

an allusion to the contents of the scroll.

108 Amulet with menorah (fig. 60, p. 97)

Morocco, 20th century
Ink on paper; iron
4¼ × 2½ in. (10.8 × 6.3 cm; with frame)
Collection of Dr. Alfred Moldovan

The menorah that is the main motif of this amulet is inscribed with Psalm 67. Above, in large letters in square *ashuri* script, is the name of God, an allusion to Psalm 16:8, "I have set the Lord always before me." The two apotropaic images below the arms of the menorah are a scorpion and a beehive, often found on amulets from countries where insect and scorpion bites were a danger.[38]

109 Amulet with names of angels and saints (fig. 60, p. 97)

Morocco, 20th century
Printed on paper; iron frame
2¼ × 2¼ in. (5.7 × 5.7 cm)
Collection of Dr. Alfred Moldovan

This modest amulet records the following holy names: Almighty, Jerusalem, six angels, and, along the sides, Rabbi Meir Ba'al haNes (Master of the Miracle) and Rabbi Simeon bar Yoḥai, considered to be the author of the Zohar. Both rabbis were buried in the Land of Israel, not in Morocco, but were venerated nevertheless. The first five angels listed, Uriel, Raphael, Gabriel, Michael, and Nuriel, are often cited on Oriental amulets.[39]

110 Amulet with names of saints of Ouezzane

Ksar es-Souk, mid-20th century
Ink on paper; glass; iron frame
2 × 2 in. (5 × 5 cm)
Collection of Dr. Paul Dahan

Ksar es-Souk is in the Atlas Mountains, north of Erfoud. Yet the amulet is inscribed not with the names of local saints, but with those of the holy men venerated at Asjen, near Ouezzane: Rabbi Amram Diwan and Rabbi David Cohen. The pilgrimage to their tombs is one of the most celebrated among Moroccan Jewry. At center is a name of God, "Almighty."[40]

111 Amulet against Lilith (fig. 60, p. 97)

Ksar es-Souk, mid-20th century
Ink on paper; glass; iron frame
1⅛ × 1¾ in. (2.9 × 4.8 cm)
Collection of Dr. Alfred Moldovan

112 Amulets for the four walls of a newborn's room

Morocco, 20th century (?)
Ink on paper
16⅛ × 22½ in. (41 × 57 cm)
Collection of Dr. Paul Dahan

These four handwritten pages of prayers and symbols were designed to restrict the movement of demons and to prevent them from harming the new mother and her offspring. The tapering of the triangles signifies the removal of evil spirits from their victims.[41]

113 Amulet for a newborn son (fig. 29, p. 57)

Morocco, 20th century
Ink on paper
12⅛ × 13¾ in. (32 × 35 cm)
Collection of Dr. Paul Dahan

The days between birth and circumcision were considered to be especially dangerous for a newborn son. To ward off evil demons, the family hung amulets such as these on the walls of the bedroom. Three protective symbols are represented: ḥamsa, Stars of David inscribed

112

114

115

"Almighty," and a tree, presumably the Tree of Life. The texts include a portion of the *Va-yehi noam* prayer, the theme of which is protection from physical danger, and three names of Elijah the Prophet at bottom.

114 Wall-hung amulet for a mother's protection

Morocco, 20th century

Ink on paper

9⅞ × 11⅞ × ⅜ in. (22 × 35 × 1 cm)

Collection of Dr. Paul Dahan

115 Broadsheet of Rabbi Ḥayyim Pinto (fig. 59, p. 96)

Ashdod, first half of the 20th century

Printed on paper

8¾ × 13¾ in. (22 × 35 cm)

Collection of Dr. Paul Dahan

Rabbi Ḥayyim Pinto moved to Essaouira when he was ten years old and died there in 1845. His synagogue, on the second floor of the house in which he lived, is still preserved, as is his tomb, which has become a place of pilgrimage. Most of Rabbi Pinto's followers now live in Ashdod, where this broadsheet was printed by a descendent, Moses Pinto, on behalf of the synagogue and *yeshiva* Or haḤayyim (Light of Ḥayyim). Moses describes himself as the son of Rabbi Ḥayyim, presumably Rabbi Ḥayyim Pinto haQatan (the lesser), the grandson of the rabbi celebrated on this broadsheet.

The text urges the reader to visit the saint's grave and to benefit from his help.

116 Broadsheet of the kabbalist Jacob Abuḥazira (fig. 75, p. 123)

Morocco, 20th century

Printed on paper

11⅞ × 8⅝ in. (30 × 22 cm)

Collection of Dr. Paul Dahan

117 Blessings for Reading the Torah from the Nahon Synagogue

Tangier, 1902

Ink on paper; copper alloy frame; iron chain

Length (chain) 3½ in. (8.9 cm); plaque 4½ × 7 in. (11.4 × 17.8 cm)

Collection of Ami Sibony

118

118 Two Jewish women

Morocco, 1860s
Photograph
12⅝ × 8¾ in. (32 × 22 cm)
Collection of Dr. Paul Dahan

This is one of the earliest known photographs of Moroccan Jewish women .

119 Cemetery at Marrakesh

Marrakesh, 1880s
Photograph
12⅝ × 9⅛ in. (32 × 23 cm)
Collection of Dr. Paul Dahan

This view was taken by photographers serving with the French.

119

120 Moshe Halioua

Marseilles, 1880s
Photograph: laquered on metal stand
6 × 3½ in. (15.3 × 8.9 cm)
Collection of Juliette Halioua

Moshe Halioua emigrated from Tangier to the Land of Israel in the 1880s. On the way, he stopped in

Marseilles, where this photograph was taken.

BIBLIOGRAPHY New York, Yeshiva University Museum 1992, no. 523.

121 Photograph of man from Tangier

Morocco, c. 1900
Photograph
6¾ × 5 in. (17.2 × 12.7 cm)
Courtesy of the Library of The Jewish Theological Seminary of America, New York

Print Collection

B3.2

123

121

123

122 *Jeune femme Juive de Tanger* (fig. 79, p. 131)

Tangier, c. 1920
Photograph on paper
13 × 15⅛ in. (33 × 39 cm)
Collection of Dr. Paul Dahan

The same woman, in identical dress, posed for a postcard c. 1920.⁴²

123 Woman seated at table in Grand Costume

Morocco, early 20th century
Photograph
12¼ × 9⅞ in. (31 × 25 cm)
Collection of Dr. Paul Dahan

124 Woman wearing Grand Costume from Tetuan

Morocco, late 19th – early 20th century
Photograph
12⅝ × 9⅛ in. (32 × 23 cm)
Collection of Dr. Paul Dahan

125 Two rabbis from the South

Morocco, c. 1950
Photograph on paper
11½ × 9½ in. (29 × 24 cm)
Collection of Dr. Paul Dahan

126 Mercedes Halioua Cohen and her nephew Marc Assayag Halioua Cohen

Tangier, 1920s
Photograph
6 × 3½ in. (15.2 × 8.9 cm)
Collection of Juliette Halioua

127 Primary class, Alliance Israélite School

Tangier, c. 1955–56
Photograph
8½ × 11 in. (21.6 × 28 cm)
Collection of Ami Sibony

124

128 Photo of Esther Play for Purim

Tangier, 1914
Copy photograph
12½ × 9 in. (31.7 × 23 cm)
Collection of Mrs. Sonia Azagury

Purim is a Jewish holiday that commemorates Persian Jewry's deliverance from the vizier Haman, who planned to annihilate them during the reign of Ahashueros, thought to be Artaxerxes II. The story is inscribed in the book of Esther, which became the basis for plays and recitations. The tradition of dressing in Grand Costumes for performances of Purim plays continued into the latter part of the twentieth century.[43]

129 *Le Detroit de Gibraltar; Le Gout Sale des Levres*

Hélène Hourmat (France, 1950–)
Paris, 1985
Gelatin silver prints; conté crayon on paper
62 × 102 in. (157.5 × 259.1 cm)
The Jewish Museum, New York
Purchased with funds provided by the Ferkauf Fund
1992-146a-e

Hélène Hourmat, a photograph archivist and an artist-photographer, conflates images from her contemporary Parisian existence with those of her Moroccan Jewish background, culled from her family's photo album. Through these two disparate cultures, she explores shifting definitions of self-identity that span East and West, past and present, masculine and feminine.

STONE

130 Tombstone of Matrona, daughter of Rabbi Judah Noah

Volubilis, 3rd century
Stone: engraved
9¼ × 14⅛ in. (25 × 35.9 cm)
Musée Archéologique, Rabat
99.4.4.1431
BIBLIOGRAPHY Goldenberg 1992, p. 52

125

128

131 Torah Mantle

Morocco, 1900–20

Silk velvet: embroidered with gilt
metallic threads, metallic fringe; lining:
cotton

31 × 9¾ in. (78.8 × 24.7 cm; top dm)

The Jewish Museum, New York

Gift of the David Elmaleh family,
Marrakesh, Morocco

1998-40

The embroidery, gilt metallic
threads on silk velvet, is typical of
work done in Moroccan cities
where Sephardim settled. The
similarity between the motifs used
on this mantle and no. 134 suggests
that both were made in the same
workshop. Three other mantles
from the same atelier are no. 151/121
in the Israel Museum, Jerusalem,
one sold by Christie's dated 1906,
and one in the Museo Sefardi,
Toledo, Spain, dated 1911/12.[44] The
inscription dates suggest that the
group stems from an atelier active
in the first two decades of the
twentieth century.

 The Elmaleh family were
custodians of one of the synagogues
in Marrakesh. When the
congregation disbanded, they took
this mantle with them to Brazil, and
then to the United States.

132 Torah Mantle

Morocco, early 20th century

Silk velvet: embroidered with gilt
metallic threads over cardboard forms,
gilt metallic fringe; lining: cotton
damask

31 × 11 in. (78.7 × 28 cm; top dm)

The Jewish Museum, New York

Purchased with funds provided by the
Sanford C. Bernstein Fund

1998-47

The floral elements and scrolls are
similar to those found on the
bodices of Grand Costumes (no.
145), but their enclosure in a wreath
suggests European influence. Bird
motifs are commonly found on
Jewish embroideries and
metalwork from Morocco (see nos.
66 and 81). On the workshop which
produced this mantle and no. 131,
see above.

132

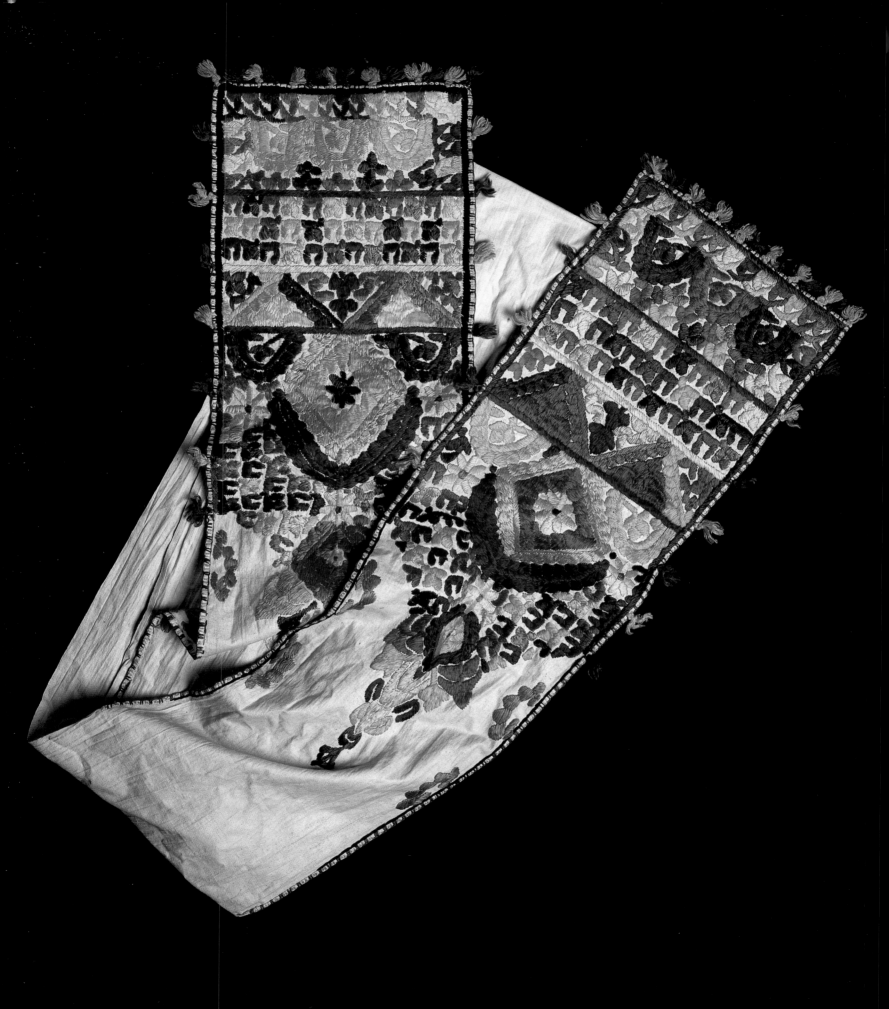

133 Torah Binder with Hebrew inscription

Rabat, 19th century
Cotton: embroidered with silk threads
7¾ × 101½ in. (19.7 × 258 cm) plus 1 in. (2.6 cm) fringe
Collection of Mrs. Sonia Azagury

This belt has a Hebrew inscription that suggests it was used for liturgical purposes, namely as a binder to hold the two staves of a Torah Scroll together when the scroll was not in use. The inscription consists of the initials [א, ת] (*aleph, tof*) repeated over and over. One interpretation is that the letters are a mnemonic device for [אור התורה] ("the light of the Torah"). Below the letters are typical nineteenth-century Rabat embroidery motifs, including a stylized bell shape and zigzag borders.

134 Antependium for the reader's desk

Fez, 1944/45
Silk velvet: embroidered with metallic threads
26¾ × 74½ in. (68 × 189.9 cm)
Collection of Dr. Paul Dahan

The reader's desks of Moroccan synagogues were generally built higher than the seats, a tradition deriving from Sephardi usage, known from fourteenth-century illuminated manuscripts. This Jewish form paralleled the raised pulpit from which the Koran was read in mosques. Probably because of the height of the reader's desk, it became customary to decorate it with an antependium. This one was made from a Torah mantle. Two tree designs flank the central panel, the concentric compostion of which is focused on a Decalogue. Above is written "Crown of Torah" and the date 5705 [1944/45] in Arabic numerals. At top, a single band of text runs across all three panels:

זה ספר תורה נדבת טהרת אשת חיל
לעטרת רבקה אל נוסיאלי בת אליהו נע
חברת אם הבנים וכות...

"This Torah Scroll is the donation

134

of the pure Woman of Valor [Proverbs 31:10], the crown of [her husband], Rebecca el-Nusaeli. The Society Em haBanim . . ." Em haBanim was an organization that built schools, for example in Fez, that promoted a comprehensive education for Jewish children, combining secular subjects, foreign language instruction, and religious studies.

135 Cover for tombs and circumcision chairs

Maker: Abraham El-Hadad
Fez, 1917
Silk velvet: embroidered with metallic fringe, metallic threads
42 × 42 in. (106.7 × 106.7 cm)
Collection of Dr. Paul Dahan

Muslims traditionally cover sacred monuments and tombs with textiles, for protection and as a sign of honor.⁴⁵ This cloth was commissioned by Jacob, son of Abraham Meloul, and was made in

Fez by Abraham El-Hadad to serve a dual purpose: to cover the tomb of Rabbi Amram Diwan in Ouzzane at the time of pilgrimages, and to cover the Chair of Elijah during circumcisions. The inscription reads:

זאת פרכת הקדש/שהתנדב והקדיש היקר
יעקב/מלול בן הזקן הכשר אברהם
יצ׳/לעתות הצריכים כגון בהילולות
הצדיקים וחופה כסא אליהו הנביא/זל
בברית דם לה׳ למנוחת נ״רו/הב״חו ן׳ חיים
מלול נ״ע נחטף ונקטף עודנו באבו קראו
רכו ביום שב״ק/י״ט ל״ח אלול ש׳ תרעו
פ״ק תנצב״ה/והיו ביום ג׳ ל״ח מרחשון
משנת/לנרצוני רחמתי״ך פא ווַאר זאן יע״א
נעשית ע״י היקר אברהם אלחצאר
בפאס יע״א

"This is the holy curtain that was donated and dedicated by . . . Jacob Meloul, son of the elder Abraham, today on the third of the month of Mar-Ḥeshvan in the year 'But in my favor I have had compassion on thee' [Isaiah 60:10 = (5)678 = 1917], here in Ouezzane, for the times when it is necessary, for example: during pilgrimages to the saints,

and as a covering for the Chair of Elijah the Prophet, because of the covenant of blood that God imposed. For the repose of the late youth Ḥayyim Meloul, snatched and plucked [away] while still with his father and tender [in years]. He was called on the holy Sabbath, the 19th of the month of Elul in the year [5]676 [1916] . . . And, this was made by the beloved Abraham Elhadad of Fez."

136 *Tefillin* bag of Moses Khalfon

Morocco, late 19th – early 20th century
Silk velvet: embroidered with gold and silver metallic threads, sequins; gilt silver appliqués; metallic thread tassels; lining: cotton over cardboard
8 × 10 × 1⅛ in. (20.3 × 25.4 × 2.9 cm)
The Jewish Museum, New York
Gift of Dr. Harry G. Friedman
F 4759

According to its inscription, this bag belonged to Moses Khalfon, son of Isaac. The initial M is on the

135

This bag's rectangular shape and the character of its embroidery suggest an early date. The centralized design of the middle field is characteristic of Islamic art. According to the inscription, which begins on the front and finishes on the reverse, the bag belonged to:

[ע״ה שלמה עמיאל/נח בר יוסף ס״ט]

"Solomon Amiel Noah son of Joseph."

139 Three *tefillin* bags

Morocco, 20th century
Cotton satin: embroidered with metallic ribbon; tassels; lining: cotton; drawstrings: cotton
Each 12 × 8½ in. (30.5 × 21.6 cm)
The Jewish Museum, New York
Gift of Mrs. Sheila Tenenbaum
JM 1-74 a–c

These three textiles and a few similar ones in other collections[47] form a small group of relatively modest *tefillin* bags that differ radically from the gold-embroidered examples. Each side is framed by metallic ribbon. In the center is one of three motifs: an eight-pointed star formed of two intersecting squares; a tree; or a house. The star is a common motif in Islamic art, as is the tree. The appearance of a house on the bags may derive from the Moroccan Hebrew *bayit*, or house.

BIBLIOGRAPHY a: New York, The Jewish Museum 1977, no. 112 (b and c are unpublished).

140 Cover for Torah from the Nahon Synagogue

Tangier, 1954
Velvet: embroidered
20 × 20 in. (50.8 × 50.8 cm)
Collection of Ami Sibony

This cover's only decoration is its inscription:

למנוחת האשה/הכ״ו ה לידיסייא/נאולבאז
שנלב״ע/ ה' אייר תשיד פ״ק/מאת בעלה
ובניה/תנצב״ה

"For the repose of the honored woman Lidicia Nailbaz, who died on 5 Iyyar [5]714 [1954]. From her husband and her children. M[ay] her s[oul] be b[ound] in the bonds of e[ternal life]."

back of the bag; the *K* is on the front. The combination of various embroidery stitches and materials lends a colorful effect.

BIBLIOGRAPHY New York, The Jewish Museum 1977, no. 118.

137 *Tefillin* bag of Abraham Solomon Abitbol

Meknes (?), 19th century
Red velvet: embroidered with gold and sequins; wool
8½ × 7 in. (21.6 × 17.8 cm)
The Jewish Museum, New York

Gift of Dr. Harry G. Friedman
F 4361

The gold metallic decoration of this bag, a flowering tree with circular foliage organized about a central axis, is similar to the decoration of the bodices of Grand Costumes from Meknes.[46] The inscription reads:

ע״ה אברהם/שלום אביט

"The Servant of God, Abraham Solomon Abit'[bol]."

The names Solomon and Abraham

appear among members of the Abitbol family who lived in the nineteenth century, suggesting a similar date for this bag.

138 *Tefillin* bag

Morocco, 19th century
Silk velvet: embroidered with gilt metallic threads and gold braid; tassels; lining: cotton
5 × 7½ in. (12.7 × 19.1 cm)
The Jewish Museum, New York
S 53

143

141 *Akhnif* (man's cape; figs. 5, 6, p. 28)

Siroua Mountains, c. 1930
Wool: woven; silk: embroidered
56¼ in. (142.9 cm; max. length including hood); 110½ in. (280.7 cm; max. width)
Collection of Linda Gross

Berber and Jewish men living in the Siroua Mountain region, the territory of the Aït-Ouaouzguite people, wore a fringed burnoose woven from dark-brown or black wool, the main feature of which was a lozenge or eye-shaped area, embroidered in red or orange, that signified the evil eye. While Muslims wore the *akhnif* with its decoration on the outside, adult Jewish males wore theirs inside out as a sign of lesser status.

142 *Ijekjad* (boots)

Ouaouzguite region, first quarter of the 20th century
Wool: woven; cotton; leather
11½ × 4¼ × 11 in. (29 × 12 × 28 cm)
Collection of Dr. Paul Dahan

The boots worn with the *akhnif* were woven of wool and generally matched the color scheme of the cape. A similar pair is in a private collection.[48]

143 Chemise and matching hood

Tafilalet region, early 20th century
Cotton: embroidered with silk
Chemise: 46 × 45 in. (117 × 112 cm)
Hood: 19½ × 11 in. (49 × 28 cm)
Collection of Dr. Paul Dahan

The elaborate embroidery of Jewish costumes from the Tafilalet region consists of intricately patterned lozenges, formed of flat and twisted silk threads, embroidered on a red or white cotton ground.[49] Similar embroidery appears on skullcaps and other headcoverings.

144 Man's belt

Morocco, c. 1930
Silk threads and fringe
157 × 16½ in. (398.8 × 42 cm)
Collection of Mrs. Sonia Azagury
No. c-21

142

143

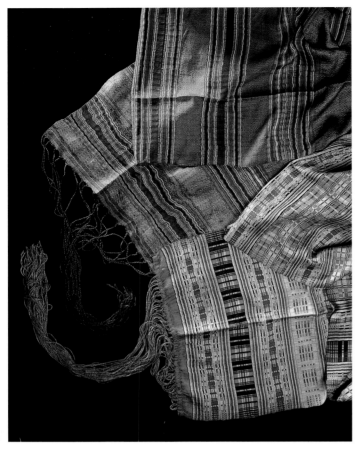

145

A nearly identically patterned belt
was worn by David ben Barukh,
president of the goldsmiths' guild
in Essaouira, in a 1935 photograph,[50]
while a later example from
Taroudant is in the collection of the
Israel Museum, Jerusalem.[51] The
provenance of this example is
Tangier, suggesting that the use of
such brightly colored belts, woven
in stripes and rectangles, was
widespread among Jewish men in
Morocco.

145 Man's belt

Morocco, c. 1930
Silk threads and fringe
97 × 5¾ in. (246 × 14.5 cm)
Collection of Mrs. Sonia Azagury

151

146 *El-keswa el-kbîra* (the Grand Costume; back: right; front: fig. 86, p. 135)

Rabat, late 19th century
Skirt: silk velvet with gold metallic
ribbon and passmenterie; lining:
polished cotton; bodice: silk velvet with
gilt metallic embroidery, leather; sleeves:
transparent silk chiffon with gold
brocade

Skirt: 118⅛ × 39½ in. (300 × 100 cm);
Jacket: 24¾ × 23⅝ in. (62.8 × 60 cm);
Bodice: 14⅛ × 18½ in. (35.8 × 47 cm);
Sleeves: 33 × 7 in. (83.8 × 17.7 cm; to
armhole end)

The Jewish Museum, New York
Purchased with funds given by the
Judaica Acquistion Fund
1993-195 a–e

This nearly complete Grand
Costume consists of a floor-length
wraparound skirt (*zeltita*) of silk
velvet embroidered with gold
metallic threads, a *plastron* or
bodice, and a waistcoat (*gombaz*) of
the same materials. Diaphanous,
billowing sleeves (*kmâm*) of striped
silk woven with gold threads were
affixed within the short sleeves of
the jacket. Such costumes were
worn by brides during the henna
ceremony that preceded the
marriage, and afterwards for
religious festivals and special
occasions. This one was made for
Mas'uda, the bride of David Ohaion
of Marrakesh, in the late nineteenth
century, and was worn by women
of the family into the twentieth
century.

The *keswa* is thought to derive
from medieval Spanish dress,
brought to Morocco by Jews after
the expulsion from Spain in 1492.
The refugees settled in the northern
part of the country and in major
cities further south. The impressive
appearance of the costume caught
the attention of eighteenth-century
European writers and of French
painters such as Delacroix, who
came to Morocco in the nineteenth
century (nos. 92–96). The same
decorative patterns appear on
pieces of a Grand Costume in the
Israel Museum, Jerusalem
(2749.12.64; 1176.72 a–b; 1403.8.66).
A parallel costume is in the Musée
National des Arts Africains et

146

147

d'Océaniens, Paris (no. M.61.10.51), and another is in the British Museum, London (Af4.1).[52]

BIBLIOGRAPHY *The Jewish Museum 1992–1994*, 1995, p. 37.

147 Grand Costume of Mrs. Levi's grandmother

Tetuan, mid-19th century
Silk shantung; embroidered with gold threads and ribbon

Skirt: 19 × 39 in. (48.3 × 99.1 cm); jacket: 18 × 17 (45.7 × 43.2 cm); sleeve: 16¼ in (41.2 cm)
Collection of Mrs. Sonia Azagury

This costume from Tetuan, consisting of a skirt and jacket, differs from the *keswa* of other cities in its materials, its mode of embroidery, and its motifs. Lacking is the sequence of nested curves radiating from the hem up the skirt that characterizes most Grand Costumes. Instead, the skirt is embroidered with zigzags and straight lines. Although the waistcoat has the usual floral motifs, they are arranged differently from those on the typical Grand Costume. Also, the silk shantung and ribbon embroidery give off a low sheen that lacks the high lustre of gold metallic-thread embroidery on silk velvet. Both types were made in Tetuan, which produced many of the finest examples of the *keswa el-kbîra*.[53] A photograph of a young Jewish woman, dated c. 1880–85, shows her wearing an embroidered silk velvet waistcoat like the one described in the previous entry, together with the type of skirt seen in this example.[54]

148

151
153
156

148 Grand Costume

Tangier, 20th century
Black silk velvet: embroidered with gold
metallic threads; buttons: silver; filigree
Length 43⅓ in. (110 cm); vest 20½ × 18⅛
in. (52 × 46 cm)
Collection of Mrs. Sonia Azagury

On either side of the front of this
jacket are three large spirals. The
same motifs, generally thought to
signify the sun or infinity and belief
in the hereafter,[55] appear on

embroidered Jewish shrouds from
Morocco and on the tombstones in
Essaouira and other cities (see
p. 137). Their presence on the bridal
costume associates marriage and
the beginning of a new phase of life
with death and entry into the
afterlife, a sober reminder at a
moment of great joy.[56]

149 Sleeves for Grand Costume

Marrakesh (?), beginning of the 20th
century

Silk; gold braid
Top width: 24 × 4½ in. (61 × 11.5 cm);
bottom width: 34½ in. (87.6 cm)
Collection of Mrs. Sonia Azagury

Similar mousseline sleeves of
striated silk with gold braid were
photographed in Marrakesh during
the first half of the 20th century.[57]

150 Hzam (belt)

Fez, 19th century
Silk; rayon; cotton and metallic threads
105 × 15 in. (266.7 × 38.1 cm), with 31 in.
(78.8 cm) fringe on each end
Lent by The Minneapolis Institute of
Arts
The Driscoll Art Accessions Endowment
Fund
93.25.2

Belts like these were produced in
Fez, in workshops largely staffed by
men. They are composed of
various patterns, arranged in two
vertical strips, that draw on a
variety of external sources.[58]
Among the models are medieval

Spanish textiles, and architectural
decoration and carpets from Persia.
For example, a concentric frame
enclosing three crossed bands may
be seen at the center of the Banner
of Los Navas de Tolosa, now in the
monastery of Las Huelgos in
Burgos, Spain, and on a textile in
the Smithsonian Institution
National Design Museum, New
York.[59] Hands at the edges of the
belt may be apotropaic symbols.

151 Hzam (belt)

Fez, 19th century
Silk and gold metallic threads
70 × 3¼ in. (177.8 × 8.2 cm), plus 21 in.
(53.3 cm) fringe on both ends
Collection of Mrs. Sonia Azagury

The palette of this belt is limited to
green, blue, and gold. The
manufacture of gold threads, such as
those in this work, was a specialty of
Moroccan Jews. Most of the motifs
on the belt are drawn from the
medieval Spanish decorative arts
that were the basis of the later arts of

152

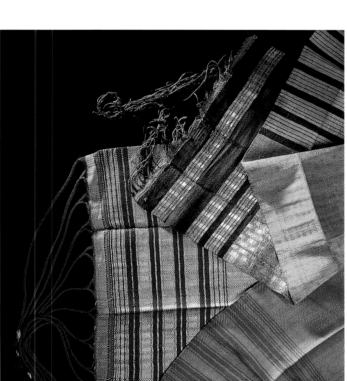

155

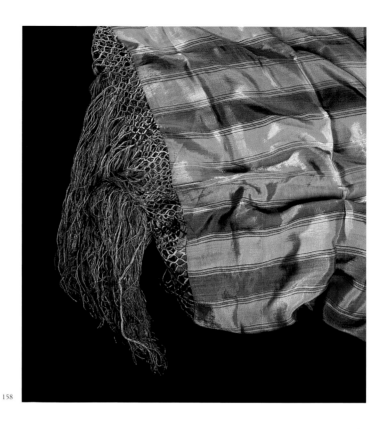

158

palette and composition, which also feature white motifs along the periphery of the main design.[61]

153 *Hzam* (belt)

Fez, early 20th century
Red and black silk; gold metallic threads, bosses, and fringe
128 × 27½ in. (325 × 70 cm)
Collection of Mrs. Sonia Azagury

Like the Fez belts, this type was folded width-wise when worn.

154 *Hzam* (belt)

Fez, early 20th century
Green silk; gold metallic threads
144 × 14 in. (35.6 × 365.8 cm)
Collection of Mrs. Sonia Azagury
C15

155 *Hzam* (belt)

Fez, early 20th century
Orange and magenta silk
158⅛ × 17 in. (402 × 43 cm)
Collection of Mrs. Sonia Azagury

156 *Hzam* (belt)

Fez, early 20th century
Purple and green silk; gold metallic threads; silk fringe
97 × 5¾ in. (246 × 14.5 cm)
Collection of Mrs. Sonia Azagury

157 *Hzam* (belt)

Fez, early 20th century
Red and black silk; gold metallic threads, bosses, and fringe
128 × 27½ in. (325 × 70 cm)
Collection of Mrs. Sonia Azagury

158 Veil

Fez, early 20th century
Orange, black, purple, and pink silk threads and fringe
124 × 15¼ in. (315 × 38.7 cm) plus fringe
Collection of Mrs. Sonia Azagury

The center of a long shawl, such as this striped example and nos. 157–59, was worn across the forehead. The remainder was wrapped around the head, falling to the floor as a double train. A bride

Morocco. Concentric eight-pointed stars are found on Iberian textiles and in nineteenth-century tiles from Fez.[60] On both ends are *hamsa* and eight-pointed stars, as on the previous example. Although the work was made in Fez, it was worn by a bride in Tetuan.

152 *Hzam* (belt)

Fez, 19th century
Silk
69¼ × 14¼ in. (177.2 × 36.2 cm), plus fringe
Collection of Linda Gross

This Fez belt reflects medieval Spanish textile designs of similar

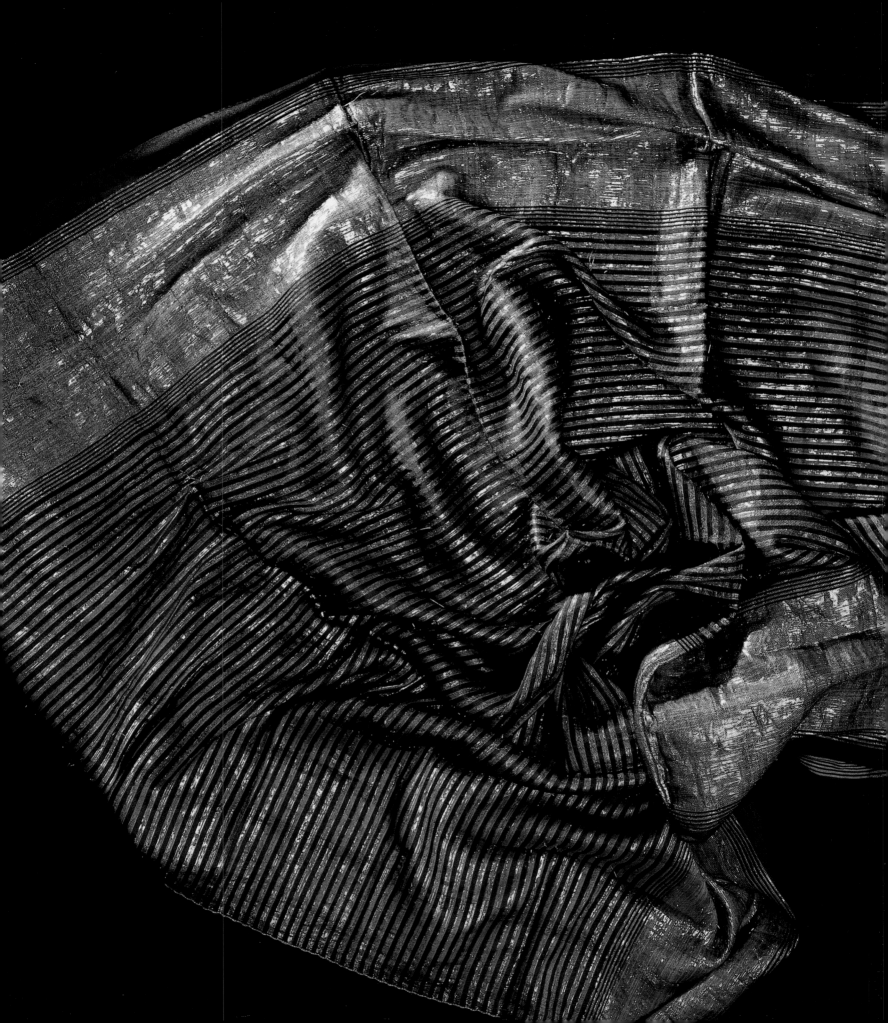

in Marrakesh is shown wearing
such a shawl in an early twentieth-
century photograph.[62]

159 Shawl

Fez, early 20th century
Green silk and gold threads
124 × 15¼ in. (315 × 38.7 cm)
Collection of Mrs. Sonia Azagury

160 Shawl

Fez, early 20th century
Pink silk and gold metallic threads
142½ × 9 in. (362 × 22.8 cm)
Collection of Mrs. Sonia Azagury

161 Shawl

Fez, early 20th century
Yellow, black, and scarlet silk threads;
gold metallic ribbon
128 × 24 in. (325 × 60.9 cm)
Collection of Mrs. Sonia Azagury

161

159

160

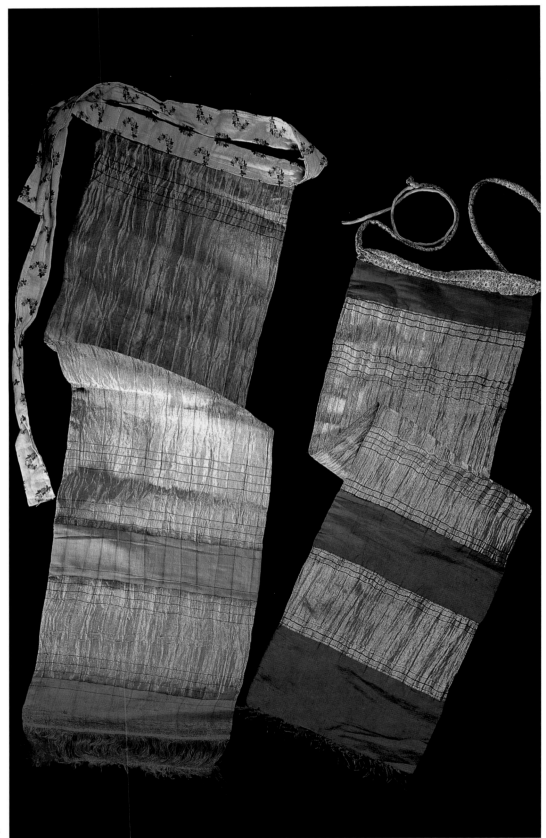

162–63

162 Pendant panel from the Azancot family

Fez and Tangier, 19th–20th century
Black and orange silk; gold metallic threads; cotton: printed
33½ × 8¾ in. (85 × 22.2 cm)
Collection of Mrs. Sonia Azagury

A panel was sometimes cut from an old shawl and furnished with a cotton belt. When worn, the panel imitated the fall of a full shawl down the lower back of the wearer.

163 Pendant panel

Fez and Tangier, early 20th century
Black and blue silk; gold metallic threads; cotton: printed
33½ × 8¾ in. (85 × 22.2 cm)
Collection of Mrs. Sonia Azagury

164 Pair of woman's shoes

Marrakesh, late 19th century
Silk embroidered with silk and gold threads; leather soles
9⅞ × 3⅞ in. (24.9 × 9.8 cm)
The Jewish Museum, New York
Purchase made with funds given by the Judaica Acquisitions Fund
1993-196 a, b

Many documentary photographs taken before the 1950s show Jewish shoemakers crafting *babouches* such as these.
BIBLIOGRAPHY New York, The Jewish Museum 1995, p. 37.

165 Pair of woman's shoes

Tangier, 20th century
Silk: embroidered with silver and gold threads; cotton lining; leather soles
10 × 3⅞ in. (26 × 9.8 cm)
Collection of Mrs. Sonia Azagury

166 Pair of woman's shoes

Morocco, 19th century
Silk: embroidered with metallic threads; leather soles
9½ × 4¾ × 1¾ in. (24 × 12 × 4.5 cm)
Collection of Dr. Paul Dahan

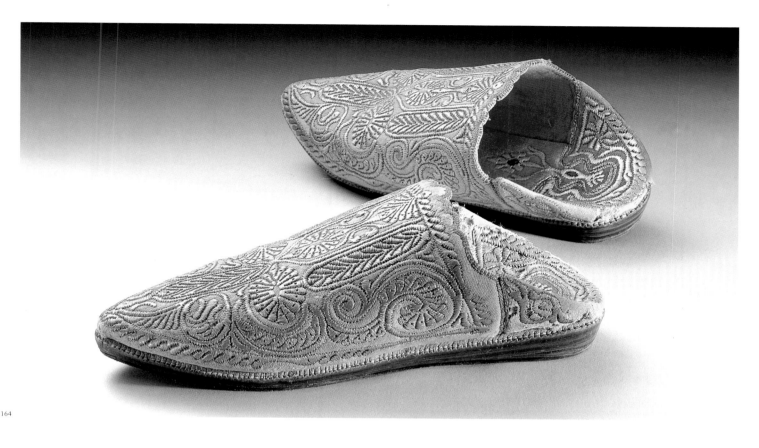

164

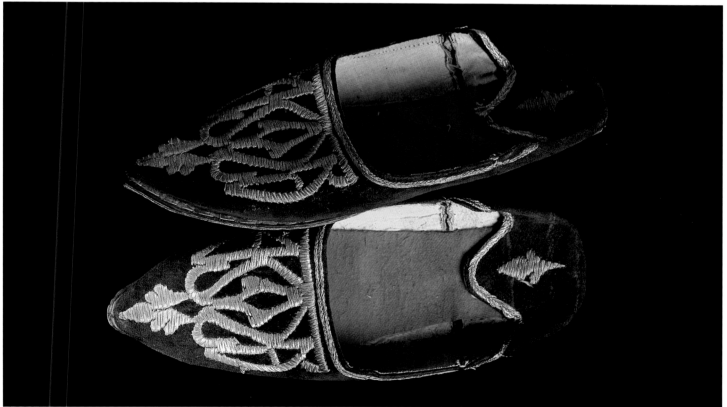

165

171

167 Bag for a new mother

Marrakesh, late 19th – early 20th century

Silk velvet: embroidered with gold metallic threads

16⅛ × 13⅛ in. (41 × 33.5 cm)

Israel Museum, Jerusalem

No. 1083/74

In Marrakesh, it was customary to present a new mother with an embroidered bag. A flowering tree with dense foliage decorates the front of this example,[63] while the reverse is embroidered with an eight-pointed star that encloses floral motifs, similar to metallic appliqués made by Jewish women of Tetuan (nos. 166–67). Both derive from medieval Spanish textile patterns. According to the Hebrew and Judeo-Spanish inscription that begins on the front and finishes on the back, this bag was:

מנחה היא שלוחה לאסתר די
מאיר אסבאג מב״ת

"a gift sent to Esther di Meir Assabagh . . ."

168

168 *Cache-matelas brodé*
(embroidered mattress cover or
***'arid*; fig. 83, p. 133)**

Tetuan and Chefchaouen, 18th century
Linen and velvet: embroidered with silk
and gold metallic threads
75½ × 15⅛ in. (192 × 39 cm)
Collection of Isabelle C. Denamur

Chefchaouen in the Rif Mountains
was one of the cities in which Jews
fleeing Spain settled. As a result,
the embroideries produced there
often incorporate Peninsular
motifs, such as eight-pointed stars
made of metallic threads.
Appliqués with these motifs were
produced by Jews in Tetuan, while
the remainder of the hanging was
embroidered in Chefchaouen. Pairs
of 'mosaics,' densely embroidered
squares with floral and geometric
motifs, frame the metallic stars.
These textiles were used as
hangings behind furniture in
reception rooms or bedrooms.
Some examples of this
composition are embroidered
entirely in silk and lack the metallic
appliqués.

BIBLIOGRAPHY Paris, Le Petit Palais
1999, no. 376.

169 *Cache-matelas brodé*
(embroidered mattress cover or
***'arid*)**

Tetuan and Chefchaouen, 18th century
Linen and velvet: embroidered with silk
and gold metallic threads
82⅔ × 70 in. (210 × 178 cm)
Musée Batha de Fès, Fez

170

170 Wall hanging

Azemmour, end of 17th century
Linen; silk, embroidery
88¼ × 49¼ in. (224.8 × 125 cm)
Collection of Isabelle C. Denamur

Azemmour, a small coastal city south of Casablanca, was ruled by the Portuguese between 1513 and 1541. This avenue of European cultural influence on Azemmour was reinforced by the arrival of Muslims and Jews from the Iberian Peninsula in 1610. As a result, the embroideries produced here, solely the works of Jews who specialized in the craft, are decorated with motifs derived from the art of Spain and Portugal. For example, the image of two birds flanking a vase appeared in early Christian and Byzantine art as a representation of the doves of the Holy Spirit, and continued to be used thereafter. In Jewish works from Azemmour, the peacock, symbol of incorruptibility, is substituted; this image appears against a red ground, characteristic

of Azemmour embroidery. This type of textile was mostly used for household purposes: as a hanging or as a border on bed linens and the like.[64] The large size of this example is unusual.

BIBLIOGRAPHY Paris, Le Petit Palais 1999, no. 383.

171 Wall hanging (hayti)

Tangier (?), 20th century
Silk velvet: appliquéd
206 × 73¼ in. (523 × 186 cm)
Collection of Mrs. Sonia Azagury

These large textiles were hung along the walls of salons, synagogues, and sukkot.[65] The arcade motif is found in both Andalusian and Moroccan architecture.

WOOD

172 Amuletic dagger (fig. 49, p. 87)

Marrakesh, late 19th century
Iron; wood
15¼ × 1⅞ in. (40 × 4.7 cm)
The Jewish Museum, New York
Purchased with funds given by the Judaica Acquisitions Fund
1993-198

One of the ways that Moroccan Jews assure the well-being of a parturient mother and her newborn is to demarcate their chamber or space, and to perform rituals (taḥdid) that prevent demons from entering.[66] Iron daggers such as this one are used in the rituals of demarcation that follow the birth of a male child. During the day, the dagger rests beneath the mattress of the mother. In the evening, people assemble in the home, and, following the recitation of prayers and portions of the Zohar, the father waves the sword and hits

each of the four walls of the chamber and each of its corners, while the assembled people recite passages from the Torah and Psalms. At the conclusion of the ceremony, a bundle of salt is placed next to the baby, and a book of Psalms at his head, to guard him against the demon Lilith.

173 Tevah (reader's desk)

Marrakesh, early 20th century
Wood: carved and turned
46 × 29 × 70 in. (123 × 77.6 × 187.2 cm)
The Jewish Museum, New York

The form of this reader's desk, a horizontal surface surrounded by a decorative superstructure on three sides, is typical of Moroccan synagogue furnishings. Most were made by local carpenters. This desk comes from a synagogue sold to Muslims by its owners, a Jewish family of Marrakesh.

OBJECTS FROM A JEWISH SCHOOL IN FEZ

The following works belong to the Musée Israélite de Fez, courtesy of Edmond Gabay:

PAPER

174 *Certificat d' instruction Juive Gabriel Cohen*

Fez, 1972
Printed on paper
12⅝ × 9¼ in. (32 × 23.5 cm)

175 First prize in Choumash

Fez, 1950s
Ink and printing on paper
12⅝ × 9¼ in. (32 × 23.5 cm)

176 *Années scolaires* (report cards) of Claudine Attias, Abraham Assayag, and Issakhar ben Chamroun

Fez, 1941
Ink and printing on paper
9½ × 7⅛ in. (24 × 18 cm)

177 *Carte: les articulations - les muscles* (Chart of Human Muscles)

France, 20th century
Printed on paper
Approx. 48 × 36 in. (122 × 91.4 cm)

178 *Bougies de Chabbat* (Sabbath candles)

Moche Hazan
Fez, 1950s
Crayon on printed paper
11 × 8 in. (28 × 20.3 cm)

The printed legend reads: "On Friday night, one lights the candles and says a blessing over the candlesticks." (Translated from the French.)

177 Drawing of a Sukkah

Fez, 1950s
Crayon on printed paper
10½ × 6¾ in. (26.4 × 17.1 cm)

180 *Carte de Hanoucca* (Hanukkah drawing)

Eliya Abuhazira

Fez, 1950s
Crayon on colored paper; brown paper
9¼ × 12¾ in. (23.5 × 32.4 cm)

PHOTOGRAPHS

181 Mohammed V

Morocco, c. 1940
Photograph on paper
19 × 17 in. (48 × 43 cm)

182 Hassan II and Rabban Monsenego

Rabat (?), 1960s
Photograph on paper

METALWORK

183 Box of pen nibs

20th century
Steel; paper
2½ × 3½ in. (6.3 × 8.9 cm)

TEXTILES

184 Banner: *Toujours Plus Haut* (Scout's banner)

Fez, mid-20th century
Felt: appliquéd
24 × 8 in. (61 × 20.3 cm)

185 Banners: *Nuit de Bienfaisance* (two banners)

Fez, mid-20th century
Felt: appliquéd
a) 91½ × 18 in. (232.4 × 45.7 cm)
b) 30½ × 8 in. (244 × 20.3 cm)

WOOD

186 Ten Commandments

Morocco, mid-20th century
Wood: painted
24 × 12 in. (60.9 × 30.4 cm)

187 Inkwell and blotter

Morocco, 20th century
Wood; glass; paper
9⅛ × 11¾ in. (23.1 × 30.1 cm; inkwell)

188 Double desk

Morocco, 20th century
Wood; steel
Depth 43⅛ × 29 × 31 in. (109.5 × 73.6 × 78.7 cm)

VIDEOS IN THE EXHIBITION

Hamid Farjad
Producer and Director

Ghasen Ebrahimian
Director of Photography

Sussan Deyhim
Sound Design

JEWISH COMMUNITIES OF
MOROCCO: HISTORY AND
IDENTITY
Daniel J. Schroeter

1. On various traditions and legends regarding the antiquity of Jews in southern Morocco, see Jacques-Meunié 1982, pp. 175–88.
2. On the Berbers, see Camps 1995, and Brett and Fentress 1996.
3. Camps 1995, pp. 31–36.
4. For the first extensive discussions of the theory of the Berber origins of the Jews, see Slouschz 1908, pp. 334–35, and idem 1927; see also Nahon 1909, p. 259. The theory was challenged by Hirschberg 1963, who found little convincing evidence of Berber origins of Jews. Most recently, in an effort to challenge the myth of the Diaspora, Wexler 1996 argues for the Berber origin of much of Sephardic Jewry. On the historical context for this debate, see Schroeter in Abitbol 1997.
5. Simon 1986, pp. 302–04.
6. Hirschberg 1974, pp. 48–52; Goulven 1921.
7. Gattefossé 1935. These traditions are preserved in two texts, one of which is published in Toledano 1911. The text may date from the fifteenth century. See Levy 1991.
8. Examples of this wide network of links between Sijilmasa and the Jewish communities of North Africa and the Middle East in the eleventh century are found in Goitein 1967, pp. 48–49, 55–56, 192, 212–13. For an overview, see Abitbol 1982, pp. 31–32, and Levtzion in Abitbol 1982, pp. 253–63.
9. Ben-Sasson in Abitbol 1997, p. 47.
10. 'Ubayd al-Bakri 1965, p. 115 [p. 226 in French trans.].
11. Corcos 1976, pp. 326–27, states that there were Jews, and even Jewish mercenaries, in Marrakesh at the time of the Almohad conquest. However, Hirschberg 1974, pp. 124–25, does not believe that Jews lived there at the time of conquest.
12. Corcos 1976, pp. 54, 320–21.
13. Hirschberg 1974, pp. 157–63; Shihatah Riyaḥ 1999, pp. 86–89.
14. Africanus 1969, p. 58.
15. Zafrani 1986, pp. 176–77; see also Goldberg 1990, and the

essay by Moshe Idel in this catalog.
16. The influx of Jews to Fez and the foundation of the mellah has been discussed in a number of studies. See especially Gerber 1980, pp. 19, 42–51, and Stillman 1970, pp. 78–81.
17. Levy 1992; Schroeter 1993.
18. Slouschz 1927, pp. 398, 403–05.
19. Aubin 1906, p. 296.
20. Deshen 1989, pp. 8–9, 99–100, 119–22.
21. Corcos 1976, p. 84ff; Brown 1981.
22. Flamand 1959–60, pp. 84–95; Bilu and Levy 1991, p. 290.
23. Lempriere 1794, p. 125.
24. Chaumeil 1953, p. 233.
25. Schroeter 1988.
26. Slouschz 1904.
27. Gerber 1977.
28. Ben-Ami 1998, pp. 41–45.
29. The subject of a massive, though not totally reliable, study by Abraham I. Laredo, Les noms des Juifs du Maroc, 1978.
30. Schroeter in Stillman and Stillman 1999, pp. 88–89.
31. Massa' ba'arav was first published in Berlin in 1792. For an English translation and edition of the book, with excellent commentary, see Stillman and Stillman 1989.
32. Stillman and Stillman 1989, p. 28.
33. Brooke 1831, p. 146.
34. Arama 1994, pp. 70–71. (See pp. 126–30 and cat. nos. 90–94).
35. This is detailed in my forthcoming book The Sultan's Jew: Morocco and the Sephardic World (Palo Alto: Stanford University Press).
36. Miège 1961–62, vol. 2, pp. 569–80, pays considerable attention to this question.
37. Ibn al-Saghir 1997, p. 61ff.
38. Consular protection has been the subject of numerous studies: for one that combines foreign with Moroccan sources, see Kenbib 1996.
39. Toufiq 1980; Kenbib 1994, pp. 235–40; Flamand 1952, pp. 18–20.
40. Frankel 1997.
41. Schroeter 1984; on the impact of the bombardment of Tangier, see Miller 1991.
42. Kenbib 1994, pp. 147–73.
43. Rodrigue 1990, pp. 17–24.
44. The subject of a comprehensive study by Michael M. Laskier, The Alliance Israélite Universelle and

the Jewish Communities of Morocco, 1862–1962, Albany: State University of New York Press, 1983.
45. Miège 1961–62, vol. 2, pp. 574–80; see also idem 1984.
46. George Borrow, The Bible in Spain, London: J. Murray, 1843, p. 31; Picciotto 1875, p. 320.
47. Leibovici 1984, pp. 287–96; Miller 1996; Liberman 1991.
48. Ma'oz 1975, pp. 142–43; Parfitt 1987, pp. 127–58.
49. Bar-Asher 1986.
50. On changes in the status of Jews brought about by the Protectorate, see Bensimon-Donath 1968, pp 102–03; Laskier 1983, pp. 163–65; Chouraqui 1950, p. 63; Kenbib 1994, pp. 407–22.
51. Schroeter and Chetrit 1995.
52. Laskier 1983, pp. 152–63; Gaudefroy-Demombynes 1928, pp. 193–95.
53. Laskier 1983, pp. 226–32, 266–68; Goldenberg 1993.
54. Laskier 1983, pp. 247–51.
55. Adam 1968, vol. 1, pp. 149, 183–204; Tsur and Hillel 1995, pp. 132–33.
56. Lughod 1980, p. 209.
57. Ktan 1990, pp. 164–69, 497–99.
58. Flamand 1959–60, pp. 214–17.
59. Adam 1968, vol. 1, pp. 152–53.
60. Flamand 1959–60 lists about 185 mellahs in the mid-1950s, primarily in the south of Morocco. His list, however, excludes most of the communities of the southeast and the central and northern parts of the country. Fieldwork from 1997 to 1999 in southwestern Morocco also revealed a number of communities not found on Flamand's list. See also Goldberg 1983.
61. Abitbol 1981, p. 69; Laskier 1983.
62. Stillman 1995, pp. 59–64.
63. Laskier 1994, pp. 102–11.
64. Bensimon-Donath 1970, pp. 91–92.
65. Bensimon-Donath 1968, pp. 91–92; Levy 1981, Tsur and Hillel 1995, pp. 225–29.
66. Laskier 1994, p. 203ff.
67. Abitbol 1989, p. 79; 1992, pp. 44–46; Assaraf 1997; Kenbib 1994, pp. 626–29.
68. Laskier 1983, pp. 330–34; Tsur 1995, pp. 229–36.
69. Stillman 1995, pp. 73–76.
70. Bilu 1987, pp. 285–313.
71. On the Moroccan-Jewish dispersion in France and North America, see Lasry and Tapia 1989; Tapia 1986;

Bensimon-Donath 1971.
72. Levy 1997, pp 25–46.
73. Addison 1675, pp. 11–12.

4
CUSTOMS OF THE JEWS OF
MOROCCO
Harvey E. Goldberg

1. Chouraqui 1952; Stillman in Ben-Ami 1982; Zafrani 1983.
2. Ben-Ami 1974, p. 30.
3. Stillman in Ben-Ami 1982, p. 361; Ben-Ami 1974, p. 31.
4. In standard Arabic, the word mushaf is the "name given to a complete text of the Koran considered as a physical object" (Encyclopaedia of Islam, vol. 7, pp. 688–89). It is possible that in the rural context, the term was applied to any printed or bound book, copies of the Koran being the most common examples of such items.
5. Ben-Ami 1981; Bilu 1987.
6. Zafrani 1983, p. 62, n. 2.
7. Toledano 1990.
8. Dobrinsky 1988, pp. 33–36.
9. Benoliel 1977.
10. Laredo 1948.
11. Bar-Asher 1978.
12. Laredo 1948.
13. Ha-Cohen 1978, p. 117.
14. The text of zeved ha-bat can be found in Gaster 1901, p. 180.
15. Zafrani 1983, p. 57.
16. Zafrani 1983, p. 63.
17. Toledano 1990, p. 98.
18. On se'udat mitzvah, and when it is appropriate, see Pollack 1971, pp. 103–04. See also the discussion in Katz 1996, pp. 31–32.
19. Toledano in Ben-Ami 1991, p. 101.
20. Zafrani 1983, pp. 60–61. A song by a popular Israeli singer, Shlomo Bar, makes reference to this custom. The song is discussed in Marcus 1996, p. 23.
21. Marcus 1996.
22. Tedgi 1994, p. 20.
23. Zafrani 1983, p. 107.
24. Encyclopaedia Judaica, vol. 10, p. 756.
25. Deshen 1989.
26. Assouline 1988.
27. Zafrani 1983, p. 101; Assouline 1988, pp. 22–24.
28. The most comprehensive discussion of the topic is found in Ben-Ami 1998; see also Bilu 1987.
29. Goldberg 1983.
30. Goldberg 1990.
31. Stillman in Ben-Ami 1982.
32. Goldziher 1971, p. 259.
33. Geertz 1968; Gellner 1969;

Eickelman 1976; Brown 1977; Rosen 1984. This is just part of the extensive literature on the subject.

34. Goldberg 1990.
35. Goldberg 1978.
36. Bénech 1940; Brunot and Malka 1939; Hirschberg 1972.
37. Zafrani 1983, p. 244.
38. Encyclopaedia Judaica, vol. 22, p. 1075.
39. Other aspects of the festival are explored in Maman in Ben-Ami 1990, pp. 85–95.
40. Ha-Cohen 1978, pp. 303, 322.
41. For a comparative perspective, see Ben-Ami 1972, p. 37; Ha-Cohen 1993, p. 47.
42. Turner 1969.
43. Brown 1977; Rosen 1984, pp. 152–53; Schroeter 1988, pp. 113–15.
44. This legend is, in fact, recorded in Hirschberg 1972, p. 211, and was told to him by one of his interlocutors in Morocco, who was explaining the festival to him.
45. Ben-Ami 1972, pp. 37, 43, n. 17; idem 1973.
46. Bilu 1987; idem 1997–98; Weingrod 1990.
47. Goldberg 1977.

5

THE KABBALAH IN MOROCCO: A SURVEY
Moshe Idel

1. From here to the end of the passage the language is Aramaic.
2. In Aramaic, 'ahiza' be-'ain.
3. MS Jerusalem, National and University Library 1959, fol. 207a. See also the much later eighteenth-century Moroccan codex New York JTS 1805, which contains this version, as mediated by another Moroccan book: Joseph al-Ashqar's Tsafenat Pa'aneah. For a different version of this passage, which does not mention the Moroccan sage, see Goldreich 1984, p. 56, and Goldreich's remarks, pp. 402–03.
4. On the kabbalistic epistle and the type of kabbalistic literature to which it belongs see Scholem 1987, pp. 309–64, especially pp. 349–52.
5. See Vajda 1954, vol. 2, pp. 483–500; idem 1974; idem 1956, pp. 25–71; and more recently Fenton 1991.
6. Idel 1990, pp. 4–15.
7. Vajda 1974, pp. 22–23, and see the important parallel on

p. 26. Idem 1954, p. 140 and n. 1; Sirat 1964, p. 77. A very similar story appears in the anonymous Perush ha-Tefillot, which is close to both Abulafia and to ibn Malka (MS Paris BN MS Hebr. 848, fol. 52b). In the last case, the recipient of the angelic revelation is described as studying, and combinations of letters and divine names are also mentioned in this context. Moreover, according to this story the revealing angel is seen solely by the recipient.

8. Vajda 1974, p. 23, and see also p. 26, where this experience is described as that of the prophets.
9. Vajda 1974, pp. 31, 41.
10. Nahon and Touati 1980, pp. 333–63.
11. Vajda 1954, p. 140, pointed out the affinity between ibn Malka's astro-magic and that of Sefer ha-Tamar, but without entering into the implications for the history of Kabbalah, since he thought that ibn Malka flourished some time in the fourteenth century.
12. Pines 1988, pp. 511–40; idem 1980, pp. 165–251. This theory recurs several times in Sefer ha-'Atzamim.
13. Sha'ar Kevod haShem, fol. 94ab.
14. Vital 1988, p. 22.
15. See note 5 above.
16. Shushan Sodot, fol. 69b; Scholem 1991, pp. 253–54; idem 1930, pp. 285–90.
17. Goldreich 1984, pp. 368, 412.
18. See, for example, MS New York, JTS 1777; MS New York JTS 1853, etc.; MS Sasson 919.
19. Scholem 1956, pp. 379–96.
20. Scholem 1924–25, p. 166; Sack 1981, p. 175; Tishby 1991, p. 19; and Elior 1985, pp. 36–38, established the nexus between this legend and Isaac of Acre.
21. Vajda 1956, pp. 89–92.
22. Elior 1985, p. 59; and Hacker 1999, pp. 597–600.
23. Gottlieb 1976, pp. 248–56.
24. Hallamish 1980, pp. 205–34; idem 1986, pp. 87–131; idem 1983, pp. 29–46.
25. Zafrani 1986.
26. Manor 1988; idem 1983, pp. 67–81; and below note 45.
27. Elior 1985.
28. Moyal 1984.
29. Idel 1992, pp. 166–68.
30. On Hallewah see Idel 1984, pp. 119–48.
31. Idel, "Inquiries in the Doctrine of Sefer ha-Meshiv," 1983,

p. 230.

32. Stahl 1980, pp. 77–86; Goldberg 1990, pp. 249–51.
33. Scholem 1929, pp. 259–76; idem 1930–31, p. 461; and note 19 above.
34. Idel 1991, pp. 21–37.
35. Elior 1985, pp. 60–64.
36. Loc. cit.
37. Ibid., pp. 60–65.
38. MS Paris, Bibliothèque nationale: MS Hebr. 598.
39. Hallamish 1998.
40. For a detailed survey of this kabbalist's books and thought see Hallamish 1990, pp. 85–110, which includes excerpts from Ifargan's books.
41. On Cordovero's influence on Azulai in general see Sack 1987, pp. 372–78, and idem 1981, pp. 164–75.
42. Moyal 1984, pp. 212–15.
43. Tishby 1954.
44. Carlebach 1990.
45. Netiv Mitzwotekha 1983, pp. 6–7. On the meeting with the double see Scholem 1991, pp. 251–60; Idel 1987, pp. 88–95. On the legends relating the Besht to Hayyim ben 'Attar see Manor 1984, pp. 88–110.
46. Rossman 1996, pp. 129–30.
47. See the detailed and informative study in Benayahu 1978, pp. 40–133.
48. See also Hallamish 1990, pp. 33–35.
49. On this book see Scholem 1934, p. 500; Elior 1985, pp. 50–63.
50. Idel, "The Kabbalistic Material . . . ," 1983, pp. 170–73.
51. Elior 1985, pp. 48–49, 60–61.
52. See, for example, Guetta 1989, pp. 79–94; See also idem 1980, p. 62.
53. Fenton 1993, pp. 92–123.
54. Ibid., pp. 94–95.
55. Ibid., pp. 105–11.
56. Zafrani 1968, pp. 366–82.
57. Elior 1985, p. 67.

6

MEMORY, MIMESIS, REALIA
Vivian B. Mann

1. Rubens 1981, fig. 88.
2. Thornton 1994, p. 4.
3. Harper in New York, The Dahesh Museum 1996, p. 61.
4. Rosenthal 1982, p. 44. The discussion following (to the end of the paragraph) is based on Rosenthal 1982, pp. 44–45.
5. "We pass our time scouring the city," [he wrote] "... precautions prohibit visits to the homes of Moors ... In compensation, the interior of

Jewish homes offer the caprice and grace of the Moorish genius ... and the women that we meet there are not the least embellishment. These women are at once beautiful and pleasing, and their habits have a certain dignity that excludes neither grace nor coquetry."

6. Lamprière 1794, pp. 194–96.
7. Fort in New York, The Dahesh Museum 1996, p. 41.
8. BenJelloun, d'Hooghe, and Sijelmassi 1999, p. 10.
9. Eugène Delacroix, Une Noce juive au Maroc, in Le Magasin Pittoresque, 1842.
10. A. Joubin. E. Delacroix. Voyage au Maroc. 1832. Lettres, aquarelles et dessins. Paris 1930, p. 71.
11. Thornton 1994, p. 69.
12. Ibid., p. 66.
13. Ben Ami 1998, pp. 62, 315–18.
14. Israel Museum nos. 304.71, 305.71, and 512.71.
15. Thornton 1994, p. 62.
16. For example, Charles Yriarte's Une Famille riche du Maroc was published in Le Journal Illustré, VI, no. 124, 1866, p. 200, with commentary on p.199; and Henriette Browne's Judenschule in Marocco was printed in Ost und West, 2, 1902, along with J. Portael's Juden aus Tetouan. Later numbers of Ost und West contain additional illustrations of European paintings of Moroccan Jews.
17. On the early history of photography in Morocco, see benJelloun, d'Hooghe, and Sijelmassi 1999.
18. Many postcards concerned with Jewish life in Morocco are reprinted in Goldenberg 1992.
19. Swarzenski 1967.
20. I wish to thank Labelle Prussin for calling my attention to Leo Africanus' references to the Jews of Morocco.
21. His reference to the new section is to the mellah, the quarter established by the king to protect the Jews of Fez by isolating their homes from those of Muslims. See above, p. 34.
22. Hasson 1987, p. 7; see also Brosh 1987, p. 137.
23. In Italy, for example, during the Renaissance, Jews were musicians, dance masters, and dealers in second-hand clothes. In the seventeenth century, the Jews of Venice took over the Ottoman trade, which had been deemed

uneconomical by the Doges.

24. Hasson 1987, p. 10.
25. Dodds 1992, cat. nos. 67–68, 70–72.
26. See Lacave 1984, p. 146.
27. Carretero 1984.
28. Rabbi Adret's text is quoted in ibn Abi Zimra 1882, no. 107 (1178). English translation in Mann 2000, p. 57.
29. Constable 1998, pp. 159–61.
30. On Islamic regulations governing the status of Jews in Muslim lands, see Cohen 1994.
31. Lancet-Muller and Champault 1986, pp. 218–19.
32. I want to thank Rica Cohen Knafo of Caracas for providing the detailed account of the berberisca ceremony (the dressing of the bride in the Grand Costume the night before the wedding ceremony) on which this description is based. My deepest gratitude to Sonia Azagury, who taught me about the costume in its many varieties.
33. Goulven 1927, pp. 32–33.
34. On Muslim practice, see, for example, Denny 1979, p. 44. The Jewish custom of laying a cloth beneath the Torah Scroll is mentioned in Meir ben Barukh 1860, no. 496.
35. Roth 1975, p. 34 of facsimile section.
36. Grammet 1998, nos. 292–94.
37. Narkiss 1982, esp. fig. 161.
38. M. Narkiss 1939, fig. 41.
39. Moscati 1988, pp. 105, 114, 166, 614 (no. 179), 615 (nos. 186, 187), 616 (no. 191), 619 (no. 207).
40. Rabaté 1996, pp. 78, 79; 107–08. I thank Dr. Ivo Grammet for bringing these works to my attention and for suggesting the link between the Jewish tombstones with anthropomorphic forms and the presence of Phoenician settlers.

CATALOG NOTES

1. On these bowls, see Naveh and Shaked 1987.
2. See New York, Yeshiva University Musuem 1992, no. 315, fig. 33.
3. On the veneration of the Zohar, see above, pp. 97–100, Goldberg 1990, pp. 233–58.
4. Paris, Le Petit-Palais 1999, p. 115.
5. Tahon 1994, p. 21, fig. 2.
6. For the Wolfson finials, see Muller-Lancet and Champault 1986, p. 51, no. 64.
7. Tahon 1994, pp. 25–27.
8. Grammet 1998, nos. 292 and 294.
9. Exodus 20:12; Psalms 137:5, and Proverbs 23:25.
10. For a later example of a thumb formed as a rooster's head, see Muller-Lancet and Champault 1986, no. 46.
11. The medieval lamps mentioned here are illustrated in Narkiss 1980, figs. 3 and 5.
12. M. Narkiss 1939, no. 39. A third lamp of this group was sold at auction in 1982 (New York, Sotheby's, *Fine Judaica: Printed Books, Manuscripts, and Works of Art*, June 2–3, 1982, no. 429). Later examples in the Israel Museum, Jerusalem, are M. Narkiss 1939, no. 39, and Muller-Lancet and Champault 1986, nos. 114–15.
13. Schrire 1966, pl. 11.
14. For a photograph of a young Jewish woman wearing such a necklace, and for other examples, see Grammet 1998, pp. 261–63.
15. Muller-Lancet and Champault 1986, p. 224.
16. Paris, Musée d'Art et d'Histoire du Judaïsme 1999, no. 16.
17. For a similar pair of pendants from Rabat, see Gotzmann 1990–91, fig. 11.
18. Grammet 1998, pp. 219 and 225.
19. For example, see Chicarro y de Dios and Fernández Gomez 1984, p. 193, no. 13, pl. 61.
20. Muller-Lancet and Champault 1986, p. 208.
21. For other examples, see *ibid.*, pp. 208–09. Another is in the collection of the Eretz Israel Museum, Tel Aviv, Judaica section. For a similar headdress, see Rabaté 1996, p. 49.
22. Hoshen 1999, p. 25.
23. Grammet 1998, no. 586.
24. For photographs of women from Ida ou Semlal wearing similar fibulae, see *ibid.*, pp. 245 and 250; for parallels, see *op. cit.*, cat. nos. 351–52 and 355.
25. For a similar pair of fibulae, see *ibid.*, cat. no. 322.
26. For similar work, see Rabaté and Goldenberg 1996, p. 160, no. 1; and Gotzmann 1990–91, fig. 4.
27. Paris, Musée d'Art et d'Histoire du Judaïsme 1999, pls. 1 and 20.
28. *Op. cit.*, pl. 19.
29. For similar silver beads, see Grammet 1998, no. 589.
30. For similar rings, see *ibid.*, pl. 264.
31. The watercolor *Un Maure et une mauresque sur leur terrasse* is in The Metropolitan Museum, New York, while the painting is in Edinburgh.
32. The second belongs to the Salander O'Reilly Gallery, New York.
33. London, Christies 1998, lot no. 88.
34. Shadur and Shadur 1994, pls. 28–32, 35.
35. See, for example, Muller-Lancet and Champault 1986, pp. 199, 216–17.
36. *Ibid.*, no. 197.
37. For a similar example, see Muller-Lancet and Champault 1986, no. 245.
38. Schrire 1966, pp. 87–89.
39. *Ibid.*, p. 104.
40. For a similar – but not identical – amulet, see Muller-Lancet and Champault 1986, no. 247.
41. Schrire 1966, p. 61.
42. Goldenberg 1992, p. 68.
43. Goldenberg 1992, p. 185.
44. "*Aquisiciones, Donaciones y Depósitos*," *Museo Sefardi Noticias*, 15, 1997, p. 4; Christies, Amsterdam 1989, no. 154, where the date is erroneously given as ?1790.
45. Golombek 1988, p. 32.
46. Spring and Hudson 1995, p. 55.
47. New York, Yeshiva University Museum 1992, no. 86.11, with motifs of a house and a lamp; Israel Museum, Jerusalem, 187/63 (star) and nos. 187/71 (star and lamp).
48. Grammat 1998, no. 238.
49. Other shirts embroidered with similar compositions are published in *ibid.*, no. 286, and Muller-Lancet and Champault 1986, p. 388.
50. *Ibid.*, p. 220.
51. Muller-Lancet and Champault 1986, no. 420.
52. Spring and Hudson 1995, p. 71.
53. Stone 1985, no. 79.
54. BenJelloun, d'Hooghe, and Sijelmassi 1999, pl. 28.
55. Spring and Hudson 1995, no. 59.
56. In a parallel custom, Ashkenazi grooms wear a white robe (*kittel*), part of the death shrouds, beneath the wedding canopy, and crush a glass in remembrance of the destruction of Jerusalem.
57. Paris, Institut du Monde Arabe, cat. no. 1553.
58. Spring and Hudson 1995, p. 57
59. Carretero 1988, p. 122. The New York textile is no. 1902-1-310.
60. For example, a textile published in Dodds 1992, no. 92, and a tile published in Sijelmassi 1986, p. 231.
61. Kühnel 1924, fig. 15.
62. Paris, Institut du Monde Arabe, cat. no. 1555.
63. Another bag with a flowering tree is in the Israel Museum, Jerusalem (Lancet-Muller and Champault 1986, p. 153).
64. For a hanging with similar red and green coloration, see Marrakesh, Medina 1999, p.60.
65. A *sukkah* (pl. *sukkot*) is a booth erected during the fall holiday of Sukkot to comemmorate the Israelites' wandering in the Wilderness of Sinai.
66. This account is based on Bensimon 1994, pp. 56–57.

BIBLIOGRAPHY

Abitbol, Michel. "Zionist Activity in the Maghreb," *The Jerusalem Quartery,* 21 (1981), p. 69.

Ed., *Communautés juives des marges sahariennes du Maghreb.* Jerusalem: Ben-Zvi Institute, 1982.

The Jews of North Africa during the Second World War. Detroit: Wayne State University Press, 1989.

Ed., *Relations judéo-musulmanes au Maroc.* Paris: Éditions Stavit, 1997.

Adam, André. *Casablanca: essai sur la transformation de la société marocaine au contact de l'Occident.* Paris: Éditions du Centre National de la Recherche Scientifique, 1968.

Addison, Lancelot. *The Present State of the Jews.* London: by J.C. for William Crooke, 1675.

Ibn Adret, Solomon. *Teshuvot u-She'a lot le-hasRashba,* Rome: 1470.

Africanus, Johannes Leo. *Description de L'Afrique.* London, 1556; 2nd ed., Amsterdam: De Capo Press, 1969.

Arama, Maurice. *Itinéraire Marocains regards de peintres.* Paris: Les Éditions Jaguar, 1991.

Assaraf, Robert. *Mohammed V et les Juifs du Maroc: L'Époque de Vichy.* Paris: Plon, 1997.

Assouline, Chalom Rotariel. "Ḥayyei haYehudim be-Mazagan," *Zivhei Elohim, leYosef Asulin* [Tunis, 1934], rev. ed. C.R. Assouline, Jerusalem: Agudat Brit Avraham – Brit Shalom, 1988, pp. 19–43.

Aubin, Eugène. *Morocco of Today.* London: J.M. Dent & Co., 1906.

Bar-Asher, Moshe. "Al hayesodot ha-ivriyim be-aravit meduberet shel Yehudei Maroko," *Leshonenu* 52 (1978), pp. 163–89.

Bar-Asher, Shalom. "The Jews of North Africa and the Land of Israel in the Eighteenth and Nineteenth Centuries: The Reversal in Attitude toward Aliyah from 1770 to 1860," *The Land of Israel: Jewish Perspectives,* ed. Lawrence A. Hoffman, Notre Dame, IN: University of Notre Dame Press, 1986, pp. 298–310.

Ben-Ami, Issachar. "Hag hamimuna shel Yehudei Tzfon Afriqa," *Yeda Am* 16 (1972), p. 37.

"Le Mariage traditionnel chez les Juifs Marocains," eds. Issachar Ben-Ami and Dov Noy, *Studies in Marriage Customs. Folklore Research Center Studies,* vol. 4, Jerusalem: The Magnes Press, 1974 (Hebrew).

"Folk Veneration of Saints among the Moroccan Jews: Continuity and Change. The Case of the Holy Man, Rabbi David u-Moshe," *Studies in Judaism and Islam,* eds. S. Morag, I. Ben-Ami, and N. Stillman, Jerusalem: The Magnes Press, 1981, pp. 283–344.

Ed., *The Sephardi and Oriental Jewish Heritage Studies.* Jerusalem: The Magnes Press, 1982 (Hebrew).

Ed., *Recherches sur la culture des Juifs d'Afrique du Nord.* Jerusalem: Communauté Israélite Nord Africaine, 1991.

Saint Veneration among the Jews in Morocco. Detroit: Wayne State University Press, 1998.

Benayahu, Meir. "R. Abraham ben Musa and his Son," *Michael,* 5 (1978), pp. 40–133. (Hebrew).

Bénech, José. *Essai d'explication d'un mellah.* Marrakech, 1940.

BenJelloun, Tahar, Alain d' Hooghe, and Mohamed Sijelmassi. *Le Désir du Maroc.* Paris: Marval, 1999.

Benoliel, Jose. *Dialecto Judeo-Hispano-Marroquí o Hakitia.* Madrid, 1977.

Bensimon-Donath, Doris. *Evolution du judaïsme marocain sous le Protectorat français, 1912–1956.* Paris: Mouton, 1968.

Immigrants d'Afrique du nord en Israel. Paris: Éditions Anthropos, 1970. *L'Intégration des Juifs nord-africains en France.* Paris: Mouton, 1971.

Bensimon, Raphael. *Le Judaïsme Marocain. Folklore: du berceau à la tombe.* Lod: Orot Yahadout haMaghreb, 1994 (Hebrew).

Bilu, Yorum. "Dreams and the Wishes of the Saint," *Judaism Viewed from Within and from Without.* ed. Harvey E. Goldberg, Albany: State University of New York Press, 1987, pp. 285–313.

"The Sanctification of Place in Israel's Civil and Traditional Religion," *Jerusalem Studies in Jewish Folklore,* 19–20 (1997–98), pp. 65–84 (Hebrew).

Bilu, Yoram, and André Levy. "Nostalgia and Ambivalence: The Reconstruction of Jewish–Muslim Relations in Oulad Mansour," *Sephardic and Middle Eastern Jewries.* Bloomington: Indiana University Press, 1991.

Borrow, George. *The Bible in Spain.* London: John Murray, 1843.

Brett, Michael, and Elizabeth Fentress. *The Berbers.* Oxford: Blackwell, 1996.

Brooke, Arthur de Capell. *Sketches in Spain and Morocco.* London: Henry Colburn and Richard Bentley, 1831.

Brown, Kenneth. "Changing Forms of Patronage in a Moroccan City," *Patrons and Clients in the Mediterranean,* ed. E. Gellner and J. Waterbury, London: Duckworth, 1977, pp. 304–28.

"Mellah and Medina: A Moroccan City and its Jewish Quarter (Salé ca. 1880–1930)," *Studies in Judaism and Islam,* ed. Shelomo Morag, *et al.,* Jerusalem: The Magnes Press, 1981, pp. 254–55.

Brunot, Louis, and Elie Malka. *Textes judéo-arabes de Fès.* Rabat, 1939.

Camps, Gabriel. *Les Berbères: mémoire et identité,* 3rd ed. Paris: Éditions Errance, 1995.

Carlebach, Elisheva. *The Pursuit of Heresy: R. Moses Hagis and the Sabbatean Controversy.* New York: Colombia 1990.

Carretero, Concha Herraro. *Museo de Telas Medievales. Monasterio de Santa Maria La Real de Huelgas.* Madrid: Editorial Patrimonio Nacional, 1988.

Chaumeil, Jean. "Le Mellah de Tahala au pays des Ammeln," *Hespéris,* 40 (1953), p. 233.

Chicago, DePaul University Gallery. *Weaving Cultures: Textiles and Jewelry of Morocco.* Exhib. bro., 2000.

Chicarro y de Dios, Fernández, and Fernández Gomez, *Catálogo del Museo Argueológico Provincial de Sevilla.* Madrid, 1984.

Chouraqui, André. *La Condition juridique de l'Israélite marocain.* Paris: Presses du Livre Français, 1950.

Marche vers l'Occident les Juifs d'Afrique du Nord. Paris: PUF, 1952.

Cohen, Mark R. *Under Crescent and Cross: The Jews in the Middle Ages.* Princeton: Princeton University Press, 1994.

Constable, Olivia Remie. *Trade and Traders in Muslim Spain.* New York: Cambridge University Press, 1998.

Corcos, David. *Studies in the History of the Jews of Morocco.* Jerusalem: Rubin Mass, 1976 (Hebrew).

Denny, Walter B. Oriental Rugs. New York: Smithsonian National Museum, 1979.

Deshen, Shlomo. *The Mellah Society: Jewish Community Life in Sherifian Morocco.* Chicago: University of Chicago Press, 1989.

Dobrinsky, Herbert. *A Treasury of Sephardic Laws and Customs.* Hoboken: Ktav, 1988.

Dodds, Jerrilyn, ed. *Al-Andalus. The Art of Islamic of Spain.* Exhib. cat. New York: Metropolitan Museum of Art, 1992.

Eickelman, D. *Moroccan Islam.* Austin: University of Texas Press, 1976.

Elior, Rachel. "The Kabbalists of Dra," *Pe'amim,* 24 (1985), p. 59 (Hebrew).

Encyclopaedia Judaica. Jerusalem: Keter Publishing House, 1972.

Encyclopaedia of Islam, new edition. Leiden: Brill, 1960.

"Exotische Juden," Ost und Ouest, 1 (1901), p. 939.

Fenton, Paul B., ed. *Judah ben Nissim ibn Malka's Judeo-Arabic Commentary on the Pirkey Rabbi Eli'ezer.* Jerusalem, 1991.

"Rabbi Makhluf Amsalem – A Morrocan Alchemist and Kabbalist," *Pe'amim,* 55 (1993), pp. 92–123 (Hebrew).

Flamand, Pierre. *Un mellah en pays berbère: Demnate.* Paris: Librairie Générale de Droit & de Jurisprudence, 1952.

Diaspora en terre d'Islam: les communautés israélites du sud marocain. Casablanca: Imprimeries réunies, 1959–60.

Frankel, Jonathan. *The Damascus Affair: "Ritual Murder," Politics, and the Jews in 1840.* New York: Cambridge University Press, 1997.

Gaster, Moses, ed. *The Book of Prayer and Order of Service According to the Custom of the Spanish and Portuguese Jews.* London: Henry Frowde, 1901.

Gattefossé, J. "Juifs et Chrétiens du Dra' avant l'Islam," *Bulletin de la Société de Préhistoire du Maroc,* 3–4 (1935), pp. 39–66.

Gaudefroy-Demombynes, R. *L'Œuvre française en matière d'enseignement au Maroc.* Paris: Librarie Orientaliste Paul Geuthner, 1928.

Geertz, Clifford. *Islam Observed.* New Haven: Yale University Press, 1968.

Gellner, E. *Saints of the Atlas.* Chicago: University of Chicago Press, 1969.

Gerber, Jane S. "Palestine and Morocco and the Bonds of Peoplehood," *Shiv' im: Essays and Studies in Honor of Ira Eisenstein,* ed. Ronald A. Brauner, Philadelphia: Reconstructionist Rabbinical College, 1977, pp. 119–25.

Jewish Society in Fez, 1450–1700. Leiden: E.J. Brill, 1980.

Goitein, S.D. *A Mediterranean Society,* 5 vols., *Economic Foundations.* Berkeley: University of California Press, 1967.

Goldberg, Harvey E. "Introduction: Culture and Ethnicity in the Study of Israeli Society," *Ethnic Groups,* 1 (1977), pp. 163–86.

"The Mimuna and the Minority Status of Moroccan Jews," *Ethnology,* 17 (1978), pp. 75–87.

"The Mellahs of Southern Morocco: Report of a Survey," *The Maghreb Review,* 8, 3–4 (1983), pp. 61–69.

"The Zohar in Southern Morocco: A Study in the Ethnography of Texts," *History of Religions,* 29, 3(1990), pp. 233–58.

Goldenberg, André, ed. *Les Juifs du Maroc. Images et Textes.* Paris: Éditions du Scribe, 1992.

"Les Juifs du Maroc et l'Alliance: Les Écoles de Bled," *Les Cahiers de l'Alliance Israélite Universelle,* 5 N.S. (1993), pp. 23–24.

Goldziher, Ignaz. "Veneration of Saints in Islam," *Muslim Studies,* vol. 2, trans. C. R. Barber and S. M. Stern, London: Allen and Unwin, 1971, pp. 255–341.

Golombek, Lisa. "The Draped Universe of Islam," *Content and Context of Visual Arts in the Islamic World,* ed. Priscilla Soucek, University Park and London: Pennsylvania State Press, 1988, pp. 25–49.

Gottlieb, Efrayyim. *Studies in the Kabbalah Literature,* ed. J. Hacker, Tel Aviv: Tel Aviv University, 1976, pp. 248–56 (Hebrew).

Gotzmann, Andreas. "Some Characteristics of Moroccan Jewish Jewelry," *Jewish Art,* 16–17 (1990–91), pp. 12–19.

Goulven, J. "Notes sur les origines anciennes des Israélites du Maroc," *Hespéris,* 1 (1921), pp. 326–29.

Les Mellahs de Rabat-Salé. Paris, 1927.

Grammet, Ivo. *Splendeurs du Maroc.* Exhib. cat. Tervuren: Musée royal de l'Afrique centrale, 1998.

Guetta, Alessandro. "Due Lettere de Aime Palliere a Elia Benamozegh," *Gli Ebrei in Toscana du Medievo al Risorgimento Fatti E Momenti.* Florence: L.S. Olschki, 1980.

"Elia Benamozegh, Un Cabbalista nel secolo dell' Idealismo," *Bailamme,* 4 (1989), pp. 79–94.

Guiffrey, J. *Le Voyage de Eugène Delacroix au Maroc,* vol. 4,Paris: 1909.

Hacker, Joseph. "Maghrebi Jews in Egypt and Jerusalem in the Late 15th Century and Intellectual Activity Under Mameluk Rule," *Studies in the Talmud and Medieval Rabbinic Literature in Honor of Professor Haim Zalman Dimitrovsky.* Jerusalem: The Magnes Press, 1999, pp. 597–600.

Ha-Cohen, Mordecai. *Higgid Mordecai: Histoire de la Libys et de ses juifs lieux d'habitation et coutumes.* Jerusalem: Ben Zvi Institute, 1978 (Hebrew).

Hallamish, Moshe. "The Kabbalists in Morocco," *MiMizrah u-Mima'arav,* 2 (1980), pp. 205–34 (Hebrew).

"On the Categories of Kabbalistic Composition in Morocco," *Pe'amim,* 15 (1983), pp. 29–46 (Hebrew).

"On the Kabbalists in Morocco (Corrections and Additions)," *Daat,* 16 (1986), pp. 87–131

"R. Jacob Ifargan and his Books," *Pe'amim,* 43 (1990): 85–110 (Hebrew). Ed., *Ginnat Beitan.* Jerusalem, 1998.

Hasson, Rachel. *Later Islamic Jewellery.* Jerusalem: L.A. Meyer Memorial Institute for Islamic Art, 1987.

Hirschberg, Haim Ze'ev. "The Problem of the Judaized Berbers," *Journal of African History,* 4 (1963), pp. 313–39

"La 'Mimouna' et les festivités de la fin de la fête de Pâques," *Zakhor le-Avraham. Memorial Volume for A. Elmaleh,* ed. H.Z. Hirschberg, Jerusalem: Vaad Adat ha-Mugrabim, 1972: 206–35.

A History of the Jews in North Africa, vol. 1: *From Antiquity to the Sixteenth Century.* Leiden, E.J. Brill, 1974.

Hoshen, Sarah Harel. *Juifs parmis les Berbères. Photographies d'Elias Harrus.* Tel-Aviv: Beth Hatefusoth, 1999.

Ibn al-Saghir, Khalid. *Al-Maghrib wa-Baritaniya al-'uzma fi al-qarn al-tasi' ashar: 1856–1886.* Rabat: Jami'a Manshawarat Kuliyat al-Adab wa-l-'Ulum al-Iñsaniyya, 1997.

Idel, Moshe. "Inquiries in the Doctrine of Sefer haMeshiv," *Sefunot,* 17 (1983), p. 230 (Hebrew).

"The Kabbalistic Material from the School of R. David ben Yehudah he-Ḥasid," *Jerusalem Studies in Jewish Thought.* 2 (1983), pp. 170–73 (Hebrew).

"R. Yehudah Halewah and his Book *Tzafnat Pa'aneaḥ,*" *Shalem,* 4 (1984), pp. 119–48 (Hebrew).

The Mystical Experience of Abraham Abulafia. Albany: State University of New York Press, 1987

"The Beginning of Kabbalah in North Africa? – A Forgotten Document by R. Yehudah ben Nissim ibn Malka," *Pe'amim,* 43 (1990):4–15 (Hebrew).

Introduction to Sefer Tsafenat Pa'aneah. Jerusalem: Misgav Yerushalayim, 1991, pp. 21–37 (Hebrew).

"Spanish Kabbalah after the Expulsion," *Moreshet Sefarad: The Sephardi Legacy,* ed. H. Beinart, Jerusalem: The Magnes Press, 1992: vol. 2., pp. 166–68.

Isaac of Acre. *Me'irat Einayyim,* ed. A. Goldreich, Jerusalem, 1984.

Jacques-Meunié, D. *Le Maroc saharien des origines au XVIe siècle.* 2 vols. Paris: Librairie Klincksieck, 1982.

Kalder, Diane. *The Collection on Samuel J. and Ethel Le Frank.* New York: The Le Frank Organization, 1988, pp. 12–14.

Katz, Jacob. "Traditional Jewish Society and Modern Society," *Jews among Muslims: Communities in the Precolonial Middle East,* ed. S. Deshen and W.P. Zenner, Basingstoke: Macmillan, 1996, pp. 31–32.

Kenbib, Mohammed. *Juifs et Musulmans au Maroc, 1859–1948.* Rabat: Université Mohammed V, Publications de la Faculté des Lettres et des Sciences Humaines, 1994.

Les Protégés: contribution à l'histoire contemporaine du Maroc. Rabat: Université Mohammed V, Publications de la Faculté des Lettres et des Sciences Humaines, 1996.

Ktan, Yvette. *Oujda, une ville frontière du Maroc (1907–1956): Musulmans, Juifs et Chrétiens en milieu Colonial.* Paris: Éditions L'Harmattan, 1990.

Kühnel, Ernst. *Maurische Kunst.* Berlin: Bruno Cassirer Verlag, 1924. Lacave, José Luis. *Sefarad, Sefarad. La España Judía,* Madrid, 1984.

La Cave, José Luis. *Sefaral, Sefarad. La España Judía.* Madrid: n.p., 1984.

Laredo, Abraham. "Las Taqqanot de los expulsados de Castilla en Marruecos y su regimen matrimonial y successoral," *Sefarad*, 8 (1948), pp. 245–76.

Les Noms des Juifs du Maroc. Madrid: Consejo Superior de Investigaciones científicas Instituto 'B. Arias Montano,' 1978.

Laskier, Michael M. *The Alliance Israélite Universelle and the Jewish Communities of Morocco, 1862–1962.* Albany: State University of New York Press, 1983.

"The Evolution of Zionist Activity in the Jewish Communities of Morocco, Tunisia and Algeria: 1897–1947," *Studies in Zionism*, 4 (1983), pp. 205–07.

Yehudei haMagreb betsel Vishi utselav ha keres. Tel-Aviv: Tel-Aviv University. HaMakhon leḥeker haTefutsot, 1992.

North African Jewry in the Twentieth Century: The Jews of Morocco, Tunisia, and Algeria. New York: New York University Press, 1994.

Lasry, Jean-Claude, and Claude Tapia, eds. *Les Juifs du Maghreb: diasporas contemporaines.* Paris: L'Harmattan, 1989.

Leibovici, Sarah. *Chronique des Juifs de Tétouan.* Paris: Éditions Maisonneuve & Larose, 1984.

Lemprière, William. *A Tour from Gibraltar to Tangier, Sallee, Mogodore, Santa Cruz, and Tarudant; and thence, over Mount Atlas to Morocco,* 3rd ed. Philadelphia: Printed by T. Dobson, 1794.

Levy, André. "To Morocco and Back: Tourism and Pilgrimage among Moroccan-Born Israelis," *Grasping Land: Space and Place in Contemporary Israeli Discourse and Experience,* ed. Eyal Ben-Ari and Yorum Bilu, Albany: State University of New York Press, 1997, pp. 25–46.

Levy, Simon. "Les Juifs et la libération nationale au Maroc," *Les Sepharades et la paix,* ed. Shalom Cohen, *et al.,* Tel Aviv: Perspectives Nouvelles. 1981, pp. 87–90.

"Légende et tradition écrite dans la Tarïh Wad Dr'a," *Les études littéraires universitaires au Maroc.* Rabat: Université Mohammed V, Publications de la Faculté des Lettres et des Sciences Humaines, 1991, pp. 55–67.

"Hara et mellah: les mots, l'histoire et l'institution," *Histoire et Linguistique,* ed. Abdelahad Sebti, Rabat: Université Mohammed V, Publications de la Faculté des Lettres et des Sciences Humaines, 1992, pp. 41–50.

Lughod, Janet L. Abu. *Rabat: Urban Apartheid in Morocco.* Princeton: Princeton University Press, 1980.

Malka, Judah ibn. "Les Observations critiques d'Isaac d'Acco sur les ouvrages de Juda ben Nissim ibn Malka," 115 [N.S. 15] (1956), pp. 25–71.

Kitab Uns we-Tafsir, ed. Georges Vajda, Ramat-Gan: Bar Ilan University, 1974.

Judaeo-Arabic Commentary on the Pirkey Rabbi Eli`ezer with a Hebrew Translation and Supercommentary by Isaac b. Samuel of Acco. ed. Paul B. Fenton, Jerusalem, 1991.

Malka, Yehudah ibn. *Kitab Uns we-Tafsir.* Ramat Gan: Bar-Ilan, 1974

Mann, Vivian B. *Jewish Texts on the Visual Arts.* Cambridge, New York, Melbourne, Madrid: Cambridge University Press, 2000.

Manor, Dan. "Kabbalah in the Homilies of R. Joseph Adhan," *Pe'amim,* 15 (1983), pp. 67–81 (Hebrew).

"R. Ḥayyim ben Attar in Ḥasidic Tradition," *Pe'amim,* 20 (1984), pp. 88–110 (Hebrew).

Exile and Redemption in Moroccan Jewish Philosphy. Lod: Habermann Institute for Literary Research, 1988 (Hebrew).

Ma'oz, Moshe. "Changes in the Position of the Jewish Community of Palestine during the Ottoman Period," *Studies on Palestine during the Ottoman Period.* Jerusalem: The Magnes Press, 1975.

Marcus, Ivan. *Rituals of Childhood: Jewish Culture and Acculturation in the Middle Ages.* New Haven and London: Yale University Press, 1996.

Marrakesh, Medina. *Points et entrelacs. Broderies et tissages du Maroc. Collections Tami Tazi and Lucien Viola.* Exhib. cat., 1999.

Meir ben Barukh of Rothenburg. *She'a lot uTeshuvot Maharam,* Lvov: 1860.

Miège, Jean-Louis. *Le Maroc et l'Europe: 1830–1894,* 4 vols. Paris: Presses Universitaires de France, 1961–62.

"Les Juifs de Gibraltar au XIXe siècle," *Les Relations intercommunautaires juives en méditerranée occidentale, XIIe–XXe siècles.* Paris: Éditions du Centre National de la Recherche Scientifique, 1984, pp. 99–103.

Miller, Susan Gilson. "Crisis and Community: The People of Tangier and the French Bombardment of 1844," *Middle Eastern Studies,* 27, 4 (1991), pp. 583–96.

"Kippur on the Amazon: Jewish Emigration from Northern Morocco in the Late Nineteenth Century," *Sephardi and Middle Eastern Jewries,* ed. Harvey E. Goldberg, Bloomington: Indiana University Press, 1996.

Moyal, Elie. *The Shabetaian Movement in Morocco – Its History and Sources.* Tel Aviv: Am Oved, 1984 (Hebrew).

Muller-Lancet, Aviva, and Dominique Champault, eds. *La Vie juive au maroc.* Exhib. cat. Jerusalem, Israel Museum, 1986.

Nahon, G., and Ch. Touati, eds. "Le Sefer haTamar et les Maggidim des Kabbalists," *Hommage Georges Vajda,* Louvain: Peeters, 1980, pp. 333–63.

Nahon, Moïse. "Les Israélites du Maroc," *Revue des Études Ethnographiques et Sociologiques,* 2 (1909), p. 259.

Narkiss, Bezalel. "Un objet de culte: la lampe de Hanuka," *Art et Archéologie des Juifs en France médiévale,* ed. Bernhard Blumenkranz, Toulouse: Privat, 1980.

Narkiss, Mordecai. *The Hanukkah Lamp.* Jerusalem: Bney Bezalel Publishing Company, 1939.

Naveh, Joseph, and Shaul Shaked. *Amulets and Magic Bowls.* Jerusalem: The Magnes Press, 1987.

New York, Dahesh Museum. *Picturing the Middle East – A Hundred Years of European Orientalism.* Exhib. cat., 1996.

New York, The Jewish Museum. *The Fabric of Jewish Life.* Exhib. cat., 1977.

The Jewish Museum 1992–1994. Pamphlet, 1995.

The Jewish Museum 1996–1998. Pamphlet, 1999.

New York, The Metropolitan Museum of Art. *The Private Collection of Edgar Degas.* Exhib. cat., 1997.

New York, Yeshiva University Museum. *The Sephardic Journey: 1492–1992.* Exhib. cat., 1992.

Parfitt, Tudor. *The Jews in Palestine.* Woodbridge, Suffolk: Boydell Press, 1987.

Paris, Institut du Monde Arabe. *Delacroix in Morocco.* Exhib. cat., Flammarion, 1994.

Paris, Le Petit-Palais. *Maroc. Les Trésors du royaume.* Exhib. cat., 1999.

Paris, Musée d'Art et d'Histoire du Judaïsme. *Parures. Bijoux des juifs du Maroc,* 1999.

Peltre, Christine. *Orientalism in Art,* trans. John Goodman, New York, London, Paris: Abbeville, 1998.

Picciotto, James. *Sketches of Anglo-Jewish History.* London: Trubner & Co., 1895.

Pines, Shlomo. "Shi'ite Terms and Conceptions in Judah Halevi's Kuzari," *Jerusalem Studies in Arabic and Islam* (1980), pp. 165–251.

"On the Term *Ruhaniyyut* and its Sources and Influence on Judah Halevi's Doctrine," *Tarbiz,* 57 (1988), pp. 511–40 (Hebrew).

Pollack, Herman. Jewish Folkways in Germanic Lands (1648–1806). Cambridge, MA: the MIT Press, 1971.

Rabaté, Jacques, and Marie-Rose Rabaté. *Bijoux du Maroc.* Aix-en-Provence: Édisud, 1999.

Rabaté, Marie-Rose and André Goldenberg. *Bijoux du Maroc.* Aix-en-Provence: Édisud/Le Fennec, 1996.

Robaut, Alfred. *L'Oeuvre complet de Eugène Delacroix.* 1885

Rochester, Memorial Art Gallery of the University of Rochester. *Orientalism. The Near East in French Painting 1800–1880.* By Donald A. Rosenthal. Exhib. cat., 1982.

Rodrigue, Aron. *French Jews, Turkish Jews: The Alliance Israélite Universelle and the Politics of Jewish Schooling in Turkey, 1860–1925,* Albany: State University of New York Press, 1983.

Rosen, Lawrence. *Bargaining for Reality: The Construction of Social Relations in a Muslim Community.* Chicago: University of Chicago Press, 1984.

Rossman, Moshe. *Founder of Hasidism.* Berkeley: University of California Press, 1996.

Roth, Cecil. *The Sarajevo Haggadah.* Belgrade: Beogradske Izdavacko-Graficki Zavod, 1975.

Rubens, Alfred. *A History of Jewish Costume,* rev. ed. London: Peter Owen Limited, 1981.

Sack, Bracha. "On the Sources of R. Abraham Azulai's book Ḥesed leAvraham," *Qiryat Sefer,* 56 (1981), pp. 164–75 (Hebrew).

"The Influence of Cordovero on Seventeenth-Century Jewish Thought," *Jewish Thought in the Seventeenth Century*. Eds. I. Laversky and B. Septimus, Cambridge, MA: Harvard University Press, 1987, pp. 372–78.

Scholem, Gershom. "An Unknown Story about the Finding of the Book of the Zohar," *Qiryat Sefer*, 1 (1924–25), p. 166 (Hebrew).

"Sefer 'Avnei Zikkaron," *Qiryat Sefer*, 6 (1929), pp. 259–76 (Hebrew).

"Eine Kabbalistische Erklaerung der Prophetie als Selbstbegenung," *MGWJ*, 74 (1930), pp. 285–90.

"An Index to the Commentaries to the Ten Sefirot," *Qiryat Sefer*, 10 (1934).

"Isaac of Acco's Commentary on the First Chapter of the Book of Formation," *Qiryat Sefer* (1956), pp. 379–96 (Hebrew).

Origins of the Kabbalah, ed. Zwi Werblowsky, trans. Allan Arkush, JPS and Princeton University Press, 1987.

On the Mystical Shape of the Godhead. New York: The Schocken Books, 1991.

Schrire, T. *Hebrew Amulets. Their Decipherment and Interpretation*. London: Routledge & Kegan Paul, 1966.

Schroeter, Daniel J. "Anglo-Jewry and Essaouira (Mogador), 1860–1900: The Social Implications of Philanthropy," *Transactions of the Jewish Historical Society of England*, 28 (1984), pp. 62–63.

Merchants of Essaouira: Urban Society and Imperialism in Southwestern Morocco, 1844–1886. Cambridge: Cambridge University Press, 1988.

"The Jewish Quarter and the Moroccan City," *New Horizons in Sephardic Studies*, ed. Yedida K. Stillman and George K. Zucker, Albany: State University of New York Press, 1993, pp. 67–81.

Schroeter, Daniel J., and Joseph Chetrit. "Reform of Jewish Institutions in Morocco at the Beginning of the Colonial Government (1912–1919)," *Miqqedem Umiyyam*, 6 (1995), pp. 71–103.

Sérullaz, Maurice. *Mémorial de l'exposition Eugène Delacroix ...* Paris: 1963.

Shadur, Joseph, and Yehudit Shadur. *Jewish Papercuts. A History and a Guide*. Berkeley and Jerusalem: The Judah L. Magnes Museum and Gefen Publishing House Ltd., 1994.

Shihatah Riyah, 'Ata 'Ali Muhammad. *al-Yahud fi bilad al-Maghrib al-Aqsa fi 'ahd al-Mariniyin wa-al-Wattasiyin*. Damascus: Dar al-Shafiq, 1999.

Sijelmassi, Mohamed. *Les Arts traditionnels au Maroc*. Paris: ACR Éditions, 1986.

Simon, Marcel. *Verus Israel*. New York: Oxford University Press, 1986.

Sirat, Colette. *Les Theories des visions surnaturelles*. Leiden: Brill, 1964.

Slouschz, Nahum. "La Colonie des Maghrabim en Palestine," *Archives Marocaines*, 2 (1904), pp. 239–56.

"Hebræo-Phéniciens et Judéo-Berbères," *Archives Marocaines* 14 (1908), pp. 334–35.

Travels in North Africa. Philadelphia: Jewish Publication Society of America, 1927.

Spring, Christopher, and Julie Hudson. *North African Textiles*. London: British Museum Press, 1995.

Stahl, Abraham. "Ritual Reading of the Zohar," *Pe'amim*, 5 (1980), pp. 77–86 (Hebrew).

Stillman, Norman A. *The Jews of Arab Lands*. Philadelphia: The Jewish Publication Society of America, 1970.

Sephardic Religious Responses to Modernity. Luxembourg: Harwood Academic Publishers, 1995.

Stillman, Norman A., and Yedida K. Stillman. *Travail in an Arab Land*. Tuscaloosa: University of Alabama Press, 1989.

Stillman, Norman A., and Yedida K. Stillman, eds. "Morocco, England, and the End of the Sephardic World Order," *From Iberia to Diaspora*, Leiden: Brill, 1999, pp. 88–89.

Stone, Caroline. *The Embroideries of North Africa*. London: Longman, 1985.

Swarzenski, Hanns. *Monuments of Romanesque Art*. Chicago: University of Chicago Press, 2nd ed., 1967.

Tahon, Dahlit. "Rifdunei ba Tapuḥim," *Rimonim*, 4 (1994), p. 21.

Tapia, Claude. *Les Juifs sépharades en France: 1965–1985*. Paris: L'Harmattan, 1986.

Tedgi, Joseph. *Le Livre et l'imprimerie hébraïque à Fes*. Jerusalem: Institute Ben-Zvi, 1994 (Hebrew).

Thornton, Lynn. *The Orientalists. Painter-Travellers*. Paris: Poche-Couleur, 1994.

Tishby, Isaiah, ed. *Tizizat Novel Tzevi*. Jerusalem: Mossad Bialik, 1954.

Wisdom of the Zohar, vol. 1. Jerusalem: 1961 (Hebrew).

Toledano, Ya'akov Moshe. *Ner haMa'arav*. Jerusalem: AML Lunts, 1911.

Toufiq, Ahmed. "Les Juifs dans la société marocaine au 19e siècle: l'exemple des Juifs de Demnate," *Juifs du Maroc: Identité et dialogue*. Grenoble: La Pensée Sauvage, 1980, pp. 152–66

Tsur, Yaron, and Hagar Hillel. *Yehudei Kazablankah: 'iyunim be-modernizatsyah shel hanhagah yehudit bitefutsah kolonyalit*. Tel-Aviv: The Open University, 1995.

Turner, Victor. *The Ritual Process*. Chicago: Aldine, 1969.

'Ubayd al-Bakri, Abu. *Description de l'Afrique septentrionale*. trans. M. de Slane, Paris: Librairie d'Amérique et d'Orient Adrien-Maisonneuve, 1965.

Vajda, Georges. *Juda ben Nissim ibn Malka, philosophe juif Marocaine*. Paris: Hesperis, 1954.

"La Doctrin Astrologique de Juda ben Nisim ibn Malka," *Hommage à Millas Vallicrosa*, vol. 2, Barcelona, 1956, pp. 483–500

"Une citation kabbalistique de Juda ben Nissim," *Revue des Études Juives*, 116 (1956), pp. 89–92.

Virch, Claus. *Master Drawings in the Collection of Walter C. Baker*. New York: 1926, no. 96

Vital, R. Hayyim. "The Fourth part of Sha'arei Qedushah," in *Ketavim Ḥadashim me-Rabbenu Hayyim Vital*. Jerusalem: 'Ahavat Shalom, 1988.

Weingrod, Alex. *The Saint of Beersheba*. Albany: State University of New York Press, 1990.

Weinstein, Jay. *A Collector's Guide to Judaica*. New York: Thames and Hudson, 1985.

Wexler, Paul. *The Non-Jewish Origins of the Sephardic Jews*. Albany: State University of New York Press, 1996.

Zafrani, Haïm. "Une Qessa de Tingir, Hymne a Bar Yohay," *Revue des Études Juives*, 127 (1968), pp. 366–82

Mille ans de vie juive au Maroc: Histoire et culture, religion et magie. Paris: Maisonneuve and Larose, 1983.

Kabbale, vie mystique et magie: Judaïsme d'occident musulman. Paris: Éditions Maisonneuve & Larose, 1986.

Ibn Abi Zimra, David. *Responsa Radbaz*, vol. 4, Warsaw: Aaron Walden, 1882.